The Complete Guide to the
ENNEAGRAM

A Modern Approach to Self-Discovery and Connecting Well with Others

Sierra Mackenzie

Founder of Enneagram Enthusiast

PAGE STREET
PUBLISHING CO.

PAGE STREET
PUBLISHING CO.

Copyright © 2022 Sierra Mackenzie

First published in 2022 by
Page Street Publishing Co.
27 Congress Street, Suite 1511
Salem, MA 01970
www.pagestreetpublishing.com

Distributed by Macmillan, sales in Canada by The Canadian Manda Group.

26   25   24   23   22   1   2   3   4   5

ISBN-13: 978-1-64567-596-9
ISBN-10: 1-64567-596-3

Library of Congress Control Number: 2022930171

Cover and book design by Rosie Stewart for Page Street Publishing Co.

Printed and bound in the United States

To Mum, for sitting down to read my
unoriginal short stories as a four-year-old
and saying, "Hey, you're a great writer."
The fact that you were biased remains
quietly sunk in the back of my head, but
those words of encouragement were all that
I needed to continue. To the moon
and back.

Also to those who think my stories and
examples are about you but the names are
different—they probably are.

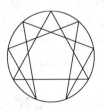

Contents

Introduction

The Importance of Self-Discovery

Before we were jaded adults, young adults, teenagers, or tweens, we were children. The ages from birth to four are what we call our formative years for a reason—they're when we develop; create our core memories; and, one could argue, when we first develop our personalities (and identifiable Enneagram numbers).

Why do we do the things we do? Respond the way we do? Act the way we do? Of course, we innately know there's a reason, even if we don't necessarily want to take the time (or have the time to take) to discover and unravel those reasons.

Without sexualizing this, what does it mean to realize and know yourself naked? If you go to a museum that specializes in paintings from the Renaissance period, there are paintings in which nakedness is equated to being fearful, easily damaged, and vulnerable. We also look at nudes and judge them based on standards of beauty and health. When visiting the Louvre in Paris, my sister and I made a point to see the famous sculpture *Psyche Revived by Cupid's Kiss* and noticed three types of passersby. As a powerfully tangible example of vulnerability on complete display, there were those who sat and looked at it for its incredible beauty and as the art that it was created to be, and then there were those who passed by almost awkwardly, looking as if they had interrupted an intimate moment. Finally, there were a few that looked at the sculpture with disgust, seeing something degrading instead of the original beauty. Unmasked, vulnerable, in a position for others to judge—which one are you? The judger? The observer of those judgments or of the sculptor themself? Or the appreciator of the sculpture for its beauty?

How we see things traces back to our first four years, which is when we learn about four simple-on-the-surface, four-letter words: home, love, work, and play.

Take a moment and think back. What was your home life like growing up? Do you associate it with feelings of warmth, consistency, and comfort? Or do you have feelings of uncertainty, strife, and internal striving? Or is it somewhere in the middle, where life was great as you recall it, but there was some disconnect with a parent, or you remember sleeping uneasily for a few months? Thinking back myself, I don't recall *that* much. But the things I do recall are the core memories that make up my childhood and why I am a 9w8 (Nine Wing Eight)—a Peacemaker with a foot in the door of a Challenger. It's complicated, but to be personally vulnerable out of the gate, a lot of my childhood was spent feeling the need to be a mediator with a strong sense of justice that would come out and yell when it wanted to. It's traceable. And it's slightly terrifying when you realize that the choices you make now reflect back on those times when you weren't half as equipped to understand or make a decision as you are now. This is not a way to place blame, but an added interior complexity that helps make up your reactors.

How about your relationships? Intimacy and how we define love start in the home. As you grow older, your capacity to love stems from your family tree as well. Love is a word we tend to throw around in English. (Get me started on a deep coversation and you'll hear me at least once declare my utmost irritation with people who say, "I love you," and "I love macaroni and cheese," with the same quickness. Have I just been loved on the same level of mac n' cheese? We're about as different as night and day. I digress.) We also tend not to understand the roots and definition of the word love. How we love someone else can greatly differ from the way they choose or even understand how to love *us*. Our definitions of love can be completely different based on how we receive and give love, and how we were taught to love ourselves as children. Were we proud of what we accomplished? Were we impressed by ourselves because we just *were*?

At work and in play, we form relationships based on how we view authority and peers . . . again, based on formative years. How did we view our parents or guardians? Did we respect them? Push their boundaries? In school, were we always trying to stick out as Hermione Granger 2.0 (perfectionist), teacher's pet (needing approval), or class clowning our way around, or were we trying to fit in with the rest of the class?

So, here we are, trying to find our own place in the midst of a world that is struggling with sickness and misunderstanding, evolving with diversity and language and cultural nuances, learning how to function anew every day. With each of us having a different motivator and working alongside others who function differently, learning how to properly understand each other is crucial.

This is where the Enneagram comes into play. Taken at face value, the Enneagram is made up of nine numbers representing different personalities interconnected and woven together through human psychology and more traditional knowledge of human nature. However, in recent years, the Enneagram has become instrumental in the modern world. From businesses and group utilization in team building, to relationships and self-help and identification, to understanding and healing.

At its most basic, the Enneagram is a useful tool to help individuals manage their emotions and interpret the world as their most whole selves. In conflict resolution, leadership styles, emotional and intellectual intelligence, loving tendencies, family life—psychology sits at the heart of it all, and learning to understand oneself has never been so necessary than in times like these.

Before we continue, have a look at the nine types, and start thinking about which one makes sense for you. Surface-level descriptions of these types aren't necessarily exactly what they sound like, and the *motivation* of each type makes all the difference in the world, but the titles are there for a reason and may have some impact or steer you in the right direction as to your own type.

Type One: The Reformer

Type Two: The Helper

Type Three: The Achiever

Type Four: The Individualist

Type Five: The Investigator

Type Six: The Loyalist

Type Seven: The Enthusiast

Type Eight: The Challenger

Type Nine: The Peacemaker

Here's another question for you: What's your biggest core motivator? What makes you tick? Honesty with yourself is essential (spend any amount of time with the challengingly honest Type Eight, and you'll get it), and motives are everything. Type Ones will show anger differently than Type Fours. It doesn't mean the anger is any less fiery; it does mean that it will sustain itself differently. Type Twos will show love differently than Type Fives. It doesn't mean their partner will feel more or less loved; it does mean that their love stems from different roots. If you've never heard of the Enneagram before, or if you've taken the test and didn't 100 percent agree with your results, your core motivation is what will help you understand and guide you in the right direction. (You'll find more on each type's core motivation in each type's chapter.) At that point, you'll be better equipped to unravel and trace back to your own childhood.

Acknowledging in advance that there's probably a lot of hurt to unravel is part of the journey. Staying tenderhearted with yourself and with others in your life and past is a massive aspect of the healing process, since many don't necessarily understand exactly what their personal actions and words bring up in another person.

Rest assured that there's also probably a lot of healing that will allow for some deep re-rooting of your own self as well. While processing the pain and frustration that may arise will take some time to understand and deal with in a healthy and vulnerable manner, I encourage you to get to the healing process quickly, as painful as it might be. Take your time in this healing. Navigate it well. Enlist a coach, a partner, or a friend to keep you accountable. Start a journal. Looking at how far you've come is an encouraging self-motivator and an indication that things can change and you can be all you were created and designed to be.

In this book, in addition to a broad overview of the Enneagram, we'll be examining the relational aspects of the types: at home, in love, at work, and at play. Each example you read here has names changed for anonymity, but they are also true-to-life circumstances. I encourage you to not only take notes on your type, but also on the types of others. It is critical to understand that people's core motivations are *theirs*, and not what we believe they might be—a seemingly obvious Type Three Achiever could be running around as a Type Eight Challenger in disguise. I ignored anything Enneagram related for two years because someone insisted I was a Type Four, and I didn't feel that the descriptions or stereotypes they kept sending me made sense at all. While I am a creative (like Type Four), I crave authenticity in my relationships and don't mind emotional vulnerability or sadness (like Type Four), and I don't mind sitting with discomfort or silence (like Type Four), I am not someone who is generally self-conscious or purposefully individualistic. I don't find myself withholding from others (in fact, I often wear my heart on my sleeve even though I'm reserved with many things), and I quite enjoy and find beauty in the simple things in life (whereas the Type Four often deems these things ordinary). Type Four just didn't fit me as much as others thought it did from the outside; and unfortunately that was enough to turn me off of the Enneagram in general. The sad thing is that this has been a consistent story for many people.

I know it can be so exciting to be able to find yourself (my own mum cried when she realized she was a Type Seven and not a Type Two because she finally felt understood and seen). For every one individual who is able figure it out immediately, there is another who is taking their time—and that's okay!

Sharing your discovery is a great opener to a conversation; don't force it down someone else's throat if they're not ready for it, and try not to type others verbally to such a drastic amount that they're turned off. You're potentially robbing them of the joy of understanding themselves.

If the Enneagram can be used as a relational tool to understand others' hearts and the way they tick—your dad's need to always be on the go for the next adventure; your friend's strangely beautiful compulsion for anything dark and morbid; your manager's overly inclusive leadership style—then you can be accepting and open, challenging and kind. That in turn builds *your* leadership skills. As you unravel each type's core motivation, your genuine approach to loving others as they are comes from taking time to understand where they're coming from with their opinions, life experience, and conflicts. Your own response to resolve any conflict as it arises can change the way people see themselves. You—yes, you—are a lot more powerful than you realize.

A closing thought behind the Enneagram and reading this book: Your type does not dictate every nuance and iota of who you are. In fact, that may be the biggest self-sabotage of learning the Enneagram; the entire point is for you to remove yourself from the blame game of, "I'm a Type Eight; of course I'm going to be angry at you!" and move to, "I'm a Type Eight; how am I really feeling right now, and how are *you* feeling?" It helps to keep you responsible, since your motivations, your desires, and your fears don't dictate you or your personality. Surprise! However, they do greatly influence your personality (not your type), and reveal more about you and why you do the things you do.

Moving oneself from bad habits to a healthy space takes

time. Recognizing your strengths and consequent weaknesses is difficult, but it's necessary. It is not a chance for manipulation of self or others, placing blame, or dramatics. Nobody wants to be friends with someone who feels superior or makes them feel unworthy; and to be transparent, it's manipulative and unhealthy if you use the information you learn as an attempt to control anyone else or make assumptions about the inner workings of their personal life.

While I recommend taking the Enneagram test for early learning and a good understanding of the Enneagram's basic structure, I also suggest you spend time in self-exploration and discovery when it comes to the Enneagram. The Riso-Hudson Enneagram Type Indicator (RHETI®) test is an official test; there are also multiple free versions just a click away online. I have also created a quick test in this book, just to get you started (find that on pages 10 to 16).

A common misconception is that people's type numbers change based on their day-to-day experiences, but you can't pick and choose the best characteristics from every single type to make up your own number Ten. You can be a Type Five and value learning and knowledge, yet come off as a Type Three because you're ambitious and charming. You can be a Type One and value precision and control over your life, yet appear as a Type Seven, because you're also bubbly and spontaneous. Your motivations, desires, and fears are only influencers of your personality—they are not the built-in tyrant that lives in the palace of your mind. You are certainly not a specific way primarily because "your type made you do it." Don't fall into the trap of self-sabotage from the start by imitating another type because you feel that type is more accepted or expected from you or your current role in life.

I'm a Type Nine, but I don't always follow the Nine stereotypes; I don't spend my free time doing vinyasa yoga and sleeping . . . or floating through old art galleries trying to discover the nuances of one time period or another (as much as I sometimes wish I had time for that). In our day and time, we all consider our identities very important and very individual. Potentially losing an identity is scary—but your type does not define you. I don't mirror the quiet, demure, soft-spoken, sleep-loving-but-still-sleep-deprived Type Nine stereotype (although I do love my beauty sleep). While I do value peace and a good cuppa in silence (and I make sure that's part of my morning ritual), I also love people and am full of life, justice oriented, and spontaneous.

And if who you are alone—when you look yourself in the mirror—isn't reflected in your daily life, what mask are you putting on? Who are you trying to be, emulate, become? Being open to new ideas, self-discovery, and discovery of others in your life takes the humility to realize that you may be mistaken or wrong. The most emphatic point of the Enneagram is to unmask who you've believed yourself to be so that you can become the most authentic, beautiful, unraveled, pure version of yourself.

If we so perfectly and precisely mirrored the personality assumptions of our type without thoroughly digging into things like our childhood, home, love, work, play, subtypes, and wings, we'd literally only know nine different kinds of people, full stop. There'd be no mutual understandings between two Type Sevens; Type Sixes wouldn't mistype so frequently; and Type Nines wouldn't relate to all these types, sometimes all at once. We are all *inherently* different, even within the same typing zone. I know a handful of Type Threes who *hate* their stereotype. "This doesn't really sound like me. The core fear of _____ fits, but everything else doesn't." Look, it doesn't mean you're less-than or even that you've mistyped, it means that no types even in their same realm are completely alike. So, if you've ever read or even skimmed a quick generalization, seen a meme, or taken an online quiz about what castle your type would live in and thought, "that's *so* not me," but related to other aspects of the type, it wouldn't necessarily mean that you've mistyped yourself, or that you're perhaps "less" this type than another type. It only means that you're authentically you, and created to be you, and that you're bringing something to the world that only you can. There's joy and worthiness found solely in the knowledge of that.

My hope is that, in learning more about yourself, you can feel more free to stand on firm ground as a confident, self-aware person—not to blame yourself (or blame your typing for the fact that you don't want to do the dishes), but to give yourself the grace space as you are, and actively grow into the healthy, thriving, fulfilled human you were created to be. As you begin to peel off the proverbial mask made up of childhood wounds, defense mechanisms, and overarching expectations, you can liberate others to be genuine with you, too. True liberation and freedom in identity is what it's all about.

Introductory Enneagram Test

Before we dig into more material, it's important to start with an overview of what number(s) you may identify with. It's equally important to note that, as with all personality tests, this test is not capable of being completely accurate. I highly encourage you to use your results as a general guideline as you read through this book and its type descriptions. Let it be a tool to help you explore the different types in more detail to lead you to determining the one that feels most true to you. All aspects of each type are not inherently "good" or "bad." They just make up you. Grab a pencil or pen and use the chart below to keep track of your answers. Below each letter, add a score line each time your answer includes that letter (and note that some answers include more than one letter). At the end, tally up the totals in each letter. Remember that your answers should reflect how you feel or behave most of the time (even if it's not *always* consistent). Be honest with yourself; try to avoid answering in the way you might wish you were, but which may not actually be true for your current self.

A	B	C	D	E	F	G	H	I

1. I strive for perfection, and people say I have a high moral compass.
Agree (I); Disagree (B, F)

2. I love being known as helpful to others.
Agree (H, A); Disagree (E)

3. I feel my emotions very strongly, or dislike hiding my true feelings from others.
Agree (B, F); Disagree (I, E)

4. I pride myself on always being prepared in case of an emergency.
Agree (D, H); Disagree (F)

5. I try to avoid any form of pain and suffering.
Agree (B, D, E); Disagree (F, H)

6. I'm pretty easygoing and don't mind if someone else makes the decisions—I'm just along for the ride!
Agree (A, H); Disagree (B, G)

7. I love staying active and keeping a full schedule. I enjoy planning and creating experiences for my family and friends!
Agree (C, H); Disagree (A, E, F)

8. Knowledge is power! I could spend hours researching a subject (from chemistry to amusement parks) and find such information helpful to any prerogative.
Agree (D, E); Disagree (A, C)

9. I'm super competitive. If you say run, I won't just ask, "How far?" I'll ask, "How fast?"
Agree (B, G); Disagree (A, F, H)

10. Rules are equal to security. I like to know the rules in advance, and plan accordingly.
Agree (D, I); Disagree (B, C)

11. I don't mind confrontation and can thrive in a challenging environment most of the time.
Agree (B, G); Disagree (H, I)

12. I am always trying to better myself so I can be my best—for myself and for others around me.
Agree (A, G, H, I); Disagree (E, F)

13. Success in appearance (job, family, image, relationships, etc.) is important to me.
Agree (C, G, I); Disagree (B, F)

14. I feel unsettled if I am thought of as "wrong" or have a misunderstanding about something.
Agree (E, I); Disagree (A, H)

15. I don't know why, but I have this feeling I don't fit in with anyone … and while I might not love it sometimes, I take intense pride in my individuality.
Agree (E, F); Disagree (A, G)

16. I like to be around people who need my assistance, and enjoy serving others as best as I can.
Agree (H, I); Disagree (E, G)

17. I am the strongest cog in the wheel of my organization. They could not function without me and my eye for detail!
Agree (E, G, I); Disagree (C, F, H)

18. People say I am a visionary! The future is exciting, makes me hopeful, and often occupies my thoughts.
Agree (C, G); Disagree (A, D, E)

19. I analyze everything and enjoy the process of making the logical choice . . . but some people think I'm over-thinking.
Agree (D, E, I); Disagree (A, C)

20. I'm a natural caregiver and am kind. Most people, kids, and animals naturally gravitate to me!
Agree (A, H); Disagree (B, E)

21. When I'm honest and alone with my thoughts, I can say I feel like I am "better" than others.
Agree (G, I); Disagree (A, F)

22. I often find myself feeling awkard in social settings and prefer to be alone if possible.
Agree (E, F); Disagree (C, G, H)

23. I enjoy relationships and friendships that feel mutually loyal and protective. Some say I over-romanticize the idea of having a rescuer, but security is one of the most important things to me.
Agree (B, D, F); Disagree (C, E)

24. I read books or listen to podcasts to help enhance what I do and empower me to be a more productive person (and leader, if it calls for it).
Agree (D, E, G, I); Disagree (C, F)

25. I believe things happen for a reason, and coincidences are not just random chance. My spirituality or belief system is important to me.
Agree (A, E, I); Disagree (B, E)

26. I am detail oriented. Fixing or bettering things, people, or ideas comes naturally to me.
Agree (D, E, I); Disagree (A, F, H)

27. I'm ALWAYS happy! I'm a positive person who finds a silver lining in almost everything, and I love that about myself.
Agree (A, C, I); Disagree (D, F)

28. I am a people pleaser. I often go above and beyond to make others happy.
Agree (A, G, H, I); Disagree (B, E, F)

Now, add up the score lines underneath the letters to get your total for each letter. Write your top three results below.

More As? You might identify with Type Nine.
More Bs? You might identify with Type Eight.
More Cs? You might identify with Type Seven.
More Ds? You might identify with Type Six.
More Es? You might identify with Type Five.
More Fs? You might identify with Type Four.
More Gs? You might identify with Type Three.
More Hs? You might identify with Type Two.
More Is? You might identify with Type One.

Date Taken: _____

Top Three Results: _____

Reflect on your results and read through the overviews of your top three results. Which one seems most accurate to your core motivations? This test might not be exactly on track with your top result, and if you're reading through and find that they're not in line at all, that's okay. You may be connected to your top results in other ways, such as a strong wing. A lot of the Enneagram is self-discovery, realizing what you do consciously versus subconsciously, what you've "trained yourself" to do as you've grown up, and how you relate to yourself and other people.

How to Read This Book: Home, Love, Work, Play

Growing up, we are all raised with a balance of home, love, work, and play. They all intertwine: when you're making home, you're also serving others (work), to show love to them. Home is where the power of example first comes into play. Maintaining this balance that we were raised with begins to take on its own show as it morphs into our own emphasis as adults. In love, we see it reflected in our relationships, in love for people and for God. In work, we see it reflected in everything from being an entrepreneur to serving your family as a young person or stay-at-home parent, or participating in your dream job where you climb the corporate ladder—that's another facet of personality. In play, we develop interactions with friends on a consistent basis. We formulated and practiced as children through play and imagination. As adults, play is creativity and anything that we perceive as "fun." You can easily spot a person who is imbalanced (a workaholic, or someone who is so codependent that they forget they have another aspect to themselves). Somehow, we learn and develop as adults what parts of ourselves are most important to our identities and mental/emotional well-being, and we invest a good bit of our time and energy into those things. All are important aspects of our "whole" person.

In those formative years, you either become a better and happier person where you are accepted in a peaceful environment, and/or you recognize early on what you need to do to be loved, approved of, accepted, and understood, and you acquiesce accordingly. These are also human and societal norms (tantrums don't bode well for most people).

But think about it: when your home life is a place where you are in charge, where you feel secure, safe, and comfortable, that spills out into how you relate to others. When your relationships (be it with friends or others) have gone to the wind, that can relate to how you trust your colleagues in your workplace. Unless you're naturally a very good compartmentalizer, these things spill over into your whole life—your physical, mental, and emotional health, and your well-being.

Enter, the Enneagram.

When we relate the Enneagram and our personality types to others, we bring it back to the original basics of home, love, work, and play. In the home and family, parent–child relationships are situational, and interesting to navigate as a case-to-case scenario. One wouldn't address a spouse the same way they would address their child, and the child wouldn't address their parent the same way they would address their teacher. With all the outer influences, it's important to recognize who is in your personal circle of influence—and if one of the family is outside of that circle of influence, how to either change *yourself* to get them back, or learn how to soften them to want to reenter. At home, *working from the inside out is crucial.* I once overheard a little boy in New York on the subway, probably about ten years old, who was being pressured by his friend into something that sounded like sneaking into a party. Curious, I eavesdropped on the conversation with my nose stuck in a book, and grinned when I heard, "I'm a Howard, man! We Howards don't do stuff like that." Clearly, there was some quality identity here, and some method to his family's madness. I didn't know his family or his grades or his ideals, but I absolutely knew that *he* knew where his value and identity was rooted. Does your family have a mission statement? Or something you "work toward" as a family? Are you playing on the same team, or on opposite ends of the field? Can you truly make a change, or are you simply caught in the paradigm of the justice trap that assumes all is fair and right?

In the follow-up to each type overview, you will find more in-depth examples of how to best love and relate to the type in each circumstance. The examples examine parent–child relationships a bit more closely and can provide ideas for situations such as how to relate to a Type Five Investigator who just doesn't want to have a lengthy conversation about how you're feeling. Respecting where each type is coming from has a lot to do with developing empathy for *their* original home, love, work, and play life. How can you better your empathy—so that you can relate to them better—and so that they can better even a small part of their life? It's a cycle that may seem vicious, but is actually a framework that relates all types back to their levels of maturity and health.

You Need Both Wings to Fly

Your wings are the two types on either side of your primary type. For example, if you're a Type Six Loyalist, your wings would be the Type Five Investigator and the Type Seven Enthusiast. While you do dominate usage in one wing primarily (you could be a Type Five winging Type Six: 5w6), you still utilize your other wing when you're doing something that draws you into that skill set. Both wings are not necessarily your entire personality; rather, they are an *extension* of your personality.

It seems to have become a common misconception that your wing is simply your second-ranking type. I have heard everyone from pastors to professors say something along the lines of, "I'm an Eight Wing Three!" The second-highest score on the test may or may not be one of the wings; and if it isn't, there are two options: that it (1) could be connected to your number via growth and heart points (which we'll unpack shortly in the "The Key Ss" section on stress, security, and subtypes; page 22), or (2) could simply be your second-ranked type (which, while contributing, honestly adds very little value in the grand scheme of things).

If you are uncertain of which is your dominant type based solely on the descriptions, have a look at the score you received on your test, and go with whichever wing has the highest score. For example, if you scored a Type Two Helper, and your second score is a Type Six Loyalist, but your next highest score is a Type Three Achiever, your dominant wing would likely be a Three (2w3). If, however, you see the traits of a Type One Reformer as the dominant role in your life and relationships, you may well be a 2w1. To quote one of my favorite Enneagram clichés, "You use both wings to fly!"

So, what exactly is a "wing?" Well, it's more of a complementary tool and asset to your personality. Sometimes it challenges the primary type, as in the case of a 4w5, in which the romantic, expressive, dramatic Type Four is paired with the isolated, perceptive, cerebrally driven Type Five. Sometimes it complements the layers. While you can't change your wings, you can learn how to tap into certain wings to help you get the job done, or to loosen up or to have fun and change your thinking. As a Type Nine, I wing Type Eight (Challenger) naturally, but you better believe that my Wing Eight was left high and dry as the Wing One (Perfectionist) kicked into influence during this writing process (ya can't challenge the facts). It's a blending of the two types that leads us to a clearer personality. Don Riso, as founder and resurrector of the Enneagram in our modern times, has noted that certain individuals who have been pursuing levels of health through psychology or spirituality have reported the development of their second wing.

Essentially, knowing your dominant wing as a guiding aspect of your type brings more fullness to the traits of your personality.

Triads: Your Heart, Your Head, Your Instincts

The nine types of the Enneagram are divided into a three-by-three structure based on the central responses of the types—instinctive or gut reaction, feeling or emotional reaction, and thinking or analytical reaction. These "centers" are based on their relationship with that very particular framework with its approach to life and its decisions, as well as the guiding liability that is at its root. Some of the centers might be deemed more "acceptable" than others; for example, historically women were thought to be in the feelings center, rather than the thinking center. However, the centers are more so based on the root emotion that is derived from the loss of contact with the child-self. The mental awareness for the 5-6-7 types, for example, is based on thinking; and each type has its own unique strengths and weaknesses that contribute to the decisions and mindset based on those strengths and weaknesses. One of Type Five's driving forces is to know and understand the world around them to remain safe—so they withdraw from the world; but the Type Seven chooses to take their fear out by keeping their minds constantly occupied and excited, to distract themselves from their fears—immersing themselves instead.

The reactor of the instinctive center (Types Eight, Nine, and One) is anger; the reactor of the thinking center (Types Five, Six, and Seven) is fear; and the reactor of the feelings center (Types Two, Three, and Four) is shame. All nine types experience all of these feelings and centers, but the types based out of a certain center and emotional theme experience them in a very intense way. They give themselves permission to relate to these feelings and share them differently with others. Do you make choices based more on a head or a heart basis? Does your type make lists and prepare in advance,

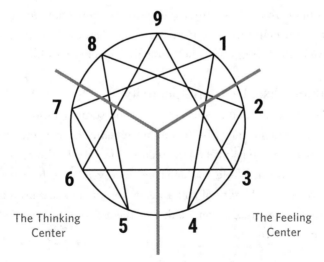

The Instinctive Center

The Thinking Center

The Feeling Center

or do they simply take things as they come and trust that it'll all be alright in the end? More passive, or more passive–aggressive? All these questions are answered within your centers of wisdom, and if they are answered in honesty and maturity, a person can grow healthier and clearer in themselves and their thought process, their emotion, and their intentionality as growth takes place.

For example, a Type Eight acts out of aggression and anger—and they are indeed in the instinctive triad that is rooted in the emotional theme of anger. However, as they grow and mature, they understand that their anger is not necessary to their very existence. Their anger helps them judge things with their keen eye for justice, and it helps enforce their place as strong leaders, but they realize that forceful and physical anger is not actualizing their existence and cause.

It's worth noting that you *can* have a dominant wing outside of your primary number that is in a differing triad—a Type Two Helper in the feelings triad can have a strong Wing One Reformer in the instinctive triad. Again, it's a blending of the two lines. You will act from your primary motivation, *but* your wing will help influence it just as much. You can have a clear drive in the feelings triad, but also have a good gut instinct.

The Key Ss: Stress and Security

When it comes to directions of stress and security (also known as "integration" and "disintegration" or "child-heart point" and "growth/stretch point") it is necessary to look at the Enneagram diagram again. While you don't necessarily *want* to be consistently stuck in the zone of stress, nor do you want to be constantly in the zone of integration, neither of them should be "avoided" as taboo, per se.

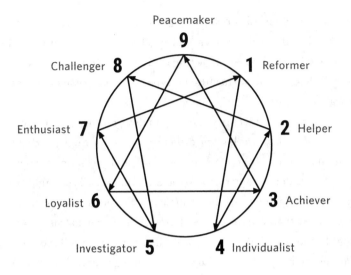

Some believe that their stress point is a thing to be avoided at all costs, but the reality is that your stress point is a reactor of sorts, and because it's outside of your primary type, you can take on the unhealthy attributes of the corresponding number more easily. While there is always a "set route" that the primary numbers move to (more on that later)—for example, Type One will always integrate to Type Seven and disintegrate to Type Four; Type Three will always integrate to Type Six and disintegrate to Type Nine—there is of course the disclaimer of consistent fluctuation of human beings based on their personality health, and their stressors and security.

Because of this, these zones can change per our circumstance or point in time. For example, a Type Eight moves to the Type Two in integration and takes on many of the healthy characteristics of a loving Type Two, but moves to Type Five Investigator in disintegration or stress, taking on the characteristics of an inquisitive, more withdrawn and cerebral type. Type Five will disintegrate to Type Seven, acting excitable and out of character, and integrate to a healthier Type Eight's passionate and vocal personality.

Your stress and security can help in determining your personality type if you are having difficulty distinguishing your true primary number. If you feel you're a 2w3, and care strongly about people, but don't really relate to the integration of Type Eight (in fact, you consider yourself a much more peaceful personality), it may be that you're a Type Three Achiever who has a very highly motivated Wing Two who disintegrates to a Type Nine Peacemaker, or a Type Six Loyalist who integrates to Type Nine).

Your primary type always comes down to your core motivation, and if you feel that the score wasn't necessarily correct, reading through the types in depth and detail may help more than hinder. My friend Brynn was a surface level Type One Reformer and tested as a Type One, with a second result being Type Three. The Type One made sense at surface level to her, her family, and her friends, but as soon as she read Type Three, she cried, "This is me!" The stress and security helped to determine her type more than many other aspects. We will go over this in more depth in each type overview.

Unlocking Instinctual Subtypes

Instinctual subtypes are another important aspect of understanding your primary number. They dig deeply into the layers of a personality and are worth looking into and examining extensively outside of this book since they create even more depth. At their most basic, they are further intelligences that contribute to our being and our mental, emotional reactions to life: the knee-jerk reaction that our unplanned instincts can seem to be (not to be confused with the "instinctual triad/center" discussed earlier).

In our brain's wiring, there are even deeper intelligences within our centers that propel our needs for survival as humans: the intimate instinct, the self-preservation instinct, and the social instinct. Think of these as a three-legged stool: while you might lean forward on one leg (your primary instinct), you still have a solid idea of which way the stool will carry you should you tip (the reliable "leg" or instinct supports the primary instinct). The third instinct is where very many of our blind spots are (and where the stool will fall right out from under you when very underdeveloped). The subtypes have everything to do with the primary number—each type has the opportunity to incline itself to one but does utilize all three at different levels.

Intimate subtypes are all about our deep connections with others: more intimate relationships and close friendships, our spirituality and connection with God, and the life within ourselves. These subtypes appreciate being fused with others, and are considered more intense people emotionally.

Self-preservation subtypes are all about our needs for the more material, basic instincts for survival: security, family, food, shelter, and warmth. They are the more practical of the types, and while enjoying a social or intimate relationship, they need to know they will be secure and prepare accordingly.

Social subtypes are all about our need for finding belonging and true membership in family in community and larger group settings. They are more interested in adapting themselves to their environment and social situation, and desire personal connection.

A Type Four Individualist that has a social instinct, for example, will have a different lease on life compared to a Type Four that has an intimate instinct. On a basic level, a social Type Four seeks to establish a more leadership-oriented role to make them fit into a group to help bring others' emotions out, whereas an intimate Type Four is more often described as "shameless" than "shameful" because they are intensely vocal about their needs and emotions.

On the one hand, these instinctual subtypes influence our personalities, but on the other hand, our approach toward our types and personalities (and the types themselves) contribute to how we prioritize and use these basic needs. A drastic life event can change the way we approach certain subtypes. (The COVID-19 pandemic certainly moved many people I know to hone in on their once more dormant self-preservation instinct.)

So now you have the full-on profile: your primary number, its wing, and your two points of security and stress (or integration and disintegration), along with its subtypes. All four numbers influence you, and you are well equipped enough to never take anyone at face value ("I'm a Type Three, full stop!") again. The ideal goal is for us to acquire and eventually utilize the healthy aspects in all the types, particularly the ones to which we immediately connect. How will you begin your journey?

Type One

The Reformer

"There are two sides to every issue: one side is right, and the other is wrong, but the middle is always evil."
—*Ayn Rand*

Type Ones: the people you recognize as soon as they walk into a room. A little bit awkward, a little bit enthusiastic, they can be the life (and sometimes death) of the party . . . until they see the one cushion out of place on the couch and won't stop thinking about it until they or someone else fixes it. Or the one mug out of place on the shelf, or the half-done dishes, or the person that did something kind to someone and then snapped at someone else a minute later. They won't even mention it when they're talking to you, but you'll *know innately* that something is out of place because they have an air of being distracted, like their attention is elsewhere, until they feel all is right in the world. Honest, morally correct, just, dependable, and maintaining a sense of order in their lives and in the lives of others, Type Ones thrive in the realm of making a difference and helping to create order in the world around them.

There is a sort of purity (not to be confused with innocence) to the Type Ones and their sense of justice, who see things as either right or wrong, black or white. Publicly, they rarely show

Type One at a Glance

Needs: To have a strong moral code of integrity; to be perceived as balanced; to be good, accurate, and orderly.
Fear: Being incorrect, having impure motivations, having their objective sense of right and wrong interrupted by personal wants.
Core Motivation: To resist criticism and condemnation by improving everything, justifying themselves and their ideals by desiring to be right and fair through integrity and suppressing their own desires.

emotions (suppressant) because they consider it wrong of themselves morally and societally to do so. Privately, they march to the beat of their own drum.

At one point, the Type Ones were called "The Perfectionists," but I prefer the change to "The Reformers," because their mission in life is to make sure everything is *right* in the world. They themselves *need* to be right—to the extent that, if they are wrong, it contributes to something deep within them that says that they are not "good," "strong," or "_____" enough. Justice oriented toward others and themselves; driven toward what they would call "a higher calling"; striving consistently toward, well, perfectionism, the Type One is the classic idealist. In fact, historical examples of supposed Type Ones often left their own comfort and homes to allow their drive toward their own personal higher calling—from the ordinary to the extraordinary—to contribute to the cause and make their own difference. In the fifteenth century, Joan of Arc left her home in France as a peasant who believed she heard from God and eventually led the French army to victory against the English, and helped restore the French dauphin to power during the Hundred Years' War. She was captured and burned at the stake a year later in 1431 at age nineteen, but her conviction, courage, and faith gave rise to and advanced the French national consciousness.

The Type One has a natural desire for accuracy, justice, precision, and order; they tend to be the lawyers, surgeons, judges, doctors, journalists, politicians, and law enforcement professionals of the world. They are often very bold advocates for others' rights and the surrounding environment—and when they're very healthy, they may challenge the status quo to push for equality. Still ethical and conscientious, but with seemingly more access to verbalizing truth instead of suppressing for the sake of it, healthy Type Ones find it easier to step out of their proverbial box. In fact, they often help to release fellow Type Ones of lesser health who have learned to or prefer to suppress their emotions or anger.

Type Ones often self-describe as being "married" to their jobs, responding to any negativity by redirecting emotions to find their footing and regain a sense of control. However, because of this, they tend to overly justify themselves because they spend a good bit of time before their decisions or conversations reflecting and rehearsing every scenario or word to make sure it doesn't reflect badly on them, or to ensure a "good" outcome.

In this self-justification process, Type Ones often look at their roadmap, lists, etc., and think of themselves as an analytical type (often mistyping themselves as a Type Five or even Type Seven) because of their tendency to overthink, overanalyze, and rationalize everything based on objective truth. However, being in the instinctive triad, they are passionate people who use *personal* judgments and convictions, not necessarily logical or people-oriented head types. Note that the terms "good" and "bad" are relative and loose, based on how each Type One has been raised and their life experience, as well as where they sit currently in their levels of health. Their own principles must come first, but to stay true to their strong moral code, the Type One often resists their personal instincts by minimizing their expression and verbalization. This comes across as highly controlled to those around them; but Type Ones *do* feel anger and passions and have hopes and expectations and dreams, although they rarely let them out and feel as if they're not authentic consistently due to the repression of their instincts. However, they're more worried about affecting anyone and everyone around them should they let the cat out of the bag that they are not perfect. PSA: They are not perfect.

Type Ones have a very strong internal critical voice, and when they find out that not everyone has this, it's surprising—and it can feel somewhat disheartening that not everyone has an internal critic consistently condemning their every word or action or thought. It can also feel unfair to a Type One to find that not everyone has a voice in their head helping them know the difference between right and wrong, or to realize that sometimes people make selfish choices.

To the Type One, being perfect or right is generally considered a one-and-the-same experience: they *hate* being wrong, but even harder is the self-deprecation that happens when they realize that sometimes, they are. The illusion of having to be perfect is a heavy weight to carry. Negative thinking or cognitive distortions are firm—either good or bad, with the all-or-nothing mindset, or the personalization trap where there is an irrational thought based on past experiences, followed by an emotional reaction to it, followed by unempowered thinking and reaction based on that initial irrational thought.

Type Ones often find it releasing when they allow themselves verbalizations, such as, "I make mistakes, and that makes me human." While some types gravitate toward affirmations that seem more positive (i.e., "My life is abundant," or "I embrace new opportunities."), this particular phrase for the Type One is freeing as the mindset switches. Capturing the reasoning behind our thought patterns really gives them a new lease on life. No longer is there a tie-up of perfectionism and being all things to all people; relaxing into vulnerability frees up the mental state to self-cultivate as a human being in the human race.

On the other hand, what would we do without the Type One's call to precision and fight for justice? The lawyers, who view each case with a detail-oriented eye to win; the neurosurgeons, who work with the end result and purpose in mind; the architects, who can build to the sky without a doubt that their building will not collapse; the detectives or police investigators, who are consistently bringing in details and matching facts with fiction; the songwriters, who make sure every rhythm is timed with precision; or even the parents, who plan a holiday without a hitch.

We desperately *need* such people in the world to keep it from getting sloppy. The trick is to ensure that perfectionism doesn't stem from what they *are* or what they do, but where they are going. Pity the human under the knife of a surgeon who doesn't have a desire for perfection in her work! The Type One has a passion for seeking personal growth and thrives in improvement-oriented, communication-driven workplaces like these; it is here they find their purpose and drive, and here where others see their incredible ideas brought to life.

When anyone—any type, any person, but especially The Reformer—sets out to be perfect, they are slipping into the trance of the impossible survival mode, hiding emotions, striving to create a subconscious defense against the world triggered by fear of showing themselves. The recognition that there is a higher perfection no one could ever attain is difficult and unnatural (particularly for a Type One). It is making true peace with purpose, noting lack of coincidence. It is understanding God's hand, as well as the inner workings of the world and the unwanted emotions of fear and misunderstanding. The higher perfection to attain isn't something we can reach as people. But the search for self-acceptance or self-love is worthy and should be treasured when we walk as if we are already loved, and we should love the people around us as they deserve to be, regardless of the standard they may take or break. Practicing the silencing of the inner voice of judgment toward oneself or another is where healing can take place. It relieves the pressure and tension not only from the Type One's own shoulders, but from the shoulders of everyone around them, replacing this with an allowance for a view of natural, unforced beauty.

Core Motivation: "If You Can't Do It Right, Don't Do It at All"

I have a confession to make: I mistyped my father. For years, I thought he was a Type Eight: difficult, with an authoritarian parenting style of "my-way-or-the-highway," a classic child of the baby boomer generation. He was the youngest son of twelve children, grew up with no opinions allowed, and started his career job at the age of seventeen, where he remained for twenty-eight years until he retired and finally started his own business: the rat race of a 3 a.m. wake-up call to a 1 p.m. finish. The years leading up to his retirement, he came home grumpy and unfulfilled, despite my mum's entreating him to quit because he was half-running a different business anyway. But in his mind, it was wrong to quit; it was wrong to show his anger toward his boss; it was wrong for him to feel discouraged. We just couldn't quite figure it out.

Looking back later, what we thought was the stubbornness and anger of a Type Eight was actually a Type One voice in my father's head differentiating the good and bad, right and wrong, true and false; because in the Type One mindset, there are no gray areas. It wasn't that my father didn't *want* to quit; it was simply that, in his mind, the fact that he *did* would mean that someone else won, that *he* did something wrong that contributed to the end of his nearly three-decade streak, that perhaps he self-sabotaged his own life work and mission. That would be enough to keep him up at night for months to come.

We've already briefly covered the core motives of a Type One: the value of their own strong moral compass and personal integrity that help with prioritizing daily life and the drive to be always perfect and always right. Creating a desire for perfection in the formative years could come from several seemingly small issues. For some children, the inner critic awakens at a very young age, grows through their school years, and manifests itself consistently in nearly every situation you could possibly imagine. People who began with a history of high achievement as a very young child, who suffered early on from an unhealthily self-inflicted fear of disapproval or inadequacy, or even the way that children seek a certain standard of praise can result in the growth of striving toward an impossible picture they've painted for themselves where everything is put together.

However, personality types are not what establish a person. Type Ones are often very visionary, mission-oriented children who desire *deeply* to improve the world around them. They love signing up for volunteering and being involved in the community, and are just as interested in setting their home right by finishing their chores on time. As their parents or guardians allow them to recognize setbacks as what they are (and not as a determining factor of success or perfection), they take initiative and grow into adulthood by believing that they *do* make a difference. As adults, those complications that contribute to a project only spur them on more, and in turn they enjoy that release of freedom that brings about greater motivation, determination, and accomplishment.

Diligent, focused, and seemingly always on the move, in each action Type Ones are reassessing their lifestyle, moral compass, values, and ethics to ensure that they are constantly doing things up to a standard as well as improving the world. They take great pride in what they do, and have a deep sense of responsibility and even love directed toward their tasks. Similar to Type Threes, Type Ones desire to be the very best at what they do, but unlike the Type Three, they will get there without cutting any corners, because to do otherwise would deconstruct their moral compass and disrupt their process of being both good and ethical in society. They are deeply self-controlled and principled, but they are harder on themselves than anyone in their immediate world.

During the early COVID-19 lockdowns in New South Wales, Australia, my friend's Type One boyfriend, James, was

so concerned with the rules of staying in one's own home that at first he was set in his mind that the two of them would not be seeing each other for the two-week period in question—even though they lived in the same general vicinity, neither of them would be seeing anyone outside of the grocery store and their housemates, and neither would be taking public transport. My friend (a healthy Type Three) was finally able to make James see past the rule and toward the logic by examining the facts outside of the goal—prior to the lockdown, they had seen each other every day; and besides, *if* one of them had COVID-19, the other would have had it by then. At that point, it also came to light in the fine print that the rules were not inclusive of a partner. By empowering (not manipulating) him to look past the rules to view the logic behind the rules instead, they were able to carry on their relationship as usual—carefully, of course, but with full confidence that they were following the rules according to the standard set by the prime minister at the time.

Sometimes, Type Ones can be *so* caught up in the act of following the rules that they completely miss the reality. Learning to look past the rules at times to understand the logic behind the rules is *key* to recognizing the justice-oriented side.

Digging deep into their gut types, Type Ones can frequently feel that they are the authority already, *without* the need to justify the why behind their feelings. This contributes to their desire and core motivation to improve in every aspect of their lives, aiming for their actions to be consistent with their personal values and principles, and work tirelessly to that aim. If perfection is in the finished building blueprint, consistent due diligence and responsibility are the cornerstones where there is a particular striving for functionality, coupled with a kind of accountability (whether self- or others-focused) in various projects. There is a systemic quality to their work due to the integrity, loyalty, and honesty that make up the moral code in a Type One lifestyle. Even if they are not bent toward spirituality or a particular religion, a Type One can easily come across as religious due to the purity and mission they commit themselves to. There is a massive sense of *mission* to each Type One's life, as they strive to play their part in something bigger than themselves.

Type One Wings and Levels of Health

The Type One's strengths are often tied to their weaknesses. While they are the perfectionist who excels at *getting it done*, they are equally driven to do the job right, creating a lot of internal stress. This can create a dramatic, high-strung monster inside (although this is suppressed, it is only for so long until an implosion occurs); unless the perfectionist learns to relax and unwind, failure is imminent. Recognizing that they cannot always be all-things-to-all-people-perfect is important, but it makes it extremely difficult to accept what they might deem failure. Failure in the Type One mind doesn't necessarily mean not accomplishing what they set out to do; it more so means not accomplishing their goals flawlessly. Helping them to step out of this trap means recognizing and verbalizing *for* them all their accomplishments and capability. A personal revelation that they can truly improve over time is essential.

I had a Type One piano student who, when we would do our quarterly workshops focused around a particular song, wanted to drop out every session. To keep the pressure low and more focused on an upbeat and lighthearted band experience, we would hand out multiple levels of the sheet music to a selected song the week before, from the beginners to the most advanced. We would then go through the sheet music with the students individually, and they would practice it throughout the week, as they would for a regular lesson. This particular student of mine would go through the agony of practicing every day for hours, even though he was only nine years old and had other school activities; then on the day of his workshop, he would nearly cry because he hadn't gotten his performance to his self-set standard of perfection.

Over time, we saw a great release as he realized the band was not focused, nor even waiting, on him. The horns made mistakes, the guitars strummed not quite in tune, the singers and other keyboarders all had their own mishaps, yet together they were all creating music, and he was a part of it. When he figured out that he wasn't carrying the entire load (while still understanding how important his part was to play), he realized that there were so many other contributors to the event, and that removed his burden. He still practiced meticulously (and I'm not mad about that!), but he wasn't a slave to the performance. My student was learning how to trust me as his teacher, how to trust others, and simply how to trust *life*. Learning how to rely on their own inner voice (*not* their inner critic) and guidance, though it may not lead them directly toward perfection, is what removes the need for Type Ones to self-justify their decisions and trust themselves just as much as others trust them.

To some extent, being a Type One can be a handicapping experience in the elementary age years, but that can continue into adult years as well. Similar to an unhealthy Type Three who tends to shy away from doing things they feel they won't be "the best" at, Type Ones shy away from things they feel that they won't be "perfect" at. There's much less of a "practice makes perfect," mindset because Type Ones would rather err on the side of perfection in things they're *already* perfect at. For example, a Type One who's already very analytical and mathematical, and knows they excel in those subjects would probably prefer to continue to do math only and not even want to try a different path (school- or career-wise). On the flip side, if they must do something as required toward their education, they will take the new subject/idea in stride to the point of self-consumption. It is no longer an activity they do for fun, but an outlet in which they *must* excel, otherwise they are "unworthy."

Broadly scoped, Type Ones are seen the most as a "pure" personality—their world as centered as their core, perfection being the driving goal of achievement. Centrality is an exceptional aspect, and neither wing would technically contradict the type's "oneness" (as opposed to a 5w4 or 8w9, for example). However, upon closer inspection, the two wings (Nine and Two) are both quite different personality aspects. Though they are both used depending on circumstance and scenario, the Type One is nearly always dominant.

The 1w9, or The Optimist/The Idealist, couples the best of the Type Nine calm with their own inner burst of frustration every so often, so while they're evenly balanced, they can detach from "imperfect" or "incorrect" people and their ideals relatively easily, and tend to attach to things that aren't necessarily humanly attainable. Pursuit of what they believe is right as an advocate for justice is a part of their strength set. In health, their views and human evaluations are objective and well balanced. In their unfit state, the perfectionistic standards hold impossible. Where general social and political opinions are addressed logically and with a black-and-white mindset (in search of infallible justice), instead of case by case, there is a tendency toward creating an unwittingly harsh view of humanity. They are highly practical creatures of habit who tend to appreciate function before beauty. They can present as cruel due to their extreme mindset of rule-supremacy, but as a Wing Nine, they strongly desire admiration, acceptance, and love from those around them. Their Wing Nine also contributes deeply to their connection to the inner workings of the world and their seeking of awareness and understanding.

A 1w2, or The Activist, gets a good deal of warmth and understanding from the Type Two wing, making them less of a perfectionist: they have an internal belief that humanity is trying, and even if failing, there is forgiveness to a certain extent. They *love* to do things for other people (although this can stem from a "because it's the right thing to do" outlook), working to improve the conditions of those less fortunate. They are sensitive to the community needs and wishes of others, and enjoy coming up with and being the solution to the problems; however, that can eventually contribute to a "do as I say, not as I do" attitude should they become more unhealthy and self-righteous. A common display in their unhealthy state is a bit of overly emotional touchiness or victimization that manifests in a cold mannerism of "they did that to me," as opposed to a healthy recognition that not everyone does things their way. While in some cases it may stack up internally, it often doesn't last for long periods of time. In their relationships, there is much more codependence, with a more likely jealous streak running from the Wing Two in hypocrisy and self-justified righteous behaviors.

At their very best, the Type Ones are discerning and accepting of what is. This doesn't off-set their desire to change the world; rather, there is a quality of realism and wisdom to their reforming ways. While conscientiously principled, they are no longer tangled up in the roots of unhealthy striving. At their worst, anger alienates them from those they are close to because of the self-righteousness blocking their view. There's a lot to show and to teach others, but expecting them to change immediately because they now know the "right" way to do things is detrimental to knowing their own self and coping mechanisms. Unmasking and choosing to recognize our inability to attain perfection is the key.

Stress and Security

Although they are in the instinctive/gut/anger triad, Type Ones are seemingly rarely angry. However, they can get so caught up with the hidden anger from self-righteousness and self-justification that it damages themselves and their relationships as they make sometimes unwelcome corrections and hold high expectations that others should change to match their expectations. I personally know several Type Ones that have a good deal of unnecessary bodily tension due to their emotional repression (neck pain, jaw clenching, etc.). Instead of the explosion (Type Eight), or the stuffing (Type Nine), their frustration surfaces as critical and judgmental—which can create immense rifts in their social circles as a result of their critical nature. Although they crave deep and loyal relationships, and bring those traits forward in their social interactions, their loved ones often don't know what to think of Ones' disapproving, critical side. When Type Ones feel that they are only giving advice because they care, this has the potential to create a boil-over of self-righteous anger when their partner or friend is more fixated on a critical delivery and takes the advice more personally than the Type One thought they were delivering it. They might not understand *why* their partners fail to demonstrate an equal sense of guilt and a compulsive need to change, despite the Type One's personal attempts to be perfect and change themselves to reach their goals. Repression of their anger is a common trait because anger is not a "right" nor "correct" emotion; unfortunately, this doesn't mean they don't *feel* the anger.

Type Ones—out of all the numbers—take criticism the most deeply because it adds to the belief that they are not perfect, not enough, and never will be. Since unhealthy Type Ones are often overly sensitive, it's worth noting that criticism may not show itself in the form of a verbal critique; it may be something simple as the Type One not receiving a text response immediately, or their friend pulling back from the relationship due to the stressors and any added dramatics involved. For a Type One, getting in touch with the unconscious and subconscious wants to attempt understanding of their tendencies as a human being is where self-condemnation ends, and development and grace begins. This doesn't mean watching the line between self-love and self-indulgence become smaller and smaller; it means recognizing that the superego is (by far) the harshest critic, and it's worth learning how to tune them out once in a while, whether through journaling, conversation, or a creative outlet (as opposed to an analytical outlet, which will just get the wheels turning again).

A particular stressor to a Type One is feeling "human" emotions and impulses. You might even say that a particular stressor is the very idea of stress itself. This isn't to say there's fragility. When I reached out to my social media networks, hundreds of answers flowed in, but they produced a short list. The number one stress trigger was undependable people—whether colleagues, friends, or even family members. Second on the list was shame and guilt focused around something they've done (and this rings true for numbers that wing One as well, Types Two and Nine). The third stressor was hypocrisy and overwhelming corruption in the world. We don't even need to mention punctuality and not living up to their own self-expectations. Stress of this kind causes the Type One to throw any sort of caution to the wind—cue potential implosion.

Going back to shame: As a whole, humanity needs to the take time to mentally detach ourselves from our roots and views of guilt versus shame. Both feelings of guilt and shame are often attached to suppressant emotions stemming from fear (or sadness, or another fairly primary emotion), and are in need of unraveling. Guilt can oftentimes be considered more adaptive and helpful than shame. As a child, guilt can mean feeling remorse for stealing candy, and the emotion, with proper counsel and training by a guardian, can lead to the conclusion, "I won't steal." This means recognizing what we value, and even as children, that's a common adaptability that contributes to being a "good" person. Shame, however, is painful—and is often based on the belief that we are *flawed* and therefore will never fall into the category of good enough, because we've done something dishonorable, out of bounds, and unforgivable. It contributes more to unjustified toxic dealings with oneself. According to Dr. Caroline Leaf, "Shame and guilt may just be a result of a deeper undealt with emotion and toxic thought."

With Type Ones falling into the body center category, often thinking something is consistently wrong with what they do, it's important they learn how to tap into their Wing Two to experience another triad (Type Two is in a feeling triad with a heart center) and taking an empathetic stance toward themselves. In reference to the Enneagram diagram arrow observation, we see that in stressful situations, the Type One arrow points toward the Type Four (the Individualist). Disintegration for them means moodiness and starkly irrational nature like the flip of a switch. In growth or security, the Type One arrow is pointed toward the Type Seven (the Enthusiast), integrating spontaneity and fun, as opposed to their generally critical default point of view.

In stress or disintegration, Type Ones borrow from the unhealthy and negative aspects of the Type Four. They seem to become truer to their stereotype, overly concerned with the black-and-white correctness of a matter. Like unhealthy Type Fours, Type Ones start to become dramatically melancholy, personally biased in their subjectiveness, participating and igniting self-destructive behaviors. They drag themselves down into a self-absorbed funk, where they are tired of being responsible and living up to an impossible (albeit self-inflicted) ideal. Like the Type Four's touch of the romantic, they can become very lost in a victim–rescue situation, in which in their disquieted stillness they are like the princess in the tower, waiting for someone to come and save them (even though at their healthiest they are oftentimes the hero). Self-loathing can occur when self-indulgence gains the upper hand. However, when recognizing this transfer to Type Four, Type Ones can also become obsessively creative, crafting each note or stick or paint stroke with a precision that far rivals Type Three's desire to be the best.

If you've ever watched or read the Lord of the Rings trilogy, there is a scene in *The Two Towers* in which the creature Gollum has an argument with himself and one half of his inner voice tells him how worthless he is, while the other side remembers who he was (as the character Sméagol) before he became overdriven by his desire for the Ring of Power. It's a powerful scene, with the creature struggling deeply with his falsified self, and he's finally able to make him be still. Upon this release, he becomes a different character—although not in appearance—and his shrill cry, "I'm free!" is enough to give you chills. Likewise, the inner critic (or falsified Gollum) comes back every so often, but just that moment is enough to help us recognize the parallel between our humanity and self-validation that comes between our true self and our broken mental state.

In security and growth, Type Ones take on the healthy side of Type Seven's enthusiastic and active mindset. Out of the window flies the overarching concern of societal norms and rules, replaced instead by a joy and unfurled energy, and zest for life. This integration is *crucial* because it allows time for refreshment, as they realize what a wild ride life truly is. During times of growth, Type Ones become playful, comfortable, self-confident people; this is where they learn and remember that they don't have the answers to everything, that some things don't quite add up to the precision of a mathematical equation, and that *they are good. Full stop.* Yes, it takes time to ensure that the Type One is truly integrating; the mental side and inner critic will be alive and well for the beginning of the journey, reminding them of all the projects and things they should be doing instead (PSA: You *should* get out there and remove yourself from the inner critic realm once in a while).

When sensing the descent into disintegration, Type Ones need to learn how to relate to their humanity again, mentally removing life as one massive goal to be accomplished and, instead, learning to laugh at themselves in hard or embarrassing situations, having fun, getting out of their comfort zone, and learning what self-care looks like for them. Tapping into the Type Seven's healthy outlook on life brings the Type One out of unintentional disintegration and integrates them into their fullness. Like most tasks, it is difficult; intentionality is *everything*.

To the Type One: I entreat you to release your perfect standards. That critical voice inside your head isn't God, or truth, or potentially even you. Rest, because you cannot make choices for others; rest, because you are not always right. You are a human being and are becoming—and that should be a breathing place of relief. Feelings are not *only* good or *only* bad, so expand the scope. You don't need to earn self-compassion, grace, forgiveness, and patience. It has already been offered to you. There *is* an intentionality behind your original purpose and placement in the world. Once you stop looking at yourself and at life as a task to be accomplished—while maintaining the balance of order and everything you know and hold dear—a much healthier, stronger, well-rounded, well-loved Type One will emerge.

Things can be both flawed and very good. The Type One isn't just known as The Perfectionist or The Reformer, but also The Visionary. They often see, hear, or observe the details that we don't, and they are working hard to make sure everybody else is catching the vision just as much as they do. Cultivate the kindness and understanding of their vision, and view just as you would hope someone would do to you—and Type Ones, allow that kindness and cultivate it for yourself. There is permission to be free and potential for beautiful growth on the other side of allowing yourself to feel loved and safe in specific company, because you're starting in secure soil. Recognizing that the middle road isn't always purely evil ground—but is perhaps another route that hasn't been taken to get to the good and add to the beauty—is a healthy choice that will only contribute to your betterment, and that of others.

Life with a Type One: Disciplined and Detail Oriented

With a drive for excellence and perfection, and a need for competition, Type Ones are among the most self-disciplined types on the Enneagram. They not only want to be right, they want to do right, and do it well and to its highest standard. But being a perfectionist is difficult because—well, let's be honest—Type Ones make their own job hard. Responsible and honest, their ethics make them stick out from the crowd, looking for ways to help and better the situation at hand.

Type Ones are principled, straight and to the point, perceptive, and effective communicators. Coming in at approximately 9 percent of the population, the Reformers are instinct-based with their emphasis on intrinsic integrity, correctness, and common sense. Because they are so responsible about knowing what is right and wrong, and following rules accordingly, they can get easily frustrated with others who don't take life with the same critical step and eye as they do. Their high standards allow them to see things as right and wrong, good and bad, true and false, and they strive to land on the "good" side for all of those categories. They are the improvers of the world—if they see something out of place, whether small or drastic, they will exert themselves to set it right, reforming everything in their path. Everything can always be better!

The Type One's uncanny eye for detail contributes to their means of improvement, giving them added insight, practicality, and the ability to offer help. But because they are (more than likely) always offering an opinion for betterment, this can come across as judgmental to the receiving party.

On the flip side, for all the critiques they so easily offer to others, Type Ones have a hard time accepting criticism from others; they take it more personally than any other number on the Enneagram. Being sensitive and kind, and apologizing if you haven't been sensitive and kind, allows them to move past it without leaving any issues unattended. Reassuring the Type One not only that they are good but *why* is the key to communication that allows Ones to be open for deeper dialogue.

Ones focus on their faults far too much for their own good; having an individual ask them what their priorities are helps to bring things back into alignment and further into their personal understanding of grace. As the Serenity Prayer prays, "God grant me the serenity to accept the things I cannot change, courage to change the things I can, and the wisdom to know the difference." Type Ones need reassurance that sometimes there is a gray area—and when someone in their inner circle reminds them that the world's burdens are not their own, wisdom and serenity can be closer than ever. Remember, Type Ones have an inner critic that almost never shuts up. It's loud and constantly picking apart everything the Type One does; and it's hardly the same as the voices of others in their lives. Don't live on the same block as that inner critic! Instead, help to silence the critic with honest affirmation, open dialogue, and acceptance. Be the person who reminds them who they are before they learned how to put the pressure on how things should be.

At Home

As children, the Type One copes with their feelings of disconnect from their protective guardian figure and critique from their parental figure by working to set things right. This manifests in early onset via people pleasing and ensuring that all is well in their personal space and with others. Developing their own ethics to defend their inner feeling of never being acceptable to themselves or others is part of their defense mechanism; they have learned early on to be responsible and improve the world around them. To be loved, they must be and appear to be good, and they believe that others must feel the same way about them.

Congratulating Type One children on what they've accomplished is important, because they need to feel acknowledged. But playing with them to teach them the beauty of spontaneity and helping them to override any negative feelings of self-worth based on their drive for perfection will help them learn how to take care of themselves; this provides them with extended energy and joy. To prove their goodness, Type One children can brag about their accomplishments to peers and can often come across as self-righteous. Reminding them that they are loved for who they are, not how well they did something or how good they are, is critical. Opening yourself up for criticism ("Oops, looks like I made a mistake on this recipe, but it tastes just as good!") is a teaching tool on vulnerability, and helps them learn to overcome perceived failure.

To help Type One children recognize that theirs is not the only way, show them historical figures (or fictional examples if they prefer) who did not have immediate success. For example, Thomas Edison failed one thousand times when developing the light bulb, but he didn't see it as failure, but as "an invention with one thousand steps." Finding a well-loved book or film and helping the kids put themselves in other characters' shoes by asking questions helps to teach other perspectives at an early age. "What would you have done if you were Lucy? Why do you think Edmund did that?" It's not about desensitizing them to their high moral compass, it's about teaching them that they have a unique perspective, and each of their friends will have their own unique perspective.

If Type One children become frustrated or angry with themselves, encourage them to take a break, and let them vent their anger. Explaining the difference between good and bad anger allows them to tap into that feeling, while keeping a rein on "bad" anger that might hurt others.

Type One parents will have their own set of beliefs, firm values, and character traits that translate into their parenting style. Certain things should be done in a particular way, and their children (not to mention their parenting partner) are expected to follow their lead and accept their principles. They can get frustrated if their child begins to pick up cues from other peers whose parents have a less-than-disciplinary approach to children, and children have a mind of their own—many of them don't come out of the womb believing that it is "right" to put their toys away when they're done playing with them, or to wipe their feet when they come in the door. The compelling voice in the Type One's head may or may not match their child's thought processes.

Type One parents give their children firm boundaries, a comforting sense of responsibility behind their work ethic, and remind them that the world is a place that needs to be made better. With these parents, children grow up knowing what is expected of them, as well as what is right and wrong, good and bad, true and false; they know what is fair and what is not, and they experience consistency and fairness at home before they recognize that the world around them is not necessarily built on that framework. When they are taught this confidence early on at home, they are far more equipped to approach the world with a sense of "how do I improve and help contribute?"

However, it's important that the child knows that they can play with a Type One parent just as much as they can rely on them. A Type One's child can often feel they are being "preached at" and not necessarily "talked to." When that swap and clarification of being "talked to" is made, the Type One parent can more easily create a welcoming space for their children to communicate, and should remind their children that it's safe to be honest with them. This can lead to a better relationship as they learn to put the toys away and wipe the mud for reasons built out of love, not resentment. Relaxing the boundaries on occasion, having bursts of spontaneity and fun, and acknowledging that there can be more than one way to see things, especially to children, allows them to grow up secure in their standing and unconditional love from their parents.

In Love

Type Ones care deeply about getting things right and maintaining their sense of order in the world and in romance, they are no different. They care about being the very best version of themselves and show it by improving themselves and their time management (i.e., spending more time with their partner). They deeply prefer that their priorities match their partner's priorities. If they feel they have failed by losing the relationship, they take it personally. Beyond the appearance of things, they want to maintain the relationship without anything too harmful to push it out of boundaries. They want to support their partner, make them happier, and contribute to their self-improvement as well, some-times to their detriment. Because they spend so much time on their own self-improvement for their partner, they assume their partner is spending just as much time improving themselves. When this is not the case, the Type One can develop resentment and pent-up frustrations toward their partner. Sometimes, instead of communicating their frustration, they prod their partner to decisions that make the partner feel condescended toward instead of supported.

However, while Type Ones are natural planners and enjoy making sure things are going well, checking in and making their partner feel loved, they can also integrate into the healthy Type Seven Enthusiast when things are going well. They enjoy making their relationships fun and joy-filled! They love bringing positivity and making their partner's life easier. But they can put loads of pressure on themselves as they try to ensure that everything is perfect.

Let's say a couple—a Type One and Type Six—are on vacation, and the Type One checks in with their partner and asks, "Is everything okay?" Receiving the answer, "Yeah, we're good; but I do feel a bit tired. Let's skip the water-skiing tonight?" may not be well received for two reasons. First, it implies that there's room for an improvement, as opposed to, "We're great, I love everything about us!" (which, while this is not an everyday answer, is still what the Type One wants to hear). Second, the Type One will naturally latch more onto what isn't good ("I do feel a bit tired"), and do everything in their power to make sure there is no problem. There is insurmountable pressure in the Type One mind to ensure that all is well, all of the time.

In relationships, letting a Type One know they're doing an incredible job in all aspects in their life, and showing them appreciation by reminding them that they're valued is highly necessary to them. When they start to feel stressed and become overwhelmed, find examples of them doing much better than they could realize: If they have done _____ in the past, you know they can accomplish even more. Bring out the positives instead of telling them to calm down. Type Ones need to feel that they are making a difference through their strong moral compass and through their actions; while they don't need to feel "empowered," they need encouragement and support.

A Type One's daily existence is perfectly planned out (like it should be). For them, the idea of romance should be their opportunity to let their inner child out to play, explore, and adventure. A healthy relationship will help ground them in their plans, while still inviting them to excitement and spontaneity— breaking them out of the mold once in a while. Here is the excuse to do that! They don't need a partner telling them to "grow up" or a partner who puts date night on the to-do list. They want to keep things silly, enjoy sharing life's conflicts and how they improve them, and create an environment of motivation and connection during times of frustration. With their partner, they hope to improve the world around them and together create a stronger moral compass for their family and friends.

Because they have very high standards, Type Ones can sometimes feel that they themselves are unworthy of their partner; because of this they can fall into habits of codependency quickly, and make their partner the very center of their worlds if they're not careful.

Although they may not show much emotion and may associate strong feelings with weakness, they feel emotions just as much as the next person. When I conducted a survey several months ago on love languages for each number, many Type Ones laid on the table that their "giving" love language was acts of service, while their "receiving" love language was words of affirmation. While they may or may not plan a massive display of romance, they show their love in everyday activities: cooking dinner after a long day, folding the laundry, doing the grocery shopping. In turn, they need to be told, "I appreciate you," or "Thank you so much for loving me so well." Telling them they made a meaningful difference to your day just by being present is what they want and need to hear, and it consciously drives away from codependence as it affirms their personal impact, worthiness, and presence.

In Work

Gestalt is a German word used in arts, design, and psychology. Its basic meaning is a sense of perception in which everything is seen as a whole, instead of as its individual parts. For example, if you listen to a song that is well written, like The Beatles' song "Yesterday," you can't imagine it any other way, because everything has been so intentionally put into place, *perfectly*. The whole idea is that things are well organized, constructed carefully, and put together flawlessly.

Type Ones desire integrity in all things. The principle comes first, and the Type One acts based on their view of what is "right" and "wrong" in the scenario. Conflict for a Type One can often take root through actively stuffing their frustration, because they see it as inherently bad to feel anger or irritation toward anyone—a colleague, a friend, a parent. The healthiest version of a Type One sees that facing a conflict head on and admitting their own faults (in this case, their frustration) keeps them in check and balanced. Instead of an impending explosion, they can diffuse the conflicts one at a time, and no one is the wiser.

Because they sit in the instinctive triad and are very body based, the Type One's primary attention is toward correction and doing the right thing. Responsible, with high standards, idealistic and improving, and the "social judge," Type Ones are the lawyers, politicians, doctors, journalists, and (literal) judges. Valuing high-quality work and demanding it from themselves and those around them is only natural, and the Type One can begin to feel resentment toward anyone they feel is not pulling their proverbial weight. When they're in an office or occupation that creates heaps of purpose for them in their life, such as volunteer work for a worthy cause or fighting for social justice, they are more highly motivated to excellence because they know others are depending on them, and they are contributing to the betterment of the world. They are energized when they are invited into the conversation, are in a workplace that values ethics and drive, and when their colleagues listen to their advice and follow through. However, if they are surrounded by negativity, feel unacknowledged and as though they have an audience that perceives them in a false light, they feel undervalued, stressed, and dissatisfied with their jobs.

The difficulty for a Type One is letting go of their non-adaptability, and overly critical tendencies when communicating. To maintain the self-image of being right, they rarely show anger, although they do feel it. To create a solid working relationship with a Type One, acknowledging and respecting their time and integrity, and taking things seriously (like having a meeting agenda in advance), will only help you and them prepare for your discussion and lean into how things can be improved. To handle conflict, asking them to be direct while challenging them to a different viewpoint will move them into their personal challenge: to accept what cannot be changed. Help them to be less critical of themselves and others, and more accepting of their own personal mistakes—asking them specifically to delegate certain matters to Susan over in the copyright department instead of trying to handle it themselves removes responsibility. However, delegation is an important form of leadership and learning to let go and build into bettering a team. Type Ones might feel threatened and feel this is you telling them they are not capable enough; the reality is, they are feeling the vulnerability of not having control in making sure everything is aligned and perfect to begin with.

Sure, who doesn't want a worker who nails their task every single time? What you don't want is a Type One who doesn't appreciate or value anyone else's point of view, feels demeaned in the workplace, or feels they are overworked and underpaid. And Ones, being justice oriented as well as idealistic, will feel this way. Obviously being meticulous is necessary to the job (a lawyer needs to know the inside and outside of their case; a surgeon needs to be precise in their surgery—absolutely no room for error without great cost). However, added stress based solely on a pursuit of perfectionism has never helped anyone in their workplace if they have no personal ways to unwind. This removes the pressure and allows them to act in their fullness of health, improve the world, and bring their principles and resilience to their desire for moral justice.

In Play

Type Ones show up on your doorstep to offer advice, honesty, and practicalities. Because they are so principled, they mean what they say, and do what they say they will do. Their ethics, reliability, and instincts allow them to empathize with your struggles and help guide their friends through any difficulties. For the Type One, a healthy relationship is built on responsibility and trust. Acknowledging their efforts to help you, reaching out even when they haven't reached out first, and reassuring them of their worth and goodness, are worth it.

Because Type Ones are their own worst critics, be sensitive when offering feedback, and apologize if you feel that you have been inconsiderate in any way. If they become angry, remind them that you are their friend and you understand; if they make a mistake, remind them that they're human and mistakes happen. Be fair and considerate when conversing with them. To help them get out of their comfort zone and into a place of creativity, plan original but comfortable activities that allow them to tap into their inner artist, but still use their gifts of precision (although choose carefully: once I took a Type One friend to a paint class that was detrimental to our friendship because she felt imperfect the entire time). To show love and encouragement to your Type One friend, help get them out of the house and away from their to-do list. Go bowling, biking, to a cooking class—anything to help them relax and bring their inner child back to life. This will ease them out of their perfectionist tendencies.

My good friend Denny, a Type One, once asked me to make breakfast: bacon and poached eggs. Now, I'm a (self-proclaimed) cook. I grew up making meals for my family every week, and I have been making poached eggs since I was about six years old, but Denny walked in five minutes later to ask if I had timed the eggs and checked the water temperature, why I hadn't started the bacon first, and essentially to "check in," to see if I was doing it right (apparently I wasn't). He had gotten poached eggs down to an *art*, and I wasn't ready to deal with it at 9 a.m. Being a 9w8 and on my *own* time of "go with the flow" and version of "right," my first instinct was to chill out, so I did, and started making coffee. When that didn't go right, I tried toast. Finally, I said, "I need a minute!" and took five.

Type Ones see the highest potential in general—and in their friends—and when they're honest about that, even if it hurts, it's because they believe in the best, and they believe you are capable of delivering above and beyond what you're giving them. *Yes, it can come off as harsh.* But the truth is, most Type Ones don't necessarily realize that they are sounding judgmental or overly critical. They care and mean well when something is brought up; and they don't understand why other people don't just see something and act on it. And, they naturally give advice and share their opinion with people. If you're feeling judged or demeaned, bring it up *gently.* Type Ones don't appreciate conflict, but they need the clarity that can come from it. If you don't need or want advice in a particular area ("Don't come at me for my poached eggs!"), clarify it in advance kindly, then show or verbalize appreciation for what feedback they give you in other areas. If you know you did something "wrong," were rude, irresponsible, or didn't appreciate the One's values, apologize.

The desire for excellence can run them ragged and into the ground, but the people around them can help lift them back up into their strengths. They will make mistakes and feel like they've failed, but that doesn't change their worth and value. Help bring them into their playful side, where they can experience spontaneity and joy, while still bringing a drive for having good fun! Asking a Type One "What *does* matter to you?" allows for open conversation about what's right in front of them in that particular season, and clarifies what they can draw excellence and perfection from, while lessening the burden of expectation. Having the right priorities will allow for them to be confident in carrying out those priorities to their fullest capacity.

Type Two

The Helper

"There are two kinds of people in the world:
those who walk into a room and say, 'Here I am,'
and those who say, 'There you are.'"
—*Abigail Van Buren*

Type Twos are the kind of people who remember everyone's birthday, even when no one remembers theirs. They love entertaining and hosting people—the more the merrier. Socially aware, adaptable, and usually the one who will "take one (or ten) for the team," the empathetic caregiver, and the listening ear—and always the one to bring cupcakes to every social gathering. Truly the Mr. Rogers of the Enneagram, who "always wanted to have a neighbor just like you . . . would you be mine?"

In their world, to be loved, Type Twos must love you first. Their attention is already naturally focused on others' needs and wants—they probably know what you need before you do. They are experiential immersers with keen senses that are equipped to predict what others desire as they alter themselves to make it happen. Type Twos thrive when giving themselves to others; supporting humanity with an exuberant, positive outlook; and considering others' needs. People depend on them and they are

Type Two at a Glance

Needs: To be loved and truly cared for; to be wanted, needed, and appreciated.

Fear: That they are unworthy of being truly loved; that they will be rejected for being their authentic self, and so disconnected.

Core Motivation: Since a Two expresses their affection through their actions and time, they are highly motivated by verbal affirmation and acknowledgment, response, and love in return.

unconditionally loving and supportive, offering attention, validation, and warmth. Their selflessness and self-sacrifice are a credit to them, and their relationship-oriented lifestyle means they can offer genuine care and compassion, easily reading a situation and room without speaking to anyone, and able to give comfort to anyone in their path. If someone needs a therapist? Type Two. Carpool parent? Type Two. Band-Aid? Guaranteed. The number of hats Type Twos are capable of wearing might seem overwhelming, but they take it all in stride and push through to get close to others just to show them that they love them . . . even if the exhaustion can cause burnout over time.

"No worries!" is, after all, the mantra of the Type Two—even if it is, in fact, a worry. For (your) better or for (their) worse, Type Twos will spend their life empowering you.

Type Twos are known as "The Helper," or "The Caregiver," or "The Companion," and they truly are all of the above, thriving on building relationships and connections above and beyond average (there is truly no such thing as an "average" connection for a Type Two). They are all-or-nothing people, and the world is their oyster as far as helping is concerned. Their mindset is based on the belief that you must give without bounds to others to be loved without bounds; therefore, they are supportive, relationship oriented, and caring. However, they can also be prideful, intrusive, and demanding (particularly of reciprocated love), even if they don't recognize it on the surface. Fulfilling the personal need (of being loved and being needed) is met through giving to others—and if others don't see and reciprocate that need, Type Twos can take it very hard.

Appreciative, generous, adaptable, and hospitable, Type Twos jump into anything and everything to help others with vivacity and deeply rooted compassion. They tend to see past the toughest exterior into the heart of the matter, and that is where they dig the deepest to plant seeds of tenderness and healing in the hearts of their connections. Their connections with others are their true life investment. In them, Type Twos find their own value and worth, and comfort that they are building the biggest and best team, existential family, friend-circle, and support group all in one. The ideal is for everyone to be there for everyone else—and the feeling that they are indispensable gives them a lilt in their step. Based in the feelings center, the Type Two relates best to people through empathy. Their highest quality is their unconditional, no-strings-attached love "in spite of." There was once a survey conducted on medical students' levels of empathy based on their Enneagram types and the Jefferson Scale of Empathy, leaving Type Twos in the top spot.

"Am I lovable? Meaningful? Needed?" Type Twos are anchored in steadfastness, but as natural nurturers, they forget almost constantly to take care of themselves and their personal needs, even when it comes to time, food, and human basics. Their core fear is rooted in being unloved or unwanted—*disconnected*—from others because of the potential rejection of their authentic self. Because of this, they can take their "helping" too far by helping too much and putting on the exterior that they believe others want to see and even expect from them. This situation can turn manipulative and martyr-like, as they overly accommodate the subject of their affections. Ironically enough, this can eventually disintegrate and disconnect the Type Two, because people recognize a false face, even when the heart is good.

Type Twos dwell in the feelings and heart-centered triad, coupled with the compliant stance of pressing into others to feel loved (unlike the Type One Reformer who complies for approval, and the Type Six Loyalist who complies for security). The compliant stance for Type Twos allows for them to turn to others to get their base needs met, and can make for a hard time setting boundaries that remove the responsibility of the relationship from their own shoulders and turn it into a two-way street.

All types have a natural inclination toward prioritizing some things before others. Having a natural inclination to prioritize others' needs before their own because they "should" doesn't necessarily allow for healthy ownership of their own emotions and motivations. Instead of waiting for someone to ask about their emotions (an unhealthy Two response), healthy Type Twos need to acknowledge and take responsibility for their feelings and differentiate someone else's feelings from their own. This is a massive step toward setting the boundaries that bring Type Twos into their fullness.

Healthy Type Twos let go of their belief that they are responsible for making everyone happy; rather, they allow a reciprocation of love in allowing others to take care of them just as much as they take care of others. Of course healthy Twos are still generous! But, they're also well-rested and take care of themselves on a physical, mental, and emotional level (they even let others take care of them). At this stage of health, they can tap into their inner creative, and recognize and verbalize their feelings in a concise, guilt-free way.

Core Motivation: "I Need to Love You, So That You Love Me (Best)"

I once conducted a bit of research questioning fellow Enneagram enthusiasts about their love language. The love languages were first introduced by Gary Chapman, with the assertion that there are five distinct ways of expressing and receiving love: quality time, words of affirmation, gifts, acts of service, and physical touch. This concept is based on the idea that each of us gravitates toward a particular way we show love; and that "speaking" our partner's/friend's/family's/coworker's love language helps to truly make them feel loved and valued. In running this poll, I was not only interested in my own correlations, but particularly what each person's experience was with the love languages and how they felt it affected their type. It was no surprise to find that Type Twos definitely landed with acts of service for their "giving" love language, and acts of service and quality time for their "receiving" language.

Type Twos thrive in joy—they love bringing joy to others. They are encouraging, relationally oriented, and highly empathetic because they so easily and naturally recognize the needs of others and want to get to know them so they can better equip and serve them. They are the world's best teachers, nurses, veterinarians, social workers, pastors, psychologists, and nonprofit organizers. They love caring for people, and because they are so patient and supportive, they make friends everywhere they go. Because they are very generous with their time, however, they can often get lost in their own depletion, and can feel used and abused, even if they're the ones who took on all the responsibilities to begin with.

Because most of their needs and core motivations center around being loved and taken care of, a Type Two can often easily fall into the mindset trap of doing things for others to feel or be needed, which can become manipulative and domineering if they're not careful. At their best, however, this mindset allows them to be unconditionally loving and generous toward others, caring for them as well as they would care for themselves. When healthy, they are invested in genuinely helping and contributing to the world and other people; when less healthy, they are invested in *seeing* themselves as helpful.

During a coaching seminar at a local church several years ago, we sent out an Enneagram test prior to our seminar to help our participants (most of whom were church staff, whether volunteer or paid). As my business partner and I watched the results come in, we were startled to realize that more than 70 percent of the tests resulted in Type Two. It's an almost laughable pattern, but the reality is church staff—and most people who take care of other people—*want* to be the Type Two on the surface, because they're always helping people in their mindset of "church"—helping things run smoothly, communicating well, being generous. While none of these traits are "bad" (and are often just traits of good people in general) it deeply affected how each person desired to be seen and not how they acted in private. Because we had gotten the opportunity to work alongside most of the staff for years, we knew from our friendships with these people that something was off and that at least half of the people were, in fact, not Type Twos.

It's interesting to note that, when I was introducing the Enneagram to a small business, everyone tended to test towards a Type Three Achiever or a Type Eight Challenger for a group training. Private versus public projection is a strong thing!

Type Twos are professionals at expressing their feelings for others. Their sensitivity to others' feelings, and their energy and willingness to stay the course even in the face of any potential disruptor, makes them an easy comfort zone for people. While on the one hand, this can cause repression of true feelings, they can encourage and motivate better than many people due to their supportive nature. Selflessness is their duty.

In Shel Silverstein's children's book *The Giving Tree*, a little boy loves a tree very much, and the tree loves him back—so much so that the tree gave him everything she had over the years until she was left a stump. "And she loved a little boy very, very much—even more than she loved herself." An active Type Two consider it a privilege to be involved in others' lives. One could say that a driving factor of the Type Two is that they *need* to be needed.

Twos can often feel that they are "used and abused" as a result of their kindness. It can be disheartening to feel that they are ever at fault for anything (even if they may be), especially when they are helping others. To mentally clear themselves from blame or accusation of any kind is another point of motivation for the Type Two. However, to "vindicate" can also be an emotional thing, where one feels either devalued or used because someone else has apparently taken advantage of them. *Vindication* is an action verb, but it's also simply a need to feel cleared of any associated guilt—not necessarily to self-justify. And vindication of oneself is going to be different for each person.

The deep fear of a Type Two is rooted in—you guessed it—love. Strangely enough, their love can often turn manipulative when a Type Two declares their intentions to someone else. Praising or giving flattery to others isn't necessarily seen as manipulative to the praiser; they believe they are doing it to make the recipient feel special (and in return, the recipient will attend to the Two's needs). It's hard to understand, but sometimes the abundance of love a Type Two brings to the table isn't necessarily welcome or wanted—and sometimes this pushes the object of their affection overboard.

For instance, think about a Type Two parent who doesn't necessarily do everything but takes good care of his child (let's call her Rosie): breakfast, lunch, and dinner are on the table, sometimes foods they like, sometimes foods they don't. Rosie doesn't have to catch the bus to school; two days a week she goes to ballet lessons; on weekends she'll have a guaranteed playdate if she does her chores. She knows she is dearly loved by both of her parents—every other week they make it a point to have a "mum date" or a "dad date." Her grades are good, she's an all-around star on her sports teams, and she's excelling at math. Her parents are so proud of her.

Rosie's dad, on the other hand, is working a full-time job as a psychologist and making it all happen at the same time—carpool, playdates, friends, ballet, baseball games. Rosie's dad is worn out. But, it's worth it; he knows that childhood isn't forever and that so long as Rosie knows she is loved and taken care of, that's what matters.

One day, Rosie turns twelve, sits down at the dinner table, and utters, "Yuck! I'm not going to eat *that!*" *The gall. The nerve. The audacity.* It's as if they've all gone back in time to Rosie's first time eating with a spoon. Suddenly Rosie's dad feels as if Rosie isn't rejecting the food on her plate; she is rejecting *him.* An unhealthy Type Two, parent or not, would take this personally, struggle internally with how to balance the years of resentment of raising an "ungrateful" child while still making sure she is feeling loved and accepted. It's a tough moment. Rosie looks stubborn. The food is not leaving her plate. And her dad feels like she'll never "love" him again.

Rosie is exhibiting a testing-of-waters, perhaps to see if she is actually loved, or perhaps as a response to a sudden feeling of being overwhelmed by the abundance of her parents' giving and unseen expectations. Multiple things can be noted at this point.

First, Rosie's dad needs to learn the importance of setting a personal boundary—leaving out the fact that he has a near-teen on his hands—giving himself space to relax and do what he needs to at certain times. While he may be great at helping others and helping Rosie get where she needs to go in her own life, building his relationship with her, and loving her well, he needs to learn how to accept help, too. It's hard to be aware of the hidden intentionality behind generosity, and focusing on Rosie and his string of clients was not helpful to himself—in fact, it was probably setting him up for overwhelming exhaustion. Perhaps more importantly, though, is that Rosie was not directing her insult of her food toward her parents. She could be having a bad day; she could be dealing with a number of other situations that are pushing her to test the authority in her life. Instead, this is an important opportunity for the Type Two parent to stay trustful in Rosie's love for them (and her potential true dislike of broccoli).

Taking this to a deeper level, this is an overarching scenario that can simmer under the surface in a Type Two on a regular basis. It may seem dramatic to others, but receiving even the slightest criticism as a personal rejection or deep wound is a more-often-than-not occurance that needs to be kept in check. Trusting that others' love for them roots deeper than their instant response to a Type Two's actions is a massive leap forward on the health scale.

Recognizing that their value doesn't stem from others' feelings about them is a massive point of integration for a Type Two. Acknowledging and working through their own emotions *instead* of replacing them with concern for others is where the core motivation for being needed goes from unhealthy to far healthier.

Type Twos *love* feeling compassionate, feeling caring, feeling nurturing, hosting, being able to love everyone through anything—it's a sense of pride they carry about themselves that they can truly meet people where they're at, and love them to wholeness. They believe their way of life is innately good; people are drawn to them naturally, which feeds into their view that helping = love.

Spirituality is deeply rooted in their "why," whether they consider themselves religious or not. But, when they feel that others don't need them anymore, they retrace their steps back to their heart/feelings triad's central fear of worthlessness. Their worth and lovability comes from self-sacrifice. If they sacrifice and love and "do" to a certain extent without feeling anything reciprocated, their repressed feelings come to an ugly head, and they have to battle with the misgivings and shame that come hand in hand with the fact that they, sadly, cannot offer unconditional love as much as they believed that they could.

Type Two Wings and Levels of Health

Early on in our childhood experiences, we are taught how to share. "Sharing is caring" is the statement we may have heard often, putting others' needs above our own. While that sentiment is not wrong, we also learned that to receive love, giving above and beyond—even if we didn't want to—was necessary. As we grew, we were asked to give our time, our space, our knowledge, our opinion . . . or to keep that opinion to ourselves to respect the other person. Hopefully, as children, we were also taught that it's okay to say no. And hopefully, there is a balance we can strike as adults to be generous but also hold our own and say "no" if we need to.

Sometimes, however, we continue to display codependent behaviors as a habit. We don't even realize we're doing it; we just feel good being perceived as a caring, generous, loving person. But, when we *don't* offer our best and do what we think others expect us to do (outside of our jobs), or go above and beyond because we "should," guilt can creep in. This is a codependent habit. If codependency becomes an addiction, you will always be performing for the other person, and when they don't respond with the same level of intensity, this causes resentment, creates shame, and can bring up abandonment issues.

Enter the (unhealthy, disintegrated) Type Two, who doesn't recognize that this is keeping them from being their fullest self. But then again, differentiating between codependency and love—especially if we were taught since childhood that sharing could only ever be caring—can be difficult to unravel.

While Type Twos are rooted in the feelings or "heart" triad and do most of what they do out of a deep sense of empathy and genuine care, this triad's chief motivator is shame, laced not with "I did wrong," but "I *am* wrong." Because Type Twos are very relationally driven, they can quickly become lost in their self-inflicted responsibilities toward others whom they love and care about, and hope to receive care from in return. However, they do receive some balance with their Type One wing in their instinctive triad, and can tap into it from a different stance.

Type Twos who have a dominant Wing One (The Reformer) in the instinctive triad are called The Servant. Those who wing Three (The Achiever) are known as The Host. While staying central to their helping tendencies, there is still plenty of balance as the Type One brings a sense of extra reason and principle, and the Type Three brings a sense of capacity and sociability. However, pride is also the root vice of the Type Two, and unhealthy Twos believe that others are dependent on their self-giving and could not function without them. This can contribute to a manipulative dynamic on the part of the Two, because they are very charming and can flatter so that others meet their base or primary needs.

The Servant (2w1) brings a beautiful motivation for serving others, coming from a stance of "principle" and "value" instead of pride, and ethics (generally) come first. Similar to the Type One, The Servant sets a high standard for themselves and for others. Instead of verbally exploding and imploding when others are not matching their level of giving, they tend to withdraw and focus inward. The personal connection is important to them when resolving conflict or receiving feedback. The healthy 2w1 is aware of their own need or potential for growth; they offer discerned but realistic support, and they are focused on tasks as well as relationships.

When in disintegration, a 2w1 can especially confuse their mission of taking care of others if their motivation comes more so from pride than deeper values; they can actually become blind to their own motives. They dominate others and situations, and justify their actions because they are "just helping!" This creates a more passive—aggressive gap between The Helper and the subject of their efforts, and their own ethics can go out the window if they happen to recognize their own selfishness because, really, they just don't want to believe that of themself.

The Host (2w3) brings on an extra dose of capability to get it all done, thanks to the achievement-oriented aspects of the Type Three. They host the most elaborate dinner party for friends, and their niece's birthday party, and their parents' upcoming wedding—not because anyone asked them to, but because, well, who else would you have as host? The drive and communication skills of the Wing Three that seeks to impress can really get it all done and bring the final touch to projects that help people. They're charming, good-natured, tend to be extroverted, and truly care; and they are capable of and enjoy balancing multiple projects at once.

When in disintegration, this wing tends to land on the emotionally controlling side of things, with pride stemming from vanity and a desire to live in their own image and what others expect of them. They can become deluded, compare themselves to others, and create a false reality or parallel life in which they deceive themselves and manipulate others.

Childhood wounds for a Type Two often come from a sense of mixed feelings or misunderstanding toward their first protector (whether a parent or caregiver) in their own homes growing up, to the point that they decided they wanted to parent themselves because they felt more qualified to take care of themselves and others in their family. Their identity stemmed from what they thought would help make their protector (guardian, parent, sibling) love them, and that stance would earn them love: through repressing their own needs, not asking for help, not asserting their presence or needs, and giving to others selflessly. This is where the quest for worth and the early tenets of codependency began: where they first believed that love was conditional. Unfortunately, this love became conditional toward themselves, too.

I once had a colleague I'll call Deb, who was a 2w3 Host, with a self-preservation subtype. When working on a project, Deb would start with the other person's agenda: only natural for a Type Two. We'd all get on with it, and as the deadline began to draw near, Deb would continue to help with her colleagues' workload, even to the point of taking it home and dealing with it herself (even if it was never her job to begin with). Her point of view was she could always work "extra" fast, "extra" hard, and put in "extra" hours—if the office was happy, she was happy. However, her colleague, Sarah, never did her the hopeful check-in of, "Are *you* happy/okay?"

It came to a point where Deb took home a project that was due the next day, realized that she had multiple reports due by the weekend, and shut down. The following day, Deb came into the office fuming. Sarah, who had never thought to check in about Deb's happiness, and who was getting a lot of her personal workload accomplished by Deb, was out partying with friends the night before, on a Tuesday! Not only that, a report had come out showing that Sarah was also up for a promotion due to all of "her" hard work—much of which had been accomplished by Deb.

Deb finally snapped. She had made so many sacrifices, worked so hard, and it would have been more than just for *her* to get the promotion, have her turn. Her self-cast image of generosity and care came tumbling to a heap on the ground. The manager had Deb take a break, and she herself had a chat with Sarah for taking advantage of a good thing. Deb quit taking on the extra work and learned through experience how to mentally rebalance, and value her own work and time enough to set personal boundaries that allowed her to accomplish her own list of tasks and priorities before assisting others. Yes, it felt selfish at first; Deb herself knew she was capable of extending herself above and beyond. However, saying no is a valuable tool that Deb hadn't quite mastered yet. Learning to utilize time management and the magic of the words "yes" and "no" in their respective boundaries pushed her into increasing personal capacity.

Asking for help is not just an option, but a necessary option. Deb's removal of herself from disintegration to integration, from stretch and stress to grace and security, was the best thing to allow her internal Type Two Helper to thrive—and it pushed her to own her own authority and keep her pride in check.

Stress and Security

For a Type Two, security comes from being wanted and needed by people. As a child, this might have manifested by doing siblings' household chores, or taking on parental responsibilities through nurturing. Similar to Type Sixes, Type Twos need to prove and see for themselves that they can be loved, and that this love is earned by self-sacrifice. Because Twos love and are actively bringing value to others, their sacrifice is engaged and presented in different ways.

I once heard that a gift is not a sacrifice unless it is something you gave up at a cost to yourself. Twos need to learn to allow for real intimacy, the kind that takes work, not just the kind that garners applause and perceived affection. The vulnerability of needing something from the world removes the Type Two from the emotional "generosity" that costs them nothing to give. Once their heart is fully involved and open, this vulnerability allows for self-security to root in an emotional groundedness that results in wholeness. This view is very apparent when it comes to the Type Two's stretch point of movement to Type Eight in stress or disintegration. The Type Two's grace point is to move to Type Four in growth and integration, staying within the Two's feeling triad, but taking on some of the introspective and built-in fine lines of the Type Four.

Integration for a Type Two looks like actively releasing pride from their sensitivities. Just because empathy is an active and strong character trait does not mean others will see what they're asking for behind the smile. When the Two moves to Type Four, there is a more authentic connection with and validation of their repressed needs, where they are able to recognize their shame and its play in their actions. At Type Four, the Two can often feel at peace: this is where the Type Two can leave a mess overnight in the kitchen. The struggle for power ceases, and as the Type Two begins to feel truly loved, the relinquishment is an easily given checkmate. When Two goes to healthy Four, they become aware of their denial and allow themselves to be stripped bare of their motivations as they accept who they truly are. They are more honest and vulnerable with themselves, and they are genuinely compassionate toward everyone. They can see without shame, with humor, and can truly support others with greater intimacy as they become more authentic and enriching.

Here is where many Type Twos can begin to feel *human—in a very good way*. Gone is the robotic response, the automatic "yes" to every question, the need to be all things to all people.

Likewise, disintegration for a Type Two is an instantaneous flip into Type Eight. Where the Type Two is normally overly compassionate and understanding, there can be a negative swap into an unbalanced demand of a Type Eight; the tone may turn harsh and blunt, and instead of being relationally focused, they become far more task oriented without patience. The outer shell is up, and they are much more confrontational—again, without paying attention to their own needs, but with very little heed to the needs of others (although they'll still generally tend to the basic needs). They can become obsessed with ensuring they can "do" everything at once, becoming less sensitive, more offensive, and more resentful under the surface toward those who are looking by without offering to help *them* in their time of need. High stress on a relationship can often come about after a long period of time without feeling gratitude from a particular person, so the disintegrating Type Two can result in removing themselves from a relationship to prove how indispensable they and their helpful nature are.

However, a stress point is also a stretch point that expands a type's initial reaction. When a Type Two moves into Type Eight, they can learn to expand their authority through the stress, impacting others even more than they could have before. They also grow a much higher task-to-people ratio. If the Type Two—or anyone for that matter—is stuck in the pattern of codependency, it's difficult to step out of this pattern because oftentimes they only see it as "helping." Moving along their growth direction toward the challenging and fiercely independent Type Eight is a helpful key for them to challenge that nature. Once one can distinguish between codependency and love, they can truly know the difference between love and obsession. The Type Two must first start by communicating supportively, without any manipulation by flattery, acknowledging that others live in their own bodies and therefore know themselves better than the Type Two wants to think they do. If you truly love someone you would be free. You would allow them to be free.

I once read that treating yourself as if you were someone you were responsible for is the beginning of learning how to love yourself well. When the Type Two can own and take responsibility for their own emotions without blaming someone else or taking pride in their indispensability, they allow themselves to speak their own needs and, in so doing, allow others to take care of them. Instead of consistently abandoning their own wants to fulfill another person, they can recognize that their true self, unmasked, will open them up to receiving more from others.

It's difficult to switch from the mentality of constantly looking after other people to focusing on your own self-care. If you have a helper in your life, work on bettering your expression and appreciation for *them*. As they have empowered you, encourage their own empowerment to say no and do it kindly. If they retaliate or feel rejected, be patient. Boundaries can be like encountering the lions' den to a Type Two—where they are open vulnerably to feelings of untrustworthiness or unwanted. Boundaries for themselves are often walked over; boundaries for others are not often clear. Clarify the boundaries on all ends. Join them in valuing contact, connection, and partnership.

For the Type Two: where does your identity lie? It's not in how much you love people, or how much people love and cherish you. It's not even in the doing of things, the push-past and hurry-scurry to anticipate someone else's needs. Take time to listen to yourself, and your mentality and heart. Remember what it feels like to be taken care of; remember what it feels like to be human. The people in your life love you beyond what you do and help them with. Your *being* in society contributes far more, and you are worthy of love before you offer to give any love away. The more you treat yourself "like someone you're responsible for," the more you can truly empower other people in a healthy way, and the more they will like you, and love you, and value you—for you. Here is where you can love them from a place of self-security and grounding, instead of fear and shame.

Life with a Type Two: The Considerate Communicator

At approximately 8.5 percent of the population, the Type Two Helpers are heart and feelings based, with their personal conviction and calling based around loving and supporting those important to them. Kind, compassionate, affectionate people, Twos constantly pick up on the emotions and needs of those around them at their own expense. They can struggle to grasp, understand, and even acknowledge their own ideas and feelings, and *hate* to admit they need help! Twos have the idea that a lovable person is a person who doesn't need anything from anyone, but as much as they desire connection and intimacy with someone else, they won't find it unless they can become vulnerable with themselves and others. They can lose themselves in their adaptability, their engagement, and their constant service to others if they don't have the right people alongside them from whom to get support.

Type Twos thrive on building relationships, teams, and communities on the solid foundation of service. Their consideration of others coupled with their incredible communication and natural people skills are their winning charm in life. Twos have the power to stretch to Type Eight Challenger, and practice their powerful and authoritative impact; and in their grace point of moving to the Type Four Individualist, they are able to connect to their authenticity and needs.

A Type Two's agreeable spirit can frequently stem from the need to build relationships with those who will *also* satisfy their own needs. It's easy for them to fall into pride or arrogance from their feeling of being "indispensable." But, when they're healthy and in a state of humility, they can give to others from a place of genuine warmth and from their *true* self who knows they are worthy of love and approval. The healthy Two is warm, expressive, and receptive. The unhealthy Two is indirect, manipulative, and possessive or clingy. Note the difference.

When communicating with a Type Two, validation and valuing is empowering. Make it a point to appreciate the little things they do, to reassure them of your love and caring for them (genuinely!), and to help *them*, even and especially when they don't ask for it. Inviting them to be vulnerable and honest, and initiating conversation is a way to reach them when they feel that they are the only ones reaching out to people. Even if they want to verbally process something, Twos can have a difficult time opening up. Don't prod, but do dig a little deeper—past the usual, "Hi, how are you?" "Fine, thank you"—to reach the heart of the matter.

Type Twos spend the greater portion of their lives prioritizing others. If they have but a few key people in their life that prioritize taking care of *them*, they can draw from a full well, motivated and energetic, and care even more genuinely and effectively. Be the person to pour into them, remind them that you care, and validate their existence.

At Home

Even as children, the Type Two wants to feel needed by people, as if they belong, and are accepted and loved to bring a sense of security. With their childhood wound of feeling a lack from their protecting or guiding figure, minimizing their needs or wants to earn love through selflessness is a natural coping and defense mechanism. Their own self-love becomes conditional on their earning their own self-worth. Similar to a Type One, Type Two children need to hear that they are loved for who they are, not what they do. Their internal dialogue often stems from an idea that if people are good and well, they don't need anything. It only makes sense to them that others would love them because of their generosity but when they are loved, they don't quite know how to receive that love.

When they are so selfless, young Twos develop and cultivate a sense of pride and superiority that others need them, so many can and do give until they forget who they are, running themselves into the ground. However, if their selflessness goes unnoticed or unacknowledged, they can become bitter and resentful. Parents need to remind their Type Two children that it's normal to have needs, and clarify for them that it's okay to say "no." Help them listen to their body when it needs to rest; as Twos integrate to Four, intentionally give them their own space to be creative and use their imagination, and encourage them when there is something unique about themselves. Twos can become addicted to the flattering, appreciative voices in their head or to external voices; using alternative types of praise or response (not just "great job!") can allow the Two to dig more deeply into sincerity and out of the pit of flattery. Above all, remind them that they are not responsible for the feelings of others, and as beautiful and kind as it is of them to want to give selflessly, there are some situations in which they need to say "no."

As mothers, many women step into the traits of a Type Two personality. Naturally nurturing, encouraging, and valuing people, nothing is too much trouble. From sending extra snacks in the lunch boxes to share with friends, to calling throughout the day just to check in, to having kids bring home their laundry when they visit (from college!); everything done for someone else contributes to the Type Two's longing to help, and their children get to the heart of that quicker than most human beings (which is saying something). Type Two parents are warm, caring, kind, and love being there for their children. "How was your day today?" is an appeal for a genuine answer about friends, teachers, school. Their children feel empathized with, understood, and heard— and this contributes greatly to the child's self-worth and value.

On the other hand, for more naturally independent children, a Type Two parent's attention can feel smothering at times. The need to be in contact and protective can be taken as the parent's lack of trust in the child as a human (even though this isn't the case at all). The childhood wound rears its head at a young age, but still reflects through parenting: putting needs on a "back burner" to earn others' love. The truth is, children always love parents, even if they don't say it all the time, and even when they become teenagers and don't want to acknowledge a parent's presence.

As children grow and mature, it can be valuable for Type Two parents to make a conscious effort to let certain things go, while their children are still at home, and you're available and right there to help them figure it out if something happens to break or fall out of place. If a child doesn't want to play with a certain friend anymore, don't force it or try to figure out "what happened," but *do* ask without prodding, and remind them that you're always there.

In Love

Type Twos care about being the supporter in a relationship: they love cooking meals, being thoughtful, making phone calls (or texting), and promoting romance in general. Relationships mean *everything* to them, and if you're in a relationship with a Type Two, you are where all their energy is focused. Because they are so nurturing, so concerned with others and their needs, and are anticipatory of the other person's wants and desires, they are an ideal partner. Type Twos are detail-oriented, and pay very close attention so as to anticipate the other's needs. Their desire to feel worthy and wanted and cared for is their *driving* force in life and in romance. I once heard my Type Two friend Kaia say she had completely "memorized" her partner—she knew his habits, the way he liked his coffee, his gym routine, his brand of sunscreen, and even the spot on his forehead he always missed when applying that sunscreen. To someone else, this level of "memorization" might seem overwhelming but to a Type Two this is a way of loving a partner as much as they deserve.

Here's the thing: we tend to love others the way *we* want to be loved . . . and yet, that doesn't work much of the time. We know full well by now that Type Twos were made to love people. *But* they're going to love people a lot differently than a Type Five, who feels more loved and respected when they're left alone because they appreciate their independence. Type Twos are *incredible* at sniffing out the other person's love language and adapting to their partner's needs, but on the flip side, they may often feel that their love language is not being reciprocated half as well.

Twos *need* affirmation and appreciation; when they don't feel they have it, it can cause tension. They spend so much of their life affirming other people, and if their partner shows that they've been thinking about them even in the smallest ways, a Two will feel it. Twos also desperately need someone who will listen carefully to them. They themselves are great listeners, but because they feel that others don't pay attention to them as much as they pay attention to others, they can feel insecure or that they are not worthy conversation partners. A reassuring ear who stays engaged in the conversation makes the Two receptive, and fills up their energy tank of motivation.

Above all else, help the Two to set limitations and boundaries, even with their partner. Twos love feeling needed and they hate saying no, but it's to their detriment that they say *yes* to anyone— partner included—when what they really need is rest. If this isn't allocated and self-care is not empowered, they can grow resentful and deeply bitter, no matter how much their partner loves them. When conflict needs to be resolved: you guessed it, continue to affirm a Two throughout the entire conversation. Healthy Twos can take difficult conversations *as long as* they know they are still cared for and valued; otherwise, a difficult conversation can feel like the end of their world. Twos simply want someone that they love to love them in return, and to know they are considered special. They cannot keep giving from an empty well, and see love (correctly) as a two-way street. They'll remain patient and kind for a long time, but sooner or later the fuse will run short, and that can challenge even their loving and agreeable nature.

When in a relationship with a Two, help them to practice independence not by leaving them alone, but by focusing on them and what *they* want. "Whatever you think!" is not an acceptable answer. Unlike the indecisive Type Nine, Twos know innately what they want, but they can become so lost in their passion to please that sometimes they need it brought out of them. They want to cultivate a completely trusting, honest connection and they want you to help *them*, and reassure them that it's okay for them to *not* be switched on all of the time.

Self-sacrificing, considerate, and caring to make their partner happy is a part of the Two's purpose in love. Putting aside their own happiness and needs is of little consequence when their significant other is made to feel . . . well, significant. What Twos really want and need is the courage to be themselves wholly and completely, vulnerably and truly and to be loved for who they are, not for their potential, not for their adaptability, and not for their absolutely amazing back rubs or homemade ice cream.

In Work

Type Twos are the helpers, but they are also phenomenal leaders when it comes to motivating others in their workplace, building cohesive and clear relationships between their teams, and using relational and strong communication styles. Their jobs bring a great deal of personal satisfaction, particularly when they can help someone through any kind of personal problem or struggle. Not only do they feel excited and purposeful, but they are helping someone with their problems. If they're able to work in a culturally rich, socially active environment, they'll feel they have a deeply rewarding quality of (work) life, which will energize and motivate them in other areas of their life (home, love, and play). When Type Twos can balance their workplace with others who are highly motivated and focused, they can help support their coworkers; if the Type Two works with others who are more laid back, they themselves need more guidance to divide responsibilities clearly without overburdening themselves.

Criticism is a trigger for the Type Two: they put a lot of heart and effort into their work, and accepting feedback is not their personal strong suit. Because they seek approval from others, when someone criticizes them, they can take it personally. Twos need to acknowledge and work through their negative emotions instead of consistently avoiding them, and the same is just as true at work as it is anywhere else. To resolve conflict with the Type Two in the workplace, it's important to address it clearly and confidently, sharing your perspective, and then inviting them to share. Listen to their opinion, validate it, and help them to feel valued and cared for through the conflict resolution.

To build rapport, give appreciation whenever possible before having to deal with the conflict. Twos are often defensive through repression to maintain their ideal of being "helpful," but can often release their anxiety through verbal processing. To handle the conflict, kindly asking a Two directly to take responsibility for what they want or need instead of making excuses or inadvertently blaming others will get to the heart of the matter, and remind them that others appreciate them for who they are.

In a swiftly moving work environment, addressing a Two with the care they desire can seem complicated, but as a natural empath, Type Twos are the humanitarians, nurses, teachers, counselors, psychologists, nonprofit leaders, nannies . . . their lives are centered around caring for others. Remember, Type Twos are highly motivated by both feeling loved and accepted, but also by being helpful and accomplishing the goals of the community. If their performance is not accomplishing the primary goal, what is the heart of the matter? Feeling overwhelmed by everyone else's jobs they've taken on? Disregarding their own personal needs or space? Feeling ignored or devalued by their peers or colleagues? Or is there a deeper heart issue that's breeding resentment and frustration? Encouraging the Two's empowerment and giving them clear boundaries gives them the freedom to say no to things they need to, but if they feel a sense of rejection or dismissal, the Two will not comply or will feel unaccepted.

Type Twos are much quicker to make decisions for the community than for themselves. Because they are helpers and caretakers, they feel that they know what's best for their groups, and can direct them to what they believe is the best choice. However, they need to remember that they are not the only one responsible for the team; although they are valuable and a good voice of influence and wisdom, each person does know themself more than the Two thinks they know them. Continuing to use a voice of kindness and clear boundaries places a value and appreciation back on the Two, so they can continue to be the best team player.

In Play

Just as much as in the workplace, Type Twos are phenomenal leaders in their friend groups or one-on-one. Considering everyone's needs, desires, and explanations, they listen and offer validation and try to find something to do that suits everyone. Sensitivity and congeniality are two of their personality focuses, and they excel at making many connections. Relationally oriented, they are natural supporters and can bring others' potential out with ease. But because they so desire to be loved, accepted, and approved of by others, their adaptability can be both their strength and their downfall, as they change themselves to make themselves more attractive and lovable to others. Unfortunately, having the approval of others does not substitute for loving themselves as they are.

When communicating or trying to resolve conflict with a Two, it's important to start by expressing appreciation for them and what they do, and encouraging their freedom to set boundaries is one of the best things you can do. Because Twos tend to soak up all the feelings from everyone around them, this can create pressure that can condense and become explosive if they're not careful. It's important for Type Twos to reacquaint themselves with their individuality; it's more important that they can connect and do so without feelings of guilt or repression. Twos need to remain open to conflict and resolution; to show martyrdom in any way, shape, or form is seen by them as manipulation and insincerity. Be gentle when giving feedback of any kind, but if you feel that the Type Two is erring on the unhealthy side, don't be afraid to (tactfully) help them take responsibility for their own feelings. Conflict resolution can seem daunting at first and can be met with overbearing actions on the Two's end, but it's worth pushing past the discomfort to help the Two recognize their intentions.

Type Twos are generous people, and highly emotionally intelligent and sensitive. In my community, there is a very Type Two friend who has done everything from drive across the city of Sydney to deliver a parcel that ended up on the wrong doorstep, to editing things for people, to teaching seniors how to use Facebook over FaceTime for six hours—without anyone asking him to. It was his compulsion to help others, and he felt that if he gave his time, others would eventually accept him for who he was (even though he had already been accepted and was loved). He didn't know his own boundaries and developed increasing resentment due to his inability to say "no," until one of his friends had a conversation with him that released him from his own self-deprecating lack of boundaries.

Giving a Type Two space to recharge and recover in their own time helps them to feel they are in charge of their recovery, while still feeling needed. Twos need friends who remind them of their own boundaries.

Let your Type Two friends know they can be open and honest with you as a safe person; removing their guilt and shame for any "venting" they may do leaves space for an open dialogue, and helps them place themselves first every so often. The fact that Twos focus on others much more than they do themselves can make them feel guilty if they think they're talking about themselves for too long. Taking an active interest in their interests, asking clarifying questions, and practicing active listening encourages them to continue the honest conversation.

Twos need to hear that you are willing to help them with something specific. Don't use the, "Let me know if I can help with anything!" Asking for help may feel embarrassing for a Two, implying that they aren't good enough to do something on their own. Instead, a direct, "I know you're moving next week! I'm cooking you some freezer meals this weekend; what food is your favorite?" will go a long way with a Type Two.

If you're lucky enough to have a Two as a friend, encourage them to pay attention to their own boundaries and needs, and whenever requesting something of them (be it their time, attention, etc.), make sure you let them know that it's okay to say no and that you'll love them anyway. Reassuring a Type Two consistently that they are loved for who they are and not for the goodness they contribute is necessary to their mental well-being and personal liberation. Reminding them to take time out for themselves and that it's okay to need things from others is humanizing, and that allows them to truly be the best they can be for themselves and for the others that they love so well.

Type Three

The Achiever

"If there was a guy who just liked being himself and didn't want to be anybody else, that guy would be the most different guy in the world—and everybody would want to be him."
—Donald Miller

"So, what makes *you* valuable?"

It's the question every employer asks their prospective employee, every self-help book asks its reader, every mirror reflection surprises its onlooker with. Everyone needs validation in their life. It's a universal human trait to desire acceptance, belonging, and affirmation. The little child in us who beams when we are told, "Good job!" never goes away as we grow up. The Type Three exemplifies this need the most. Threes are driven, self-assured, strategic visionaries who dream big and have a foolproof plan of attack to reach their goals. Action and task oriented, motivated, and competitive (with themselves and with others), and known as The Performer and The Achiever, Threes are adaptable to *any* situation. They know how great it feels to develop themselves and others, to contribute to the world and its needs, and they believe in themselves more than any other number, acting as the role model of their group because of their personal charm and extraordinary

Type Three at a Glance

Needs: To feel valued and accepted, adapting to each scenario to achieve success and validation for their goals.

Fear: Unworthiness of love and acceptance based primarily on their failures and successes.

Core Motivation: To be admired, singled out through validation, and affirmed in their actions and the impressions they make on others.

effort to be the best they can be. In their search to be the best and put in the work, they inspire others to invest in themselves and what's important around them. Social status is no different: investment is necessary to achieve it, and achievement of social status contributes to their ideology of success.

Unlike the Sevens or Eights (their near counterparts of the Enneagram), Type Threes don't need encouragement to be motivated to aim for independence or success, but much of their motivation can derive from fear of potential worthlessness that is attached to lack of accomplishment. When thriving in their niche, Type Threes emerge with purpose: luminous, ethereal, energetic. They are bringing home a paycheck; people are applauding their tasks; they are known for having "done it again!" They are useful, performing, fulfilling, achieving, bringing things to life like no one else. But without acknowledgment, they feel as if they've disappeared, or that they are "nobody."

And Type Threes were not born to be nobody.

The thing is, success looks different according to each family background. I often joke that if you were born in the United States, being a Type Three is pretty much built into your DNA. Being somebody in *your* family would look different than being somebody in *my* family. My friend Lexa is a professional photographer who thrives in her career and calling. She loves to tell stories through images. It killed her for years when her parents suggested she go to school for a different, more financially stable career; it wasn't until her father realized how much money she made photographing a weekend wedding that he deemed her successful in her career and was reportedly "proud" of her achievements. To Lexa's dad, as long as she was bringing home a steady paycheck, she was successful. Whether the steady paycheck was brought in by being a writer, a photographer, a lawyer, or a professor was meaningless. However, in another family, success could come through fame as a professional actor, or through power being a CEO of a company. To be seen and become noteworthy, whether in the eyes of their family or their social circle or the world, is a Type Three's own personal, everyday achievement. Because of this, cultivating what is attractive is what adds to the Type Three as a performer.

With adaptability being the key, Type Threes learn to live up to whatever standards are set, swapping masks based on the situation, playing the crowd to give them what they want to see ... sometimes even to the extent that the Three will lose their own focal point, feelings, and heart song. This makes Threes attractive to others because they can be all things to all people, and do all things relatively well, even if they don't necessarily want to; they can become codependent on the attention and rewards from others. This is what makes the actors, singers, and sports stars of the world good performers: think Taylor Swift, Brooke Shields, Tom Cruise, Lady Gaga, Whitney Houston, Sting, Elvis Presley, Paul McCartney, Tiger Woods, Oprah Winfrey. They sink their teeth into the character because they have spent their lives waiting for this moment to perform. It is far easier to play the character that people want to see, or the character that they are paid to play, rather than to play or be themselves.

Type Threes are their own star. They are gracious, fully accomplished, and when healthy, they can influence and do incredible things. They are enthusiastic in their behavior, adjusting their roles and expressions to fit the moment, and able to adapt to their environment while reading the room with ease. They have an almost innate desire to be the hero in not only their own story, but in everyone else's story as well.

Obviously, again, there is something in all of us that wants to be noticed and recognized and seen. The difference is, most people don't feel unloved or undesirable if we don't meet all the expectations of a "doer." Meryl Streep plays a near caricature of an unhealthy Three, Miranda Priestly, in the iconic movie *The Devil Wears Prada*. She is the epitome of a workaholic, fashionista editor-in-chief with higher than high standards that she not only sets for herself, but for everyone within her reach. As the film rolls, it's clear that she is focused more on her image and presentation, and being the best . . . but struggles constantly with her personal relationships and goes through a series of divorces. However, we only ever see her internal and familiar warfare in a couple of different scenes, because throughout the film there is a continuous thread of disvalue: To Miranda, people are nothing outside of what they accomplish.

It's not that Type Threes have difficulty with all feelings. As the center of the feelings triad, they are really good at positive feelings, great with releasing and communicating their anger or frustration, but struggle deeply with vulnerability and sadness. Because they are far more task oriented, when a Type Three attempts to relate to someone expressing vulnerability or sadness, they can be seen as lacking empathy. This can show up as a mindset of, "don't waste this space or time," and can even carry over into a lack of empathy toward themselves and their own feelings. Understanding that others can and do care about and respect them even if they feel bad and are not 100 percent switched on to the task at hand is necessary to develop from not only a motivational Type Three human, but an empathetic and emotionally healthy human. To feel deeply is to be a human, not a workaholic machine—and high sensitivity is not a liability, it's a gift.

Type Threes are hyperaware of how they are perceived by others, to the point that they may not be truly aware of how much this shapes and forms who they are, sometimes confusing their own goals and aspirations with what others would expect for them and want them to be doing. In the untraditional sense, Type Threes would choose productivity and achievement as their suit-and-tie, and voluntarily jump on the treadmill/hamster wheel/rat race that never ends. If something needs to be done, the Type Three is the one to do it. Whether it's doing it for their image or because something else in their life feels like it's falling apart, you can't argue with the one who has already accomplished so much.

Type Threes want to succeed. They want to go do something. They are amazing cheerleaders for their friends as they join them on the journey, people love to be around them, and they are extremely efficient in their thinking skills. They are the consultants, the marketers, the entrepreneurs, the coaches, the politicians—and of course, the actors. Creating new goals means creating a new form of energy; meeting new people means meeting new investments. Learning to take time to pause and reflect in the midst of a drawn out, busy day to connect with oneself and with others is where empathy and appreciation starts, and doing this creates a much more loving, lovable, and faithful individual. Developing social awareness beyond the task at hand and toward goals that are outside of personal interest and availability is where many Type Threes can find their true value and reconnect with who they are, not *only* what they do.

Core Motivation: "I Can Do It Better"

"So, what do you want to do?" When I was fourteen or fifteen, the cliché questions from relatives and family friends started coming. Being fourteen, I was slightly taken aback. *Did they mean for dinner? Ohhh, for life. Okay.*

"I want to study English and acting."

"But what do you want to be?"

My response, "A good person?" was probably cheekier than originally intended (but was smart enough that my mum has never forgotten to remind me of it).

However, I was raised in an entrepreneurial-minded family, in which my parents did their jobs for years, and then changed their careers and started a new business just like that—multiple times over. It was only natural to have never felt it necessary to lock into a career, and knowing what one thing I wanted to do for the rest of my life when I didn't even know how to operate a car put pressure on my mind that previously didn't exist. I knew what things I wanted to do. I had a goal list (as a Type Nine, my growth zone is Type Three); I had completed all high school work by the time I was sixteen years old, was a natural performer, and had already begun my teaching business two years earlier. Having someone ask what I wanted to be, like it was my identity, felt insulting to everything I had "done" already, as if it didn't matter.

When children are very young and people ask, "What do you want to be when you grow up?" they might respond, "a pirate!" or "an astronaut!" or "an actress!" or "a mummy!" Adults might say things like, "Oh, she's such a ball of energy! She'll be famous!" Or, to a child learning fine motor skills playing with building blocks or puzzles, "Oh, he's so analytical! Future architect right there!" To a child who is pitching their third tantrum of the day they might say, "What a sensitive one." Even as children, what we do and how we work is commented upon and becomes an extension of our personalities.

Children also often live for attention from adults, vying to gain approval or catch a glimpse of a secret smile from someone in the room (whether that's through a tantrum to gain attention, or a run around a café, or starting a conversation with a gentleman in line at the store). As the comedian Steve Martin advised when asked how he has been so successful in his career, "Be so good they can't ignore you."

Figuring out who you are when you're in places where you don't shine is necessary, but especially to all Type Threes stepping out of their existential purpose to focus on their internal *why*. I'm a firm believer that work was created to be good and purposeful. Based on the subtype of the Type Three, there is an internal self-competition coupled with an external competition of *doing*. When Threes are healthy, they are highly capable, adaptable, and easygoing. The career need in the Type Three world is recognition and approval in the task. But *why* would they pursue X, Y, Z without purpose? For example, I once lived with two Type Three girls, both on different bents. The first saw the Type Three manifest in her career goals: her highest motivation and competition was with *herself*. In her view, it was up to her own stamina and achievement to climb the corporate ladder. It wasn't for show (she rarely talked about her job), but for her own internal confidence to prove that she was capable. If the job had no advancement available, she didn't give it a second glance. The second girl saw her Type Three manifest in achievement and competition with others; she walked into a room, and people knew it because of her magnetic and powerful presence and stance. In her view, her success was driven by outward appearance and what she did to contribute to her external image. There isn't anything wrong with either approach; they simply give a good view of how different Type Threes can be based on their personal why and purpose (and this traces back to our instinctual subtypes and how they come into play as well).

With an assertive stance that moves against the flow to get the task complete, Type Threes move toward their goals, sometimes struggling to respect the boundaries of others.

The utmost goal of the high-capacity Type Three is to be remembered for their discoveries, contributions, creations, ambitions—to be the best in their field. Being success-driven, they don't want to just succeed *themselves*, they want to inspire and help motivate others to succeed as well. They are charismatic and know how to easily connect with other people's needs through their natural charm, innate understanding of expectations placed on them, and ability to adapt to multiple social environments.

Going back to the example of children from earlier—the personality type more than likely developed and learned early on that "achievement" (whether building an original block tower masterpiece or learning how to read) resulted in verbal approval, love, and was considered "success," so it was likely that their identity was established from attention and continuously projected from there. There was a favor of the ego opposed to their true selves, rejecting their core. The seven-year-old beauty/ drama queen I couldn't stand when I was a child often started conversations on the playground with, "This many boys like me this week. How many boys like *you*?" I often ended up falling out of trees and playing with her little brother instead, but there was a tug on my heart every so often when I looked over to her surrounded by a little circle of admirers. This memory followed our friendship through the years as we competed in speech and debate, acting, and for who could get the highest grades. It wasn't a learned behavior; her actions as a child stemmed from a projected image of herself as she learned to repress her internal feelings. Though we were tiny people when we met each other, and were friends for the next fifteen years, I would also say that we never actually *knew* each other.

My friend Elissa once ran a young adults' small group, in which a few girls gathered each week to chat about life. Elissa (a Type Three) was struggling particularly with one of the girls, a Type Seven Enthusiast named Skye, who was having a hard time differentiating what she believed in and matching what others expected from her with what her values were. Elissa felt it was her duty to motivate and inspire our Enthusiast friend, but didn't know how to go about it without causing conflict. She didn't understand why Skye would connect with me outside of the small group when we were only coworkers. When she brought this up with me and we verbally processed it, we recognized that Elissa was looking at Skye like a problem to fix or a goal to achieve, not necessarily a person simply to listen to and love. Once Elissa worked on genuine connection and understanding herself and Skye's point of view—as opposed to taking a leadership and motivational stance—Skye was much more open to listening to her thoughts. As a result, she connected in return. Their opposing perspectives on multiple topics brought up some incredible dialogue and conversation as they invested in each other.

In her book *Daring Greatly*, Brené Brown defines the difference between connection and belonging according to her research data. She remarks on connection as the energy that is created between people when they feel seen, heard, and valued; when they can give and receive without judgment. She says that belonging is "the innate human desire to be part of something larger than us," and that "we often try to acquire [this feeling] by fitting in and seeking approval, which are not only hollow substitutes for belonging, but often barriers to it." She goes on to explain that our sense of belonging is never greater than our own level of self-acceptance. What is the passion behind the purposeful doing? Who are you behind what you do?

The core motivation of a Type Three is a deep longing for acceptance of who they are, by a need for admiration and for making a good impression on others. Their deepest fear is that they will be unworthy of love and acceptance; projection of certain characteristics that people find attractive is therefore a natural place to progress to in order to "earn their place." The thing is, Type Threes are incredibly strong people that thrive in their leadership, self-control, and encouragement. Using their natural strengths of presence and innate leadership—instead of using all the strengths that they believe others expect from them—is evidence that their mere presence changes the dynamic of the room. So how do Type Threes switch into the mode of empowered thinking? Having a solid boundary line and living by their own code of values is a strong asset to knowing who they are and ensuring that their actions match.

Type Three Wings and Levels of Health

It's almost too easy to overstress your body: coffee, calories, sixteen-hour days in the office (and then out of the office), working out to the point of exhaustion, excessive self-improvement (yes, it's possible), and adapting to multiple habits and scenarios to prove oneself. Even though the last item is more mental than physical, it is particularly relevant for Type Threes. Like the Type One perfectionist, Type Threes are very concerned with doing their jobs well, and are consistently driven to achieve their goals. However, there is much less of a "do it right" and "be perceived as perfect" motivation; the Type Three *will* cut a corner here and there if it doesn't affect their team or the outcome, and they still look good. That kind of attitude would drive a Type One insane! When a Type Three exposes their vulnerable places, they find their weak points touch a nerve of unworthiness that they would much rather make up for by *doing*, because at least in *doing*, one can forget about any shame connected with being unworthiness and weakness that are exposed by "just being."

Having boundaries, such as strict office hours, can be a turning point in the Type Three life. Asking, "What are [my] unmet needs contributing to this image-focused desire?" is a question that can only be thought through and answered during non-working hours. On a flight, when the flight attendants go through the "in case of emergency" step by step, they emphasize putting your own mask on before helping others. Allowing for space to actively learn how to connect with oneself brings deep and sincere connection to thrive with others who, before this point, may have only respected and looked up to the Type Three—not necessarily connected with them. Now think of this in context of a Type Three, who is incredibly capable of carrying around multiple "masks" for different situations, and is a professional at swapping them in and out. When a mask is utilized carefully and wielded wisely, the Type Three shows their true vulnerability and personality. This not only deepens levels of empathy and E.Q., it also contributes greatly to the task at hand, because people attach to their leader and the task, not the task alone.

In *Developing the Leader Within You*, John C. Maxwell aptly states, "Leaders become great not because of their power, but because of their ability to empower others." While motivating others is a consistent driving force and influence credited to the Type Three, equally as important is ensuring that they are empowering their team, believing in them more than the team members believe in themselves. When the Type Three is so focused on the task, it's easy to lose the heart of team dynamics.

Type Threes are central, or the anchor point, to the "feeling" or heart triad. Therefore, it only follows that their wings are called The Charmer (3w2) or The Professional (3w4). They *love* being everyone's inspiration and leading the pack—and they're *good* at it. That being said, Type Threes swing and tap into their Wings Four and Two, but it can be difficult to switch into other mental or instinctive gears because both of their wings remain in the feelings triad. This often results in their feeling a bit more or less cut off from the center of intelligence, affecting how they experience shame. A *very* unhealthy Type Three, for example, would lack all shame, prefer to put the figurative mask on, and would quit caring about how genuine they are so they can accomplish the task and still appear to be "the best."

The Charmers (3w2) are highly sociable people, with a tendency to play their ideal persona in real life. You know influencers who say things like, "Live the life you've always imagined"? That's a hardcore Charmer thing to say! They gravitate toward others who have a social image. When healthy, The Charmers have a beautifully enchanting warmth, and their strong leadership qualities make them a naturally easy person to follow and listen to; if they achieve some measure of success they are happy to share and mentor others (even if they aren't necessarily professionals in the area), because they generally have a sincere desire to help and do well by others (Wing Two). Their motivation of others is less than their own self-motivation. However, The Achiever is also known as *the Performer* for a reason—they *may* be genuine, but in certain circumstances, they may not.

Type Threes are often mistyped by others as Type Ones, until they dig into the Three's core values. While Type Ones need to be perceived as perfect, Type Three's prefer to be perceived, full stop. Where Type Ones are motivated by the fear of messing up, Type Threes are motivated by the fear of failing and thus being seen as incompetent. This plays into their relationships, because they want to be seen as the *perfect* spouse, parent, friend, employee, child, sibling—and the list goes on. When unhealthy, the Three Wing Two is preoccupied with seeming ideal to those around them, without care to whether or not they are falsifying feelings and relationships, and there is a social focus in that they *need* validation from others. They can become boastful and egotistical, jealous, and overly competitive, and may try to impersonate others that they admire. This could be something as indirect as picking up someone's revelation and applying it to themselves to pass along to others; or as complex as trying to imitate to the point where they lose their own emotional self-recognition.

On the other hand, the Three Wing Four, The Professional, is slightly less image conscious and will try to project an image based on subtle simplicity, because the Wing Four brings a much less bubbly side to the table than the Wing Two. Their measurement of success is their social or artistic creations, and they compete more with themselves than with other people, contributing to their own healthy self-motivation. Here, they conquer everything they set out to do with their still-competitive side, but then slink into a self-analysis to understand *why* they do what they do. They still enjoy a challenge and competition, but are deeply thoughtful, intuitive, and much less concerned with winning or being the best in the room.

On the unhealthy side of this wing, they are more self-tormented by what *could* have been, slipping into a pretentious jealousy toward those who seemingly have accomplished what they have not. They may come across as snobby and unconcerned, but personally they can often feel more accusative of anyone who is overly direct or honest by being too familial to appreciate their point of view. Eventually, without the pressure of people around, the Wing Four emerges with a melodramatic moodiness, self-questioning, and personal aspirations.

A real estate agent and acquaintance of mine, Levi, was a strong 3w4 Professional—thoroughly task oriented, especially in terms of his clients. Any emotion and anxiety he had toward the client–seller relationship he would bottle into doing a task, even if that task wasn't necessarily helpful. He recalled a time he was working with a retired couple in Los Angeles, and before they signed the papers they wanted to have a glass of champagne with him to celebrate. Up to this point, he had seen them as a goal to be achieved (they buy the house = he pays his rent); but when they wanted to get to know him, he cried. Even though *they* had seen him past his work for them, he hadn't been honest or truthful with himself about what was going on internally. Following this experience, he made a point of truly connecting with his clients and finding the best home *for them*, not necessarily just selling them the best house.

Upon his discovery of the Enneagram and his journey into identifying with Type Three, he remembered this experience and tapped into finding the emotions behind his actions. His bag of emotions that was once contained or channeled into an immovable machine settled into a good place where he can recognize his feelings and understand where the pressure is building. He remains a professional, but also knows how to swing into his Wing Two Charmer, staying centered neither by his doings, nor by his feelings, but by his acknowledgment that both are natural, and he doesn't need to feel shame for one or the other.

Stress and Security

Being in the heart center, where feelings reign as the wisdom zone, Type Threes cross over into shame on a fairly consistent basis. Just as we covered in Type One's overview of guilt versus shame, Type Three constantly struggles with shame's, "I am wrong" as opposed to guilt's, "I did wrong." Shame is a painful experience, and without proper harnessing it can become toxic. Shame is based solely on the belief that we are flawed and therefore will never fall into the category of good enough. This is where the Type Three's deeply innate desire for acceptance enacted through their actions makes complete sense. Shame is attached to suppressing of emotions that stem from something that's quite easy to unravel in the first place, but is stuffed to ensure acceptance. So what triggers this?

Unhealthy Threes—like my friend Levi once was—often verbalize that they feel resentment when they realize that they are "just" hollow shells after building up a projected image over many years. While there's external admiration for a time, there's almost no longevity to the image. For example, think of the many child stars who were expected to live up to a certain image for many years. At some point or other, most of them had to deal with their own projected image versus their vulnerable personalities and decide if it was worth it to continue as is, or instead to run their own course. While there's plenty of "making it," there's just as much "faking it," which leads to an uncertainty about whether they've actually done something that is worthwhile or praiseworthy. Referencing the Enneagram diagram arrows in stressful situations, the Type Three arrow points toward the Type Nine (The Peacemaker). Disintegration for them means quick disengagement and lack of concern for people and situations around them. In growth or security, the Type Three arrow is pointed toward the Type Six (The Loyalist), and Type Threes shed their masks and self-absorption to become more committed to others and the cause—two opposite ends of the spectrum that contribute to the same things.

In security and growth, Type Threes take on all the healthy attributes of Type Six. They acknowledge and begin to understand that their life values don't lie solely in their public image or what they've done and contributed to society; in fact, they become more committed to being themselves instead of what they believe others want them to be. This brings about the healthy side of The Loyalist, where they are committed to connecting with others, enthusiastic and enacting their natural communication skills even more effectively. They become more committed to family and friends, valuing what's best for the team, and learn to value and incorporate vulnerability; sharing the spotlight becomes easier, and this opens up their emotional health to a different degree. However, they can still take on the paralysis of decision-making based on people's opinions, borrowing from Type Six.

In stress or disintegration, Type Threes that borrow from Type Nine borrow all the unhealthy, apathetic sides of a Type Nine—losing touch with or bringing on all the noise to avoid their own feelings, strengthening the walls around them to keep from being perceived as overly sensitive. While they do remember to slow down and peacefully process and receive what's occurring around them, they also begin to procrastinate, encounter paralysis in decision-making due to their confusion, become passive–aggressive, and may even drift further into self-neglect by setting even higher goals or feeding an already-addictive personality. Instead of remaining focused on getting important things done, they take on random tasks that don't contribute much at all. They lack passion, they are drawn to busywork to avoid thinking about anything, and become much more laid back and numb to it all.

When sensing the descent into disintegration triggered by disconnection or lack of passion, Type Threes need to step back, take some time to recharge, and let go of their own expectations of themselves. Caring about accomplishment of goals and being efficient is an important aspect of life, but it can add a lot of weight to the burdens they carry. Learning what the point of disintegration is allows for an easier comeback from that disintegration, and they need to develop an understanding of what a break would look like, whether that's a mental health day or a weekend getaway, or the simple step of creating office hours.

In his book *A Million Miles in a Thousand Years*, Type Three Donald Miller writes, "If you watched a movie about a guy who wanted a Volvo and worked for years to get it, you wouldn't cry at the end. . . . But we spend years actually living those stories, and expect our lives to be meaningful. The truth is, if what we choose to do with our lives won't make a story meaningful, it won't make a life meaningful either."

Type Three: your worth is not attached to what you accomplish. There is acceptance despite a failure. At your best, you are authentic, self- and other-accepting, empathetic, and committed to others and the cause just as much as you are committed to learning about yourself without the mask, without the ego. Allow others to be kind to you, and share the workload. If we establish that passion without purpose is "dead," what do we end up with? Don't be the one who chases the car and the prestige that comes with it but only lasts for a little while. A life is so much more meaningful if we choose to look past the accomplishments, past the trophies and the relationships that appear to be perfect. What kind of story do you want to tell with your life? What kind of legacy will you leave behind? Leaving a lasting impression and influence on others starts in the everyday experience of choosing to be vulnerable with yourself, and then honestly, carefully, letting others in, one at a time.

Life with a Type Three: Daring and Motivated

Type Threes are driven by the desire to stand out in a crowd, living above and beyond others' expectations. At approximately 10.5 percent of the population, Type Three achievers are heart- and feelings-based, and built to get things done, accomplishing their goals and taking initiative like a boss (and they probably are a literal boss). They aim to excel past the status quo, and they absolutely love being acknowledged as the person that gets everything done. Unlike the Type One perfectionist, they don't care how perfectly they accomplish the task at hand, just as long as they and their team look great doing it.

When communicating with a Type Three, be direct and tactful, and don't leave room for misunderstanding. As the motivational speaker of their friend groups, Threes thrive in a relationship built on enthusiasm and goals, shared dreams, shared objectives. They will be the person in the group who believes in everyone else more than the group members believe in themselves. Threes have high social awareness and emotional intelligence. They love to help others, and with a strong Wing Two (Helper), they are excellent mentors. Backed up with their achieving mindset, they can find fulfillment when working for a higher cause.

A lot of the Type Threes' conflicts stem from being misunderstood. For example, Type Threes seem to change personalities depending on the day, time, situation; for some it may appear that they are fake and inconsistent. They see it as being adaptable and doing what's necessary (people pleasing = approval; adaptability = goal achievement). When they refuse to be transparent, to some it may appear they are being false and dishonest; to them, they haven't figured the situation out completely and want to avoid the pressure-cooker heat to their image, or they don't feel ready to trust the other person quite yet. Their strength and resilience are the things that makes them inspiring, but half the time, they feel as if they're not doing enough. Highly concerned with improvement and growth, they need to hear that they are loved outside of what they do, and they need to be reminded to slow down. Hurry is their default mode! As natural leaders, they can be prone to take off running immediately for a good cause, and the risk is usually what makes the reward greater. This is why they spend time strategizing, but their adaptability is their immediate strategy.

Active and on the go, Type Threes are hard to slow down. However, their driving focus can be on receiving praise (vanity) for accomplishing so much, and in so doing, they can lose themselves as they perform for the crowd. Deciding for themselves what they want is important—but it is so hard to speak to their inner child once they've fed the addiction of doing to avoid listening to what they truly need. If you can commit to being someone in a Type Three's life who will encourage them toward introspection, place value on them as a person because of who they are, and assure them, then you are contributing to their overall well-being and sense of humanity and worth.

At Home

Type Three children are born to win. Driven by the need for achievement, it's as if they're wired from an early age to think that what they *do* equals approval, which equals being worthy of love and acceptance. With siblings, they can compete for the spotlight to gain their parents' affection as if it's their security—and in their mind, it may as well be.

As a natural leader, the Threes feel it is their *responsibility* (and their right) to be the best; they'll pull whatever tricks necessary to impress their friends and family, and keep them coming back as a member of their personal fan club. Depending on their levels of security and maturity, Three children can be friendly, enthusiastic, and appear to be loving life, *or* they can be arrogant and overly competitive.

Threes have an innate fear of being vulnerable, and if their family is built of "winners," they can feel shame about perceived incompetence or uncertainty. Are they truly valued for who they are? Or are they valued for what they *do*? Creating a place where honesty is a character trait to be admired and expectations are guidelines and not the end-all-be-all will encourage vulnerability and allow a Three to take pride in who they are. "I'm so proud to be your mum!" takes the focus off of them doing and on to them *being*—especially if they did their best, but their best wasn't counted as the "winner." Some Threes place others' expectations for action on themselves so quickly that they can self-sabotage in their efforts to be the fastest, best, or most accomplished. Teaching them to listen to their instincts and creating a safe place to ask questions and chat through their day helps Type Three children tap into their stretch point as a Type Nine, where they can take their time and listen carefully to the world around them.

Type Three parents are goal oriented personally, and it makes absolute sense that they would pass along this character trait to their children. Success and winning is *important*! It's exciting! It makes them feel full of life, and yes, it's challenging. Success to the Type Three parents may look like sending their children to extra tennis practices and classes to fuel their college scholarship, to piano lessons to help with their coordination and SAT scores, to tutoring to help them receive straight As . . . and as naturally self-motivated and hard workers, Type Three parents expect their children to live up to their expectations. I used to nanny three children whose parents woke them up every morning about 6 a.m., so they could go over the family affirmations and motto, and make sure they all worked out together (weights and all) before school started. While this was admirable, one of the children was often openly resentful about being caught up in this expectation—for him it had not become a place of safety. Some mornings he'd rather have had a snuggle than have to go for a swim.

The Type Three parental emphasis is on the belief that with hard work, *everything* (and anything) is possible. Because Type Threes are already high-capacity people, parenting will look no different for them: it's an all-or-nothing relationship with their children. A Three parent has a natural skill set of encouragement of and dependability for their children. Keeping it tangible with sticker charts and a goal system immerses their children in an early-life experience that, in turn, manifests in their habits. Some children will thrive on the same goal orientation and being told they are the best. Some children will constantly berate themselves for feeling that they are simply not living up to the expectations of the Type Three parent. Making sure the home is a space for fun as well as competition, and where honesty and authenticity are just as celebrated as a first-prize medal, will keep the expectations realistic and allow children to slow down and breathe in the present moment.

In Love

The energetic, charismatic Threes are attractive people, and they know it—bringing their spirit into their relationships is a natural part of what they do. While part of this stems from having a goal of being the "best" partner, the other part stems from wanting intimacy and vulnerability. Because they are committed and reliable, their relationships are serious, although they are not the most emotional, being more focused on acts of service to please their partner because they care about how their partner views and perceives them.

Type Threes want to *dream* with their partner as a way of connecting with them. Chances are, they have already dreamed *about* them, and the romantic side of them is excited that they can finally do the real thing together. When they share their feelings, it's imperative to be gentle and reassuring; Threes don't open up to anyone readily, and when they open up to their partner they are making an effort to practice vulnerability, however hard it may be. If you're trustworthy, genuine, and put emphasis on being interested in who they are as a person, not only what they do, you will be their confidante and a place of security for them.

It's often difficult for a Type Three to believe or adjust their mindset to recognize that when someone loves them well, they don't have to perform or achieve or earn the other's love, and they'll need reminders of this. Healthy Threes need to have a partner who is somewhat independent. While comfortable with vulnerability and intimacy, they appreciate their alone time working on projects and get irritated when they are interrupted with other people's relatively insignificant problems and emotions. They can get even more frustrated when their partner gets in the way of their efficiency. Showing the Type Three love means giving them the adequate freedom to get their jobs done and fulfill their responsibilities so they then feel they have the personal freedom to play.

Because they value image and status, Threes can take on stress in the relationship in regard to losing their street credit and value—unhealthy Threes in particular are more concerned that their flaws will show their vulnerability. The primary fear of a Type Three in a relationship is being humiliated and left because they weren't enough, and they tend to avoid partners who have a lack of vision, are inefficient or incompetent, overtly critical, and negative. They know that their temper doesn't need *any* of that in their lives, and they act accordingly when it comes to allowing people to get close to them. Type Three Kayla walks into a room ready to turn on the charm and flirt—and she does well at this—but she doesn't care about the many interactions that might occur from it, and may "feel bad" for the guy she had a long conversation with that evening when he misinterprets their interaction and reaches out later. She had no intention of pursuing or being pursued by any of the men she talked to, but a lot of her value and worth comes from having a string of admirers and being able to turn heads—that comes from her focus on an image. She believes in being pursued, but even when she is, she doesn't want to completely commit because she feels that she is worthy of more.

On the flip side, when a Type Three *is* interested in someone, they aren't afraid of being direct about their intentions—they won't tiptoe around the topic, and they are often seen as intense and aggressive if they're not careful. Type Three Mark is on the go and wrapped up in his own business. An attractive man, he always has girls around him, but he remains uninterested and stays in his lane. But when he sees the girl he likes, he's already decided that if things go well, he'll marry her.

As conflict arises when the Type Three doesn't place importance on their emotions, they can feel overwhelmed and strained in their relationships, living up to an imaginary standard that they have set for themselves. When in a relationship with a Type Three, it's extremely important to encourage them to tune into their emotions. Inner conflict specifically surfaces when they are figuring out whether they're capable and choose to speak their own opinions and values, or live out the truth of those around them—the government, the culture, other people.

What a Type Three really needs to hear from their loved ones is that they have the freedom to be courageously authentic. They need to know and trust that their partner is unconditionally going to love them both because of and despite their weaknesses, while still admiring their many strengths. They desire someone they can connect with emotionally and mentally, and someone strong enough to hold their own, with their own ambition and goals. When a Type Three learns how to speak their own truth in a healthy, well-thought-through, simple way—not to gain attention or to force it on anyone—they become even more attractive as a leader and as an individual.

In Work

One of the Type Three's natural gifts is helping others identify their strengths and encourage their true potential. However, without any incentive, Threes can become aversive and neglectful of people around them when they don't associate them with goals or projects. When Threes work in a job in which they have an opportunity to "climb a ladder" with new opportunities, responsibility, and placements, they feel energized and motivated. When their colleagues and peers admire their work and listen well to their feedback, and when they are developing relationships with new clients or new people, they are in their element. Their drive to success, natural charisma and self-confidence, and practical thought process make them an ideal workplace candidate, and when they find a job they love, they excel.

Type Threes can be a bit tunneled in their vision when it comes to achieving above and beyond their goal. When it comes to the workplace, they are natural leaders, want to be well perceived, and want to perform all kinds of roles. Threes are leaders, motivators, mentors, public speakers, lawyers, politicians, entrepreneurs, marketers. It's no wonder that Threes are performers and some become celebrities: Beyoncé, Justin Bieber, Oprah Winfrey. They want to stick out from the crowd, have the charm of Wing Two and the artistry of the Wing Four, and are bound and determined to be the best at what they do. "You say run, I'll ask, 'how fast?'" is a common mantra of a Type Three musician friend of mine.

Competitive, energetic, efficient, motivating to their team, optimistic, and *efficient*, they thrive on getting results. Ticking the boxes on a list is a high for a Type Three—but it's a common mechanism that keeps them busy so they don't have to feel things that they don't want to feel. With their tendency toward making action-oriented decisions, they can eliminate any kind of wall, and with their keen eye and adaptability, they can change direction when necessary. However, they can sometimes lose perspective, and in their quick movements they can often make uninformed decisions.

My friend Lillian often bemoans that she could have had different opportunities if she had only taken a job or internship at a bigger company that originally offered her a job, rather than taking a job at a smaller company because at the smaller company she felt more well-liked and had more prestige right out of the gate. Although the company served her well and she accomplished her personal purposes there, Lillian was constantly comparing the prestige of the larger company to her growth and relationships at the smaller company. She knew that she made the best choice for her—but mentally the struggle continued for several years as she watched other friends get offered jobs at the larger company. Unfortunately, this is a constant frustration of the Type Three: because they are more image oriented, their fast decisions aren't necessarily best in the long run, but rather only serve the short-term goal at hand. While some prefer to compete with themselves and colleagues to climb the corporate ladder, others prefer immediate gratification and the accolades that come with it. Then, when they take time to look back and reflect on their true emotions, they realize the "mistake" and feel as if they missed out on what *could have been* (whether or not that "could have been" is obvious).

In healthy conflict, the Type Three will slow down and listen; in unhealthy conflict, the Three may become angry and impatient at their opponent's slower pace, believing that the opponent is the reason they're not meeting goals and achieving their usual success. Resolving conflict with a Type Three requires knowing *exactly* what you're going to say, and allowing for tension and aggression as you flow through a longer conversation while maintaining company or business goals. The Three needs to feel that they have the opportunity to "save face" while still taking responsibility. They need to be reminded that *people are important* and can help their growth at the company. Starting with acknowledgment of their work and what they have done thus far is what the Three *wants* to hear; following it up with affirmations of their value as a human being is what they *need* to hear. Catching them at a time when they don't have a hundred things on hand is an ideal situation, but because that's not a likely scenario with a Type Three, starting with feedback on the original company goals will help them to stop and listen.

If failure of any kind seems imminent, Type Threes, who put entire baskets of eggs into results, can build up a lot of tension. In the face of failure, they'll become insensitive, unlikable, and phony in appearance and tone. Under their tension, there is a deep layer of hollow melancholy that comes from loss of contact with their inner child and self. Because of their heavily image-centered way of life, their main psychological defense when they sense failure is to fall back on their identification to maintain "success" for themselves. When they are pushed to develop authenticity, it's a challenge for them, but their work ethic comes into play as they navigate skills of delegation and teamwork and they recognize that they don't have to do it all. And when Threes are honest with themselves, they become much more honest and approachable to their colleagues and those around them: their natural leadership characteristics bring out the *true* leader within them.

In Play

As the visionary of a friend group, Type Threes help bring to life every goal you could hope to achieve. Their energy and zest for life, and their on-the-go strategy and thought process makes them magnetic and attractive to others. Motivating others to achieve their full potential helps the Type Three feel successful, and their bright optimism helps lift others up. Threes were the popular kid in school, and they are more than likely still that popular friend in your social circle—the social butterfly who is the influential, persuasive, charismatic instigator of most (if not all) of the activities and game nights.

Threes are future oriented, working well in the present to get where they believe they (and everyone else) need to go. When healthy, they are responsible, open to feedback, inspiring, and empowering. When unhealthy, they are pretentious, self-absorbed, opportunistic, and vain. If they don't feel like you're with them for the long run, they can convince themselves that they have outgrown you.

When communicating with a Type Three, acknowledging their high levels of success while being sensitive to their feelings makes space for an open and honest dialogue. If, however, they aren't open to discussing feelings in the moment, it's important that you don't push past the opening, "How are you?" It's enough for them that you took an interest in their feelings; but it could be perceived as too much if you poke and prod, and that only makes them want to run away from you. Threes prefer to stay busy, and if you're keeping them from something at the forefront of their mind, you have to realize it's not you they're upset with if they express annoyance.

Resolving conflict and giving feedback needs to be done with consideration; as an overachiever, failures come with hurt pride for a Three. When you are trustworthy, they know innately they can talk with you about anything. Being genuine makes them believe that they can be genuine in return. Join them in their activity, and while you are doing something (this is very important), have those conversations that encourage them to tell the truth about themselves. Ask about their sensitivities, and listen. Threes are generally open to feedback because it can help lead to improvement, but if the feedback feels unjust or is about something outside of their control, critique can be detrimental.

Type Threes are in the middle of the feelings center, regulating emotion as their primary energy. Because Type Threes are generally image-focused, it may seem backward or completely wrong, but it's important to remember that their constant activity stems from deep within, in their hope for acceptance and love. They do because they want to be loved. Threes are rooted in shame because they believe that without their list of goals and accomplishments they remain unworthy of approval.

Threes need to hear from you that they are valuable, period. Encourage them to slow down every so often, and help them when you observe that they need it—and maybe even a little before they need it. Like a Type Two, Threes will rarely ask for help, because they are afraid doing so will ruin your view of them. When they can feel their own emotions and recognize why they do what they do, they are able to become vulnerable with themselves and connect more deeply to their personal meaning instead of running around in circles on a hamster wheel, being watched through the window. If they can do that, Threes are able to be kind to themselves and connect to those around them more deeply.

Type Four

The Individualist

"Once we recognize what it is that we are feeling, once we recognize we can feel deeply, love deeply, can feel joy, then we will demand that all parts of our lives produce that kind of joy."
—*Audre Lorde*

My friend Monica was once hoping to find the perfect coffee shop—one that was not on social media, that no one we knew had gone to, and that sold *good* coffee. She also wanted the shop to have a good atmosphere—slightly dark and moody. Finally, she wanted it to be within ten minutes' walking distance from our classroom. If any one of these rules was not met, she'd rather pass on the coffee altogether.

Monica is a solid Type Four, and she actually had a massive breakdown when we first explored possible Enneagram outcomes because she realized she actually matched with a type . . . and Monica was *not* a "type" to be matched with anything. Having a type was nearly insulting to her—and once she acknowledged there were indeed other people in the world who were more or less like her, a wave of emotions ensued. This revelation was both a relief and a distress to her.

Type Four at a Glance

Needs: To create a meaningful life and identity through the journey of searching and finding themselves.

Fear: Lack of identity and significance in the world.

Core Motivation: To express their individuality, to create beautiful things (whether an idea or something tangible), maintain and understand their emotions, and to be worthy of attracting a rescuer or savior.

No one wants to be put in a box, and maybe that's why I love the Enneagram so much. In its diversity with the numerical identification process, you are not confined to one number, one type, one "predictable" brain or framework of mind. For Type Fours, this is reassuring, because it is a driving force and strong motivation for them to be "unlike" anyone else, most authentic to themselves and individuality . . . and they are *dedicated* individualists. They navigate life through the beautifully dark fog of emotions, nostalgia, and preservation of the past translating into modern life. Sensitive, introspective, and melancholic, Type Fours, known as The Romantic, or The Artist, or The Individual, have a creative flair—and all creatives *want* to be the Type Four. From Edgar Allan Poe's dark and morbid poetry (*"Nevermore!"*), to Frida Kahlo's out-of-the-box artistic creations with a message, to Amy Winehouse's deep, expressive, uniquely toned vocals, Type Fours are temperamental and emotional, moving through life without shame about their identity . . . or so they hope. Type Fours' identity lies rooted in the idea that they are fundamentally their own person, and so no one would *ever* be able to love them or know them or understand them. (They are melodramatic, but they acknowledge and embrace this about themselves.) They *are* The Individualist, after all.

Although they can tend toward being overly self-absorbed and temperamental about their emotions, healthy Type Fours are honest with themselves and their loved ones about their emotions. Stepping out of their mode of rationalization and into their zone of empowering thought contributes greatly to their integration and growth. They desire to have a unique identity and an empowering, significant life; so healthy Fours, instead of having a tendency to emotionally reason their way through things, realize that they can be both seen and understood when they acknowledge that their feelings are not facts.

Similar to a Type Three Achiever, Type Fours put on a "false self" (or a fantasy self), which is made up of their "if only" self that they fantasize about being; but this false self can stem from their shame about themselves (and their feeling that they are unworthy of love), and this projected image often comes up short. This differs from Type Threes in a couple of different ways; first the Type Four is often caught up in what *is* versus what *could be* (but unlike the Type Three, not in a visionary sense)—they feel unloved, or that they will never fit in. Their "if only" self focuses more on unworthiness or lack: "If only so-and-so loved me," etc. Type Threes spend time creating a projected image; their strategy allows them to live through a perfectionist image so well that they are prone to losing touch with their feelings and their true self. However, Type Fours keep it authentic. Their strategy is particularly rooted in feeling "different" or "special" (hence The Individualist) to compensate or defend themselves from their perceived unworthiness, shortcomings, or flaws. It's not that the Type Four makes themselves out to be better (dissimilar to Type Three); rather they focus on what their personal missing piece is as they idealize what's "perfect" that they may never be able to have.

Generally speaking, the false self is often created in childhood as a means of protection from stress, shock, or even developmental or childhood trauma. The projected self-creation begins very early on within many people.

For example, my Type Four friend Sam is often very deeply in his feelings. As a creative, I've seen it be a beautiful thing; but I've also seen it eat him alive. He has gone through bouts of singing, "Isn't She Lovely?" and painting incredible portraits of his current lady love . . . to the following week where he competes with Picasso's Blue Period. Somehow he went from feeling on top of the world to feeling completely unworthy of anything at all and breaking things off before the girl leaves (fear of rejection)—even if things were going well. From this sadness, however, spring the most fascinating bouts of creativity. Sam is not obsessed with the perfection or beauty that comes out of his romance. He is obsessed with the originality that it first peaks in him. When it starts to lose the originality, he immediately slips into a mindset of the fantasy self: that he is unlovable, shameful, perhaps "too" different. While this can definitely be traced back to abandonment, there is also a key statement that Sam makes, not out of self-pity, but quite matter-of-factly: "It felt like there was less than 100 percent authenticity."

Being in the feelings center, Type Fours project their common emotion of shame by trying to prove their worth to themselves. They can see and experience the light and dark sides of life, and internalize the meaning that both hold. They rarely see "coincidences" because they are so in tune with their own sense of self and emotions, looking inwardly for connection to the unknown and deeper side of life. Sensitive, creative, and gentle, their compassionate nature lies in a distinct awareness of their own personal vulnerabilities and differences, and they *want* to live honestly and vulnerably within themselves so that they can acknowledge and understand the why behind their existence, and their emotional stability or instability. While they do view themselves as "special," they also see themselves as "specially defective." This is where Type Fours can lose themselves in longing for belonging, as they yearn for *more* and for something outside of their own space, but neglect the joy that comes from appreciating the present moment. They're unsure of what "more" entails, but they often think they see it in others, leading to a slightly jealous nature and a belief in their self-appointed role as a sufferer. In their suffering, however, they have a strong and quiet strength, and as they are generally internal processors, they are rarely overwhelmed (though easily sucked into their own romantic story).

As The Individualist, Type Fours *thrive* on consistently creating their own identity . . . around just how *unlike* everyone else they are. There may be a box, but Type Fours don't want to fit in it! Although they can feel misunderstood relatively often, they are known as the hopeful (or hopeless, depending on the day) romantics, longing for a rescuer of some kind. This rescuer is the one they deeply desire connection with and mutual understanding from, and with whom they can share their own originality, out of the box and free.

With an innate desire to be authentic, Type Fours spend a good portion of their time in artistic pursuits they hope will make a tangible mark on the world. Their canvas becomes the metaphoric world around them; their pottery molds significance and stance; their voice gives unique expression to the important things they have to say. Their art is how they emotionally ground themselves. Type Fours are imaginative, creative, and authentic, and they need people in their lives who are optimistic, and who encourage them to share their voice and feelings. Learning self-acceptance, even if it wears the Type Four out, is important.

The challenge is to maintain perspective—no matter what is going on in the mental or physical realm in the here and now—and to *live in the now*, not always in the past and not always in the future.

Core Motivation: "I Liked _____ Before It Was Cool!" (the OG Hipster)

Creating beautiful things is natural to Type Fours—which is potentially a reason so many of those who are "creatives" want to identify as a Type Four artist even if they aren't motivated by the same things. In fact, creating beauty is one of the instinctive core motivations of a Type Four—it's key to expressing themselves and protecting their own self-image while allowing for vulnerability in a tangible way. Setting aside time to be creative is a significant aspect of the Four's artistic freedom, and where the Type Four spends a good deal of time finding their originality, their honesty, and their self-expression.

It can be far too easy to become stuck on the hamster wheel of emotional turmoil, especially if the interior emotions are what can be perceived as "negative." Suppressing feelings is an alienating experience for the Type Four, and it leads to the feeling of being a flawed human who is an outsider in their own society. Men may have a much more difficult time than women with *feeling* their emotions and looking inward because this goes against the grain of a traditional societal norm, and suppressing is an attempt to be rational. However, in suppressing, most people, but especially the Type Four, can find that the emotional cutoff leaks into unintentional separation from the instinctive aspects of their personality. Withdrawing to protect their self-image and take care of their emotions before anything else is a strong pull for a Type Four, but this can be deeply detrimental when learning when and how to hold back.

Being in the feelings center, the Type Four's vital energy is drawn from others' opinions of them. "Am I special to you?" "Do you see me?" Their individuality drives them to be exceptional, or eccentric, or quirky, or striking, or outlandish, or outrageous, or even unconventional—anything to keep from being considered ordinary. Striving for authenticity, their life can be built up by a constant longing for beauty, paradise, love, something that's perceived as lost to them, although they truly desire to picture it as "whole." J.M. Barrie's classic novel *Peter Pan* is about a boy who is so scared of losing his individuality and originality and innocence, that he refuses to grow up—and he also wants to be the hero of his story as the "rescuer."

Speaking of "the rescuer," . . . deep connection with a "rescuer" or "savior" figure is an aspect of being a Type Four. This doesn't mean a princess sitting in her tower waiting for her prince or rescuer. It's more the idea that a person will come along who will just *fit* and make sense in the Four's world, to embrace them, and be constantly fascinated by them because they're just so complicated and hard to figure out. Attracting this person to their life also has something to do with a Four's level of health.

If a Four is at a lower level in their development (disintegrating consistently), they may lack self-confidence and look for someone to "rescue" them from the situation so they can get back into a healthy state again. Obviously, this is not a good place to stay for long periods of time. It's worth it to note that looking for a rescuer does not mean the Type Four is weak, because Fours are actually very strong people, particularly emotionally and particularly when they wield their mental capacity well. However, there comes a point where that stern detachment means that they do not admit that they need someone, which is just as dangerous as relying solely on the rescuer, because it leads to—you guessed it—withdrawal from others.

Withdrawing with a goal of provoking people into coming to their rescue is what makes Type Fours a reactive type. This is a slightly passive–aggressive technique used to get others to prove that they care by following the Four and reassuring them that they matter. Type Fours move away from others, through a sense that they lack something, and this is why their thought process turns inward. Many Type Fours would identify as an internal processor and can come off as an introvert, even if some are more extroverted by nature. The fact of the matter is that Fours also need quality time with their loved ones alongside their own "alone time" to withdraw. Their alone time is where they take time to learn and understand themselves better, so that you can understand them better.

At some point in their childhood, the unity between beauty and serenity were broken. The childhood wound of the Type Four lies in the rejection of identity. Something happened when they were very young that made them feel disconnected from their families or a parent, for either extreme or simple reasons—ranging anywhere from the middle child who does not feel "seen," to a child who feels as though their parents' advice is too generic and doesn't apply to them, and all the way to a child who is abused in some way. Creating an outer world of balance and symmetry was the only way this child could cope. Feeling out of place in their family may contribute to a coping mechanism of isolation to dealing with what they perceive as a rejection of their identity as children. It's a loneliness that may have plagued a Type Four their entire life.

Because Type Fours equate loneliness with originality, they also desire most things around them to be unique and to have an origin story. The character Phoebe (Lisa Kudrow) from the sitcom *Friends* is a great example of this in the episode titled "The One with the Apothecary Table." Phoebe hates the store Pottery Barn on principle, because everything in it is mass manufactured and there's no originality to the store's furniture. Knowing this, Rachel (Jennifer Aniston) tells Phoebe she bought an apothecary table for the apartment from a flea market (though it was actually from Pottery Barn) and claims the table is an antique. Phoebe imagines the herbs and potions that were mixed on the table, thus creating a "story" behind the product.

The deepest fear of a Type Four is a lack of identity and living an unfulfilled life without leaving a significant mark on the world. They are not intimidated by other people's complexities or seemingly morbid-on-the-surface nature, because they have lived through their own complexities and believe it contributes to depth of identity and "humanness." Based on that mindset, however, there is still an internal struggle that occurs in which the Four homes in on missing pieces when other people don't fully complete a thought or can't give the Four the time they feel they need to be alone or develop their *own* thoughts. Because of this, Fours can appear self-absorbed (even if they aren't). A Four's internal conflict often stems from identity unworthiness—an unhealthy Four is more likely to discredit compliments and dwell on the negative, but they don't mind being "frustrated" because part of their identity is based on needing a "rescuer." Dwelling alongside the fear of identity significance is the belief that the world is best lived through emotions—and that in itself is an aspect of identity that contributes to the creativity.

Type Four Wings and Levels of Health

It is no surprise that Type Fours are rooted in the feeling or "heart" triad. Emotions are very important to a Four, and are what contribute to their empathetic sensitivity. However, there is an escape hatch of sorts for them, because they are such an emotional type, that one of their wings leans into the thinking of "head" triad, where thoughts and mental logic are just as important as decisions made based on feelings. On the one wing, we have the Type Five Investigator, and the Type Three Achiever on the other. Type Fours who wing Type Three are called The Aristocrat, and those who wing to Type Five are called The Bohemian. Through both wing types, Type Fours tend to stay in their own heart zone, but based on their level of integration and disintegration, this can change.

The Aristocrats (4w3) are often confused with Type Sevens: generally outgoing, with a witty sense of humor and imagination. They deeply value being creative, but borrowing from Type Three, are also intuitive and ambitious, and desire to be effective in the world (in addition to wanting their identity to have significance). They *want* to make an impression and may see that as their ticket to finding belonging, trying to do so with their style and their artistic side. Their emotionally adept self combines well with others socially, but they also have a strong element of organization; however, they can also have a split personality between when they're out then coming home feeling lonely, as if they've just put on a "face" and hidden their true feelings. Also borrowing from the Wing Three, they might throw themselves into work and then feel unfortunate in love or as though there is no one to take care of them. Even if they aren't drawn to outward style and appearance, The Aristocrats are more highly aware of how they present than are the Bohemians.

In disintegration, the 4w3 Aristocrat can often come off as very competitive, and very fickle. They may at first want to commit to a relationship that they have projected onto someone, then pull away at the very last second when they begin to see the reality doesn't live up to the fantasy. Their personal or public achievements can be tainted by an envy that others in their world fit in easily (and the Fours feel they never will, despite how hard they may try) or by a deeply rooted desire to prove the crowd wrong.

On the other hand, the 4w5 Bohemian is very much less image-conscious, although perhaps equally or more withdrawn than an Aristocrat. In growth, this wing has a complex and deep creativity; they are intellectual in their art, but have an emotionally driven determination in their creativity: a method behind the madness. This combination is *very* much their own person, with an individualistic spiritualism and aesthetic about them. Like a Type Nine, The Bohemian will generally find several layers of meaning to events, or art, or stories; and there is a strong pull to pour themselves into artistic projects. Borrowing from the Type Five, they can be very lonely but they enjoy it, using it as a defense mechanism but also just to "be" special, appearing to be externally reserved while remaining internally intact. However, when they *do* open up, it's nearly sudden and surprising—and they feel freer to lay everything on the table when they do.

When in a state of disintegration, The Bohemian actually enjoys the feeling of being alienated and even depressed. They have a sense of un-belonging; their internal process and emotion takes precedence above all logic. They cling to past experiences when they knew what was happening, because evidence and understanding contribute to security (particularly as a Wing Five). The shame aspect of the feelings triad rears its head often, and can often create a morbidness and disappointment with themselves, and events are magnified out of proportion.

Something to be noted and aware of in levels of health for a Type Four is that the aforementioned need for a rescuer isn't something that a healthy Four constantly focuses on. Instead, they begin to take responsibility to work toward their own integration and growth, and in the process, learn to let go of a constant overhang of shame—that they are not inherently bad anymore. In fact, they never were. In *The Wisdom of the Enneagram*, Don Richard Riso and Russ Hudson write about the process of transformation in which Type Fours not only let go of their self-image as being based on their flaws and thoughts of missing out on what others have, but also actively switch to the mindset that there is, in fact, nothing inherently wrong with them. They write, "If there is nothing wrong with them, then no one needs to rescue them. They are entirely able to show up for themselves and create their own lives." This can make it easier to remove oneself from the spectrum of shame and realize they are a part of everything, and are not always alone.

A Type Four (primary Wing Five) I worked with several years ago had two specific areas that challenged them. The first was doing what needs to be done as opposed to doing what felt right (emotions) or what they wanted to do. The second challenge was allowing feelings to run rampant in their imaginations, and then talking them out with others who then deemed them too intense. First, we made a list of people (friends, colleagues, trusted family members) that were considered part of the "support group," to encourage action when all he wanted to do was sit in his feelings and think about it. Second, we got artistic. I asked him to create a series of paintings that either said exactly what we were affirming in his life or that evoked emotions in him such as "I am strong," "I am courageous," "I have the ability to take action," "I am good," "I am authentic and valuable."

For the second challenge, we intentionally set some strong boundaries that would create a balance when it came to emotions. Instead of constantly digging in the past (either through reading old journals or listening to a playlist that was made up of his childhood songs) and then feeling shame, first he was to focus on being content and intentional with a morning routine—wake up, *feel* the yoga stretch, *smell* and brew the coffee, *smile* at your paintings, water your plants, check the weather, write a gratitude list—and adding other routines (i.e., lunch at home or afternoon walk) to get him out of a rut. Incorporating bodily senses like scent and touch allowed for a tangible "embrace" of the present moment. As "hippie" as it may sound, it really is "the little things." Consciously working to stay connected with oneself is one of the keys to a Type Four learning how to connect with others.

Don't get me wrong, I am the *last* person to encourage making lists over reacting spontaneously; and by no means am

I encouraging people to lean on a substitute for understanding emotions. However, suppressing emotions and drowning in sorrow isn't a normal thing for any human being. You can have an expressive therapist who encourages you to go to a boxing class, or to even scream into your pillow, allowing any grief or rage out, *and* you can incorporate bodily practices that help to re-center. This advice goes for anyone, not just Type Fours.

Stress and Security

While the Type Four can wing Five, it's important to note that one of its stressor zones is in its own triad. The Type Two Helper is where the Type Four leans in disintegration and stress, whereas the instinctive Type One perfectionist is where the Type Four goes in growth and integration.

Disintegration in a stressed-out Type Four can often lead to mistyping because they become so unlike their true self. A good friend of mine, Lany, often struggled with self-acceptance growing up, even when we were in primary school. When we reconnected in our early twenties and chatted about the Enneagram, discussing which type she thought she was, we realized that far before she knew anything about being a "Type Four," she had frequently experienced moving to her heart point of Type One perfectionism, and stress point of Type Two Helper. Working in social media and management, she frequently "made up for herself" with an excessive social life to feel loved and to make sure people loved her, often doing tasks that she didn't necessarily feel good about to make others love her more (which would have gone against the grain of her internal desire for authenticity). On the other hand, she nearly identified with the Type One, because as she grew older, she recognized how good it felt to be equipped with the toolbox of a Type One—the budget, the schedule, the self-restrictions; however, she didn't understand the confusion she felt behind the perfectionist entrapment that felt good in the moment, but didn't help her understand her emotional side and flow. It came to a point where she couldn't accept herself and was frustrated with others for not understanding her, leading to her losing her empathy (a character trait that she loved), and getting aggravated with herself and the fact that she couldn't just "be perfect." It's not that she even had an innate desire for perfection—more or less; because she struggled with self-acceptance, that was often enough to send her into the search for acceptance in general. While that hurt her deep want for authenticity, it certainly fed her inner "fantasy self." Her childhood abandonment issues contributed deeply to her self-acceptance issues, sending her almost constantly into Type Two when she was young. To quote Lany, "It was almost as if I were living in two different worlds."

Recognizing that before she was a Type Four, she was also a human being who just needed some time off to have her own creative projects and to be alone was the key. Consistently trying to connect with others wasn't her issue—connecting with herself and her tendencies was like unlocking a world where she could be all aspects of herself.

In security and growth, Type Fours take on most of the healthy attributes of Type Ones. Instead of being on an emotional roller coaster, their heart/security center allows for more objective viewpoints of principle and habit, similar to a healthy and centered Type One. They enjoy sharing profound experiences with others, telling personal stories, and are honest with themselves: they see themselves as they are, celebrate their humanity, and don't try to deny or overlook their faults. Moving into Type One, Fours become more objective and disciplined; instead of focusing too much on their mood or becoming bored with their tasks, the Type One brings the Type Four back into the present. Additionally, movement to Type One finds Type Fours focusing less on themselves and finding deep personal significance in the belief that they do have a higher purpose.

Going to Type One balances out Type Four. When the Type Four understands how to tap into the Wing Five and is in the growth stance of Type One, there is a heart center in Four, the wing in the head, and the instinctive center in Type One stability. This is a powerful place to be situated.

In stress or disintegration, Type Fours that borrow from Type Two take all the unhealthy, clingy sides of a Type Two—being stressed and drained by casual or meaningless conversations, lacking enough personal creative projects, and being interrupted or facing some kind of conflict can all be triggers into the disintegration and pressure to please other people. Instead of an internal process, they create a stress-driven existence where they pick up on the behaviors around them. They feel themselves slipping away and "help" others in a passive–aggressive way to cement their place in the group and make them feel indispensable to the project (giving them purpose and significance); they may also develop feelings of self-righteousness, putting themselves on a self-made pedestal believing they are so special but that no one else will understand them. Creating a bridge and gap between themselves and their support group is the ultimate way of testing the waters to make sure that they are truly valuable to others.

Avoiding disintegration means the Type Four needs to be aware of themselves enough to realize when their beautiful authenticity is starting to slip out the back door under serious stress *before* becoming completely overwhelmed. Secluding themselves for too long makes them become even more private and secluded than is good for them. Ensuring consistent connection with their loved ones and their support system keeps them grounded; recognizing their internal significance and mark on the world simply by taking part in others' lives is a quick and tangible way to connect in the face of uncertainty. Having a clear set of values, purpose, and vision in routine brings the Type Four back to its heart center of Type One, but also back to themselves.

Integration is ultimately about understanding the high and low side of both Type One and Type Two. And yes, even though Type Two is a stress point, there should be a healthy association with going there, learning from the stance, and returning to centrality. Stressors are a part of life; learning that they contribute to personal capacity is often taught as a leadership tool. Going to a stress point should never be perceived as an obstacle.

When I was writing poetry based on the number types for a project, I penned this for the start of Type Four:

"I try so hard to recreate nostalgia as I remember it. A newspaper half-read in the morning and left lying open to the sports page.

A second cup of coffee with lipstick stains around the rim in the back bathroom.

And yet sometimes I doubt myself in that in-between creation:

is this how I remember it now, or simply how I choose to remember it? Am I trying to recreate a feeling, or am I actually living in something that isn't my own?

What if the present moment isn't something I can feel, but is something tangible if I only looked past the kaleidoscope mirror of my stained-glass window?"

As an artist, individualist, creative, it's easy to often feel the pressure of being a "one-man show" when trying to connect with others. It's even easier—natural, almost—to recollect a certain time in your life when you remember feeling love and belonging, and to try to recreate that scene in your life through art and beauty. Whether that's as simple as lighting a candle, or going on a picnic, find time to embrace yourself and realize the significance in the world is whatever you choose. Belief that you're missing something pulls the focus inward, and how could you truly be significant if you were missing something? Shifting the focus outward from time to time, in moderation, makes you realize that maybe you experienced this feeling for a reason. The inner suffering is valid, but don't stay so focused on that aspect of yourself that you can't see anything else.

The inner counselor in you is allowed to shine brighter, and focusing on what you can contribute takes some of the pressure off —you *are* a part of something bigger, and your presence has significance. The meaning that you could be seeking in yourself and from the world could be (figuratively) right under your nose, or under your sofa, or in a conversation with a trusted friend. Walk in the fullness of your personal significance. Recognizing what you're feeling, enjoying the sorrow along with the beauty, and then putting that into words, into your artistry, into your creativity, plugging that into other people—that's where joy beyond the sorrow begins. As a Type Four, that's where you find your place in this world. That's where you can allow your imagination to dance.

Life with a Type Four: Authentically Original

Despite the rap they get for being moody and inconsistent, the Type Four Individualist isn't necessarily *all* dark, deep, and serious; in fact, they often surprise others who see beneath their surface with their humor, wit, and rebellious nature. The status quo is not for them—and they're not interested in the so-called box that everyone seems so intent on fitting into. Coming in at approximately 15 percent of the population, The Individualists are feelings oriented, romantic, creative, intuitive, and empathetic. In a world that accepts fitting in as, well, normal, the Four dares to feel *all* the feelings in all of their glory, even though that might make them feel misunderstood.

As the creators in the Enneagram, Fours bring depth to the world. While most other types are consumed by the image focus of their identity, Fours face their darker side head on, deeply self-accepting and in touch with their true core being; they see their flaws, their insecurities, and embrace them for the sake of honesty. Because of this, it is disheartening that most people in the world live with a public persona that doesn't match their private personalities. They can feel lost in the crowd of people who are all alike and have it all together, and this can contribute to Four's vice of envy: "Why does Susan have what I want?" Yet, they can never quite tell what it is they're missing. Their search for identity leaves them feeling lacking, but when unhealthy, they feel that whatever it is, it is destined to be forever missing. Comparison is the thief of joy, and falling into that trap can be all too easy for a Four.

Type Fours are drawn to the creative route as their best means of self-expression. But because this is one of their best forms of expression, and creativity surfaces most often when they're dealing with intense emotions, they fear that without turmoil they won't be able to create. It takes practice for a Four to recognize that their creativity is an innate gift, and it can be used without staying on their own island of romanticized despair. Being able to embrace their vision, style, and flair for the original is vital to their life work. Traditionally, coloring outside the lines could get any employee into trouble. But now, it's more celebrated to be uniquely expressive, and a creative director is often a sought-after asset to many companies: authentic, real, and tangible.

Fours need to remember and to hear often that the most powerful feelings they may feel are not always reality. Infusing their days with positivity and healthy choices helps them look onward and upward, staying realistic keeps them grounded, and having someone along on the journey to remind them that there is *not* something fundamentally *wrong* with them keeps them in check to acknowledge their good qualities. It removes themselves from the story they have created for themselves, that "beauty is pain," and puts them into the role of who they are here and now.

At Home

Because they are so deeply aware of their feelings, it is natural for the Type Four child to empathize with the feelings of others, and Fours can often take on the moods of others. Highly self-aware, their depth and honesty as children encourages others—adults and children alike—to be fearlessly authentic, too. They are creative "old souls," and can see beauty in the unseen things. Their imagination is vivid, and they can play for hours on their own.

Four children are highly sensitive and emotional, beyond the normal heightened emotions of childhood. Their sensitivity can be a strength that allows them to stand up for others and an empathy that allows them to call out things they believe are "wrong." Allowing a Four child to express their fits of emotion and helping them learn how to channel that through creativity will set them up for life.

The Type Four childhood wound is feeling unseen and disconnected from their parents or guardians or feeling that others don't see their true selves. If you have a Four child, it is imperative that they know they are a valued, nurtured, sought-after member of the family.

The most common irritation of the Four child is feeling misunderstood. They need to know their parents see what *they* are seeing and need an atmosphere at home in which everyone feels free to express all emotions, both joy and sorrow.

Four children can be easily overwhelmed by social gatherings. I used to teach piano to a beautiful Type Four twelve-year-old aspiring composer, who recalled hating going to primary school because it felt like too much pressure to sit on a stool all day surrounded by other people, other ideas to conform to, and other children to fit in with.

Type Fours need help transitioning from one thing to another; from one class to the next, or from a family gathering to dinner time. Letting them know the plan for the week can help a Four manage anxiety, and having a structured bedtime routine will help keep the conflict at a minimum. Encourage the Four child to release their inner world into the real world, balancing their preferred alone time to help them connect with others and just get out in nature. Finding things that are unique to them and appreciating those things, or asking them specifically about how they "felt" about the day shows interest. Offer solutions when they ask for help with problems. Above all else, reassure them that they are loved unconditionally.

Type Four parents are natural creators and believers in the arts as a form of self-expression, and will pass their love and inspiration for the arts onto their children. Whether through the theatrical and film arts, cooking or baking, painting and pottery, whatever makes their children get their hands into something they can make beautiful, the Type Four seeks to give their child a love of all things artistic and creative. This can make their children feel supported in their individuality and uniqueness, and be proud of these attributes. With a Four parent's deeply sensitive and caring nature, their children are raised to understand and value their own feelings, and be empathetic to the feelings and needs of others.

However, because Type Fours are given to bouts of sentimentality and depression (co-existing of course with the upbeat and fun), some of the Four's children may feel discontinuity and anxiety; some may even take on the responsibility for their parent's moodiness. Using practiced and personal intuition, making time to reassure their children if and when the Four parent is feeling a bit more melancholy and down will add value to the parent's relationship with their children, as the child navigates their own feelings and understands that what another person is experiencing is not their fault.

In Love

The Type Four Individualists are also known as The Romantics. Deep, introspective, creative, and passionate, Fours long for an authentic relationship filled with empathy and understanding. As natural romantics, they want to connect with someone and immerse themselves completely in those feelings, often falling hard and passionately, which then inspires them in their art and expression. When they are in a relationship with someone, a Four often becomes caught up in thinking of their own identity, how that identity relates and attaches to their partner, and creating their own idealist lines in the relationship.

Being in the heart or feelings triad, Fours are expressive of their moods, they won't leave their partners guessing, and hope to together cultivate a meaningful experience. Because being "normal" has always been seen as a horror to them, the Type Four wants to stand apart both individually and in their relationship. Love will never be normal to them; they want a love that is truly unique and special to them.

When less aware or unhealthy, Fours can detach from reality, and in so doing accidentally ignore their partner. Fours are emotionally reactive in conflict, because they believe they can solve the conflict if they express their authentic feelings; but, as an internal processor, this can often depend on how demanding the conflict is. However, to the Four's partner, their idealistic and romantic nature can sometimes become irritating. The Four is constantly trying to find ways to keep the spark on fire, surprising their partner and aiming to make their relationship special. Ordinary and safe just will not do.

At times, a Four's stubbornness can distract them when they feel they are being misunderstood, and they can revert back to childhood wounds and then need a good deal of space from their partner. Their abandonment strikes hard and fast, and can zap a relationship, landing the Four in a push-and-pull battle both with themselves and with others when they feel uncertain or unsafe.

Fours need a partner who really and truly does understand their melancholy and desire to create beauty in everything, who is supportive of their emotions, but can draw them out of their .

depths of despair. A partner who can verbalize their positive feelings toward the Four, instead of throwing the jab of "you're too sensitive," allows the Four to feel safe to be themselves. They recognize the ways in which they need to grow, and they can put their attention toward the betterment of the relationship. As giving, loving, and self-aware people who are only too cognizant of their flaws, Fours need someone who appreciates what they do bring to the table, and shows that appreciation.

For a Four, the fear of being unseen and unknown for who they are is not about needing constant attention from their partner, but lies in feeling unappreciated for their authentic selves. The very last thing they want in a relationship is someone who only likes the idea of them, the potential of the relationship, or sees them at surface value. They'd much rather be alone than be misunderstood or feel as if they don't have the approval of their partner. Fours need to be acknowledged and have their uniqueness affirmed. They are unashamed of their individuality, and want their partners to appreciate their specialness.

If a Four is "in hiding," a reminder that their needs are not too much and that you'll be there when they're feeling ready to share means the world to them. It's verbalizing love, and putting in the effort and work that the Four needs to feel seen, heard, and worthy.

In Work

As creatives, Fours wish to be self-sufficient and do things on their terms and timelines. They love the uniqueness they bring to the table of a workplace, and enjoy the kind of careers that allow them to steep in their creativity and dramatics, or reservations and individuality as an artist. They are the actors, personal trainers, writers, photographers, designers, dance instructors, and artists: thriving in an environment that allows room for creativity and building relationships with colleagues-turned-friends. Fours look for opportunities for growth in their work, exploring new areas relevant to their work and beyond, and growing in ways that increase their uniqueness and identity.

For Type Fours, their work peers are not seen as colleagues, they are seen as people with their own stories to tell. Fours want to be independent and self-sufficient, but they also appreciate relationships with people who are genuine. When the Type Four's work colleagues are themselves independent, then the Four can feel safe to focus, enhancing their creative skills. A toxic workplace where everyone is always stabbing someone else in the back is mentally exhausting. The Four neither wants nor needs that extra bit of drama. When Type Fours work with others who are logical, they can provide the creative inspiration; but if they work with another individualist or creative, the key is to focus on connecting to each other via their creativity.

Building a relationship with a Type Four means asking them questions about themselves and their personal life, and appreciating their self-expression. They appreciate it when their manager or lead takes the time to get to know them on a friendly level. On the one hand (if they are winging Type Three), they want to have a good image and build strong rapport; on the other hand, they want to be seen and known as they are. To create rapport, coworkers should try to appreciate the Four's emotions and creativity they bring. To support a Four, help them stay emotionally strong and intact, perhaps referring them to a counselor, if necessary. Help them to consider their personal impact on the world to resist internalizing the world's blame and garnering the small irritations as their lot in life.

One of a Type Four's fears is that they lack significance, and one of their drives is leaving a lasting impression on the world. Do you see where this connects? When communicating with a Type Four, it's important to tune into their voice and connection with their emotions. In growth, Fours need to recognize and redirect their motivations that may be more self-centered to develop them toward the team agenda and goals. This may feel like assimilating; assure them that it is not. In comparison to others on their teams and in their lives, Fours can experience jealousy or envy toward those they feel have what they do not, be it rapport, extended creativity, or deep relationship.

When stressed, Fours can distance themselves and overreact to feedback. In conflict resolution and giving feedback, sensitivity is a must. First, share encouragement and appreciation for the Type Four. Openly share your feelings and connect with the Type Four emotionally. Empathize with where they're coming from. "I hear you, and I understand!" is a great way to start (ensuring, of course, that you do indeed understand). Without agreeing completely with their point of view, frame any negative feedback as an opportunity for growth. "Hey, Jenn! You've been doing such an incredible job bringing originality back to this side of the dance team. Unfortunately, one of the girls is having trouble with the dance because _____. I know you've been working hard to help them get it, and I can see where you're coming from. But, I think this is also a really beautiful opportunity to allow for _____ to grow! What do you think?" Leaving room for dialogue and conversation is necessary, and ending with a question allows the Four to communicate as they see fit. Let them receive the idea, take it in, and explore it for its possibilities.

In Play

Fours crave authentic, genuine relationships, with shared depth of understanding and space for imaginative ideals. Compassionate and with emotional depth, Fours desire, as Anne Shirley of *Anne of Green Gables* so distinctively puts it, "a bosom friend." As excellent artists who are in touch with the emotions of the world through music, dance, and the arts, their attention and ideation can move swiftly from empathizing with others to comparing their own inner voice and experience. They are the friend to whom others bring their darkest secrets without shame; Fours appreciate that others trust them and appreciate pain as one of the many emotions of life. Listening attentively to another person is how Fours show love.

Just as in love, Type Fours aren't looking for surface-level acquaintances with minimal interaction. They are perfectly fine being by themselves. But, being The Individualist, they also want to know they can connect. Although they can be inwardly dramatic and outwardly reserved, their dark side can rear its head when they are left to themselves for too long. Because they are often told they are "too intense," Type Fours can feel that they have to hold part of themselves at bay so that others don't misunderstand them and find them to be "too much." While they crave depth to their friendships, being misunderstood is overwhelming to them and feeds into the lie that they are deficient.

Creating a safe place for the Four to share their "darker" state of mind without them feeling judged is like offering a Four a seat at their own table, which they set and prepared the food for, but refrained from sitting at because they wanted to be sure that they were welcomed by everyone before they took their rightful place.

As a feeling type who appreciates their personal melancholy and finds it exceedingly comfortable, it's important to remove a Four friend from any place of despondency and help them to look for the meaning they so seek in their life. To encourage a Four toward growth, they need to learn to balance sadness with the capacity for joy. Appreciate their ideas and depth of feeling; don't distract them from their more difficult feelings (unless they ask you to!), but make sure they know that you are a safe space and are readily available when they want to talk some things out. When they're vulnerable, just sit with them. They can benefit from people who can respond with tact to their emotions, balancing out their waves with some stability.

Conflict for a Type Four feels like being trapped in a world that doesn't understand them; that they are the only ones experiencing true emotional suffering. Healthy Type Fours can set their emotions aside and support others in their journey with their inherent strength.

If they're sharing how they're feeling, Fours can get extremely passionate. Try mirroring their body language or sharing honestly to encourage dialogue; withdrawing makes the Four feel as if you think they're too intense, and that causes them to withdraw because they no longer feel safe to share. Above all else, make sure that the Four knows they are valid and valued, and that their feelings are valid and merited.

Type Five

The Investigator

*"If you don't know, the thing to do is not to
get scared, but to learn."*
—Ayn Rand

It's said that playwright George Bernard Shaw had a "writing hut" that he would use to escape from people. The hut itself was constructed on a turntable mechanism so it was easy to rotate, and so he could catch and follow the natural sunlight coming in through the windows any time of day. This writing hut had everything necessary, no more, no less: a typewriter, heater, telephone, and bed. Shaw was quoted to have said, "People bother me. I came here to hide from them." He nicknamed his beloved shed London, and if anyone came by to ask for (read: bother) him, they were only told that he was in London. Honest. Functional. Private.

If this isn't a Type Five thing, I don't know what is.

Type Fives are the analysts of the Enneagram. Their logic, intellect, and perception are natural gifts, and they usually cannot remember a time where they weren't in touch with their mental faculty. Their capacity and thirst for knowledge keep them sharp and perceptive about the world, and they are constantly taking "mental notes" or observations to better understand human

Type Five at a Glance

Needs: To be capable and considered competent.

Fear: Inadequacy and incompetence, lack of privacy, not having enough to offer (differentiating from "being" enough).

Core Motivation: Being self-reliant, to know "enough" to understand their environment and protect themselves, to ask "why" as they observe the world around them.

nature. They are naturally alert, bright, and driven—they can focus for long periods of time on study and learning, or developing a new idea or complex model. They love being left by themselves and having the quiet to allow for new ideas, and look at the world from a completely different angle.

Known as The Investigator, The Observer, or The Thinker (among many other names), one of the main goals of a Type Five is to understand *why* things are the way they are. Because they are so independent and easily detach with others, they tend to become preoccupied with what's right in front of them. They deeply appreciate their privacy, because it leads to invigorated energy; but that can often lead to their withdrawal from engaging with anyone because they need to continue their observations, and they fear being depleted of the energy that comes from their observations. Fives can come across as domineering and proud, when in fact they're just worried that they are losing control of their mental state or capacity, which is seen by them as their most priceless coping mechanism.

On the other hand, Fives are also very detail-oriented and love to collect new ideas. Their active mental life and capacity is where they find their strength, their individuality, their personal control, and their confidence. With Type Fives in the thinking triad, their main obstruction is fear-based. When they are in a withdrawn stance, Fives wave their white flag inward, feeling that they are inadequate. Their knowledge base supports their understanding of people and contributes to their understanding of why something could or would happen so, hypothetically speaking, the more they know, the more they can defend themselves (and their loved ones) against things in the world that might disrupt or disturb them.

The renowned mystery writer (and proposed Type Five) Agatha Christie wrote multiple novels starring her own beloved set of detective characters in the early 1900s. The basis for many of her characters, but particularly for her elderly female detective, Miss Marple, was that human nature never changes: "Really, I have no gifts—no gifts at all—except perhaps a certain knowledge of human nature." "Human nature is much the same everywhere, and of course, one has opportunities of observing it at closer quarters in a village." Of Miss Marple herself, Christie says, "There was no unkindness in Miss Marple, she just did not trust people." It's not that Type Fives don't trust people, it's simply that their use of knowledge acts as a shield, to protect them. (If a Type Five lets you into their world, it's a privilege—that means they know you're a safe person.)

Type Fives can often be misunderstood—they are seen as too demanding and private, although that is not their true nature. Too much emotional input from others (or even from themselves) can often be a hindrance from their main task or current train of thought. It can also trigger the idea that people are dependent on them, limiting the Five's need for privacy. They're not fond at all of emotions, considering them a weakness that can lead to destruction, while also viewing them as an explainable phenomenon of the brain. Fives truly desire predictability, as that adds to their self-reliance and motivation to defend themselves against the environment. If they can "learn" and anticipate the people and relationships in their lives, they can feel free to allow them into their quiet zone.

Calm in crisis, thoughtful and respectful of others, and appreciative of the simple things in life, healthy Fives can truly experience release and minimize their vice of selfishness (with time, energy, and resources). In this release, their emotional dynamics are restored, and an understanding takes place in which their basic need of understanding meets with the flow of understanding life—that emotions are just as necessary as the mind and body. Without a need to hoard all the knowledge and understanding in the world, they can function with a looser grip and lessened fear of life and its many unexpected paths and challenges.

Core Motivation: "I've Already Analyzed That"

Type Fives have a fear that they're going to go dormant if they stop their consumption of information or knowledge. Their inner avarice rears its head, but not in the traditional way; their greed extends past want of riches, and into greed for knowledge and space that will prevent any feelings of "emptiness." As the thinkers and observers, Fives believe they are a scarcity. But, they also don't feel that they are quite as capable of functioning as are others, which creates insecurity and is part of the reason that they tend to disengage with others rather than try to move past that fear. Their minds are where they feel most capable, because in their minds they can control everything. Sir Arthur Conan Doyle's detective Sherlock Holmes called this concept his "mind palace," where he receives information to instantly connect one circumstance or person to another, and then stashes it away. Holmes can create a number of scenarios in his mind based on this information and connects it much more quickly than others might, due to practice and heightened thought process.

When other people praise Fives or deem them competent, it fulfills one of their core motivations of being seen as capable and understanding: they are competent, they are intelligent, they are smart.

Children who ask "Why?" every five minutes are playing the part of the Type Five, who are motivated by wanting to understand the environment and world around them. It's part of their need to not only "have" knowledge, but to own it with every ounce of their being—it's what grounds and settles them because it's explainable. Because they're called The Investigator, it's literally written into their identity to want to know.

The Netflix series *The Queen's Gambit* is a prime example of a Five: an orphaned chess prodigy named Beth Harmon follows her personal quest to become a professional chess player. We see multiple scenes of her not only asking questions about chess, but reading about chess, replaying famous plays, mastering all of the differing moves—her whole world is built around the game of chess. She is, quite literally, an expert. During an interview after winning an important tournament, a journalist asks her how close her genius is to madness. In her answer, Beth talks about her initial draw-in and recognition of the game that she loves and knows, completely. "Chess can be beautiful. It was the board I noticed first. It's an entire world of just 64 squares. I feel safe in it. I can control it; I can dominate it. And it's predictable, so if I get hurt, I only have myself to blame." Maybe it was the fear and instability of her early years as an orphan that pushed Beth into this world; she pushes the people around her away as she feels invaded, and has moments of disintegration as she encounters emotions and anger, and tries to silence those feelings. At one point, her one friend from the orphanage comments to her, "You've been the best at what you do for so long, you don't even know what it's like for the rest of us."

Type Fives also desire to be recognized and acknowledged for their "knowing," just as Beth desired to win in order to prove to herself that she was in full control of the board and her inner domain. For their own self-security, Type Fives need to have a few—or at least one—areas in which they feel masterdom to allow for that connection with their surroundings or others. For Beth Harmon, this was chess; for my friend Christine, it was science; for Sherlock Holmes, it was his mind palace. But sometimes it's not all analytical—my friend Ryan's Type Five passion was poetry and theater. While he didn't want to be an actor, he made it a point to study and know everything there was to know about film, theater, pentameter and rhythm, screenwriting, and techniques ranging from Meisner to Method. While his understanding didn't necessarily protect him from the practical challenges of life, his knowledge was his connection to the outside world and his talking point with people around him, as well as his characters to take refuge in when he felt a conversation was becoming too fierce. Fives have a motivation to have everything "figured out."

To gain knowledge and maintain their privacy, Type Fives have no problem closing the doors of their proverbial closet. Their analytical ability is their strength, but if they are not alone, they can feel that their terms are cut short and they've lost control of their mental situation. They are naturally much more rational and detached, and use isolation (both emotional and physical) as a type of psychological defense to maintain the self-sufficiency ideal, zoning out if they can't physically leave the situation. Because they have difficulty relating to others' emotions, they are often seen as condescending and unfriendly. However, time alone is the Type Five's opportunity to unwind and reconnect with themselves—they just have a shorter fuse than some people. It's not simply an introverted-ness, it's the way they can prove to themselves that they can take care of themselves.

Learning a new skill energizes the Type Five greatly, and when they are given room to work independently it contributes to their skills and desire to understand (and then improve) what's around them with the hope that they will eventually be more confident as long as they are thorough in their research and understanding, able to fully interact in the world. Their thought process and keen perception give them a knack for thinking things through beyond the surface, thinking of life as a puzzle and challenging every move. They *love* the chance to get out of their bubble, so long as they feel aware (and thus in charge) of their mental state. Knowledge accumulation in a minimalist atmosphere, in which everything is neat and to the point, is a strong environment for a Five; anything that threatens to pull their attention outward is immediately compartmentalized into the "threat" tab.

As the pioneers of critical thought, Type Fives are inquisitive by nature. It is not enough to just "know" but to also *understand*. They seek out patterns in their analysis of information, motivated by their response to fear: avoidance of anxiety through careful protection of their resources. Freedom is at the heart of a Type

Five. They seek to remain pure from alternative influences in their pursuit of knowledge, seeking only truth. They want to fit in and enjoy relationships, but also refrain from relationships that they are uncertain of, lest they hurt or hinder their pursuits. The Five plays the part, but growth occurs when they find themselves trusting someone (or two someones) enough to open up to them.

Type Five Wings and Levels of Health

Childhood wounds for a Type Five often stem from the feeling of estrangement or unbelonging, whether in their own family units or in a personal place, such as school. They weren't necessarily disengaged from their proverbial "worlds," they just felt as though they were viewed as an outsider, rather than accepted for who they were.

To cope, the young Five retreats, hiding away to find a subject they could master that was unique to themselves and shared by no one else in their immediate circles. Young Fives distanced themselves from their feelings or from emotions that made them feel uncomfortable or were hard to navigate, and tapped into their *thoughts* as their identity. Because of this, others who are closely physical can feel demanding and intrusive to a Five. The world they have created is their domain; the outside world, unless understood, does not value them. The thing is, while they don't necessarily feel excluded (or included), they feel more as if they are always looking on, as the observer.

One of my good friends, Ellie, was a hardcore Type Five growing up. When we were little girls, I always wanted to be her friend, but she always told me—and others—that she didn't know enough about us to be friends. Hanging around her for years must have finally changed her mind, because once we were friends, we were friends for good (we still are). I became aware of her Type Five tendencies (without knowing anything of the Enneagram at the time) early on and knowing how everything worked for her led to an understanding of who she was. When we were together for more than an hour, she would retreat immediately and almost offensively. She valued her intellect far above her personality, and often took pride in the fact that in her opinion, she "was not pretty; she was smart," and that smart outlasts pretty any day.

Type Fives are rooted (quite deeply, I might add) in the thinking triad, and they don't necessarily take as much stock in relationships as they do in knowledge. When the two of these marry in a healthy relationship that doesn't stem from fear and the Five's vice of hoarding (wisdom and understanding), a beautiful assimilation can form. We can see this in the marriage of "art" and "science" in Fives that wing Four (The Individualist), or The Iconoclast. This is the wing that drives the Five out of the cognitive triad to meet with the feeling triad, bringing out more of an E.Q. than an I.Q. When the Five wings Six (to The Loyalist), we end up with The Problem Solver, as the Five mingles with the traits of the relationally loyal—but still wary—Type Six.

For the 5w4 Iconoclast, the Type Four brings a more creative, abstract trait of thought. While the Five might originally think best in numbers or letters, the Four wing introduces shapes and colors, more kinesthetic in their learning style; their mastering may lie in the arts, whether painting a canvas or learning poetry or having philosophical conversation. Fours are still withdrawers by nature, and 5w4s are no different; they can fluctuate quickly between impersonality and sudden kindness and warmth. Although their deep relationship with their feelings acts as a good medium for the usually cognitive Five to find some relief (whether welcome or not), they can still be perceived as a bit airy and superior in their mannerisms. They are extremely sensitive to their environment, and can often be easily overwhelmed if they feel intruded upon or as if they're not being given their proper space.

When in disintegration, The Iconoclast can be touchy when criticized (and critical themselves), and can be overly dramatic and isolate for days if given the reason. They can also be very much in their own world, without heed for someone else's opinion.

Fives that wing Six, The Problem Solvers, are detail-oriented and logistically sequenced (and are often mistaken as a Type One). Combining these cognitive triad numbers leaves one with an intellectual, *far* more analytical yet still deeply loyal friend; they are kind and patient people, and experts in what they do. While they still prefer to be more behind the scenes, they work hard and are very sensitive to the world around them. While they more often than not like other people, they still can practice avoidance and dislike anyone that puts too many expectations on them. Because they prefer to be self-sufficient, they aren't very gracious when someone makes an effort with them; their Wing Six asks all the questions to develop information but lacks decision-making skills.

When in disintegration, The Problem Solver can be skeptical and bluntly sarcastic. Their experimental fashion leads them to push their limits with authority to find exactly where the line is drawn in the sand and then they dance around it.

A 5w4 acquaintance of mine, Brett, often struggled as an adult with others viewing him as "selfish." We had the opportunity to chat about that in a coaching group and went over the why. During this discussion, Brett verbalized that many

Type Fives must feel out of sync with cultural norms and values, because they prefer to retreat instead of feel the need to be seen and heard to be validated. They validate *themselves*, are self-sufficient, and don't need anyone—so why would this make them (in particular, Brett) selfish? We got to the heart of what others said about him, and in the end, he wasn't very aware of what others thought—and why would he want to be, as it was based on their opinions, not facts? He said it felt as though he had a way of telling people that they didn't belong around him, and he probably didn't acknowledge people properly or give them the emotional fulfillment he felt they were expecting from him.

As we continued to discuss the disconnect between introverted tendencies and the desire for opportunity in the Westernized world, we got to the heart of fear. While Brett did not feel as though his actions were fear based, he did feel fear that he would never truly step out of the role of observer and truly belong, and this is where we circled back to the original thought of perceived selfishness. With the world being considered the *outside*, and not technically something Brett even wanted to take part in, he began to realize how his friends saw him as selfish or acting out of greed—the drive to push himself as a rule. He wanted to fit in, but he played the part of fitting in so well that it came across as ungenuine.

Brett began to put into practice the letting go of his ideas and ideals, and began to recognize how to consciously use and express his emotions—holding on to what was necessary, letting go of all the rest. It didn't mean giving up his intellect, or his friends, or even lessening himself so that others could be more comfortable. Instead, it meant seeing through the veils to where he wanted to connect, and recognizing that emotions were part of how he would get there. His gift of observing and understanding others did not give him permission to predict another's actions or deem them boring; instead, it could open up empathy and help another feel understood.

Stress and Security

"What are we doing tomorrow?" My sister Alexa is a through-and-through Type Eight, but as a little girl was almost constantly in her zone of Type Five. She was our resident investigator from the time that she could talk. Alert, insightful, curious, independent, Alexa had a strong sense of judgment and steadiness in her planning. Her "what are we doing tomorrow?" was coupled with her own personal layout of the day. Plans were her best friend, as were systems and charts, color-coded to boot. Extremely protective of her privacy and independence, taking pride in her logical and analytical system, and observing nature's extraordinariness in science with the best of them, I thought she was a Type Five disguised for years.

For the Type Five, their disintegration zone leads them into the traits of a Type Seven Enthusiast in their fellow thinking triad, which brings out some of their key fears and obstacles, while their integration leads them into the traits of a Type Eight Challenger in the instinctive triad, bringing out some of their core motivations and obstacle removal. It's an enjoyable little puzzle for a Five who thrives in an observational environment, and once they understand all aspects of their stress and securities (and what their triggers are), there will be a far more conscious discernment about why they land in these areas.

When a Type Five finds themselves stressed, their usual system of problem solving may or may not work well for them. In disintegration toward Type Seven, Type Fives can become more scatter brained and misunderstood, which induces the need for escapism, potentially using whatever stimulating activity they find on hand to help. Instead of the healthy aspect of Eight where the Five becomes more open-minded, the Five instead uses all their knowledge as a defense mechanism. Their intelligence, instead of garnering them a string of admirers, eventually pushes them away even more; their worth is no longer based on their knowledge, but based on any awards or high accolades they may receive—they no longer understand why their usual problem-solving skills are proving worthless at this point. They become more impulsive in their decisions instead of their usual thorough analysis, using anything to keep their minds active, busy, and distracted.

However, moving to Type Seven means that the Type Five can actively use the Type Seven's creative enthusiasm and zest for life to get out of their own zone, and connect with others and the world outside their own window. It allows them to reach past their usual logic into emotions.

The real problem here is that many Type Fives don't often acknowledge their emotions. They may analyze why they're feeling a certain way in a practical sense so they can add these emotions to their pie chart and know what to expect (remember, research is a shield)—and that may work for a while—but without truly learning what it means to understand one's emotions and inner workings, this only sends them into stress mode, where their emotions come to the surface is very unhealthy ways. Instead of allowing your Type Five friends to isolate, try to reach out to them.

Integration for a Type Five's move to Type Eight means that the Five can tap back into their childhood in their search to act without fear, actively stripping back their internal concerns that contribute to that fear in the first place. The Type Five generally prefers to stay solely in their mental state, but balancing between the Five, and the assertive and instinctive Eight qualities allow them to connect more with their physical expression, pulling them out of their heads and more into their heart and body zones. In this assertive zone, they become more confident and self-assured; they are, in fact, capable of both leading and researching. They understand when it's the best scenario for either logic or emotions or both (and use their instincts to determine instead of worrying about the facts). Their intuition, still confident in Type Five, explodes to great lengths, and they become the comfortable leader—humble, insightful, and willing to engage with other people to broaden their research—and also become more open-minded. People love seeing their Type Five friends find this integration because they go from being stuck in their own heads and mentality to a different place entirely.

Similar to *wabi-sabi*, a Japenese concept of acceptance of and beauty in imperfection in nature, *kintsugi* is a beautiful tradition in Japanese art. Kintsugi is literally the art of joining with gold, where broken pieces (usually ceramic) are repaired with a golden, silver, or platinum binding or lacquer. At its most basic philosophy, kintsugi is a metaphor that embraces authenticity and the scars of a life well lived, rather than a perfectly formed piece of clay. The marks where the pieces are joined are seen as a part of the object's history, not the end of its use. Kintsugi is about living with grace as well as beauty, recognizing that the golden "scars" solidify and strengthen the pot.

A lot of the stress triggers for Type Five can come from learning how to trust their body's intelligence and experience, just as much as they trust their intellectual intelligence. When we are aware of emotions, they have a much more difficult time hiding in the subconscious. Practically releasing and practicing emotions allows for release of the control over emotions: letting out grief, sadness, anger, joy—all the numbed emotions—and recognizing the beauty in the story behind them as with the vulnerability of the cracks in the kintsugi. Through the practice of emotional awareness, it's much easier to realize that most people are not the true object of fear and anger; rather, it's generally coming from someone or some scenario internalized long before. Sadness and fear make us vulnerable. Learning how to sit with these emotions instead of hiding them in a pit of intellectual reasoning is where true and real freedom begins to take place.

You don't have to be a thinker, only. Like my friend Brett in the example earlier in this chapter, half of the work is understanding where the fear stems from—from the fear of not belonging, or the fear of being misunderstood, or the fear that you are not competent or won't have enough—and what the reaction of retreat looks like. Separating those emotions and breaking them down into actual experiences as opposed to people with the emotions subconsciously projected onto them is one of the first steps into integration and self-acknowledgement. It's where the true freedom starts.

Let those around you love and support you as well. Sometimes you win; in all things, you can learn. You have permission to be a private person. You also have permission to develop connections; just note that if you truly want a connection to be deep and meaningful, it takes time to make it so. Quiet and connection are often at opposite ends of the spectrum, but it doesn't have to be that complicated. Stripping back layers and walls to allow for knowledge to be shared and communicated with another person is where even more understanding begins. As a non-conforming person, being unconventional is far more natural—and those unconventional ideas are nothing to be ashamed or concerned or shy or fearful about. You never bought the performance from someone else in the first place. Why would you play a part or give a performance now? Feel free to bring a different perspective to the table, a different intelligence and mindset—and a different emotion. You'll feel more alive and connected because of it.

Life with a Type Five: Thoughtful and Perceptive

Type Five Investigators are the Enneagram's experts. Cerebral, innovative, alert, and curious, they are the rarest type, making up approximately 4.8 percent of the population, at 7 percent men and 3 percent women.

As a head type, their inquisitiveness is their driving point; their exploratory and analytical approach to life keep their interest piqued and their isolation consistent. They have a hunger for mastery, and their explorative nature is evidenced in their desire to learn new skills.

Fives care deeply about people, but they are not the most likely to verbalize how they feel or why. Instead, they can get sucked into an endless void of analysis, letting the real world drift beyond their recognition. When communicating with a Type Five, it's important to be as straight and to the point as you can be. Repeating things excessively discredits them as they feel you didn't think they understand (they did); asking too much about their personal lives makes them feel (a) that you either haven't listened actively, or (b) purely uncomfortable. Interrupting them is like interrupting their sacred time and space with trivial things. Alone time is extremely important to the Type Five because this is where they can process their thoughts in an otherwise busy world. Because they take time to process, sometimes they may not have an immediate solution or answer to a question.

Similar to a Type Four Individualist, Fives can often feel misunderstood. Many Fives grew up with unpredictable people, and their coping mechanism was to gather information to gain mastery over what they could control, thus gaining their sense of self back little by little, and feel safe and secure. Fives crave immersion in what they would consider a "real" experience, but their mind insists on detaching from what is present, to attach instead to what is decipherable and understandable (think back to Sherlock Holmes's mind palace). If it's not logical and present, it's a lot more difficult to attach. Fives can become lonely without people around them, and yet, they are not often very fond of people being around them as it feels intrusive on their space. Being asked questions like, "What are you thinking?" makes them feel like a deer in the headlights; questions like, "What do you think about X?" are much more manageable. But sometimes, the Five doesn't want to be pressured to participate in any conversations. They're still processing and haven't made a decision, they're enjoying their well-cultivated art of observation, or they're listening to gather all the facts. But a Type Five's silence does not by any means imply that they agree. You've been forewarned.

For their own security and sense of self, Fives need at least one area of expertise that allows them to connect with others. Their identity is often based around ideas and concepts, and they are more inclined to connect with someone who has something unique and insightful to share. They want to think about things that no one has spent enough time on before. To come alongside them, listen carefully to what they express, and appreciate their knowledge and depth of understanding about their subjects of expertise. Ask *good* questions—and be patient for an answer. Their time is one of the best gifts a Five can give. Make sure they know it is valued.

At Home

Five children are curious, alert, and hungry for knowledge. While their siblings may chase each other around and vie for attention, the Five will observe and try to figure out the psychology behind attention, or spend time understanding how different familial roles intersect. Very independent from a young age, they are adept at occupying their time and don't want anyone to disturb them; they can disappear for hours at a time doing research for something that piques their interest, reading or looking at books, or using their imagination.

As a withdrawn type, Type Fives tend to be more reserved by nature. They are the original lovers of learning, taking a book everywhere (even to the dentist office), and using their imagination fueled by observation. Although not given to emotions, their observation keeps them in sync with their parents because they see and catch on quickly to what's occurring, and have the intellect to put the "pieces of the puzzle" together. To connect on a deeper level, ask them what they've been learning lately or what they're finding interesting, and engage with them—they'll open up remarkably fast.

I once tutored two brothers, and when I asked the younger one—six years old at the time—what he had been learning at school, he did not care to tell me. He had a more important project of his own going on, learning about the many species of sharks. Apparently he had caught a glimpse of Shark Week on TV, and that was enough to set him off on a nine-month hunt to learn everything he could about sharks, just in case (so much so that he also needed to know the temperature of the water every time his family went swimming in the ocean so that he'd know if it was optimal shark temperature). The greatest source of anxiety was not knowing everything he could know about sharks, but in the very thought of being unprepared because there was something he may not have been able to calculate.

Because they are observers, Fives can often struggle to connect with others: they look at them, watch them, and understand why they're doing what they're doing, but never quite feel that they fit in. The Wing Four keeps them individualistic; they don't want to be influenced by anyone, and their core fear of being incompetent is activated by their desire to learn as much as they can. The thing is, Fives generally want to fit in; they avoid disagreements, but just like love, conflicts in any relationships or friendships stir up avoidable emotions as well as become a reason for others to have an expectation of the Five.

Reminding Five children that you are proud of them and their desire for knowledge, but actively balancing their alone time with helpful interaction (for example, having an extracurricular class, or a playdate with a science-loving friend they can bond with) will help them change gears. However, respecting their alone time is critical to keeping a good relationship; bursting into their space or interrupting is perceived as rude and devaluing to them.

Fives also want to know *why*. When making a rule, explain the reason behind it. They'll listen; they just want to understand that it's fair (and well-calculated).

Above all else, make sure Fives are validated (in all things, but particularly their feelings); listen to the details of their life, and encourage them to continue their research. Connect with them in their interests is a high-profile love language that the Five child will carry on into their life.

Type Five parents are the complete antithesis to the emotionally charged Type Four. It can be difficult for them to connect with their children outside of their own subjects of interest. Although they can learn everything there is to know about raising children, they may struggle with overly emotional children, withdrawing to their own mind palace. The difficulty is helping a child who just skinned their knee or got into an argument with their best friend to cope beyond showing them kindness. Five parents are not given to natural socialization with their children, because they are often busy working or researching, and can feel disturbed when having a conversation like, "How's your day?" However, if they can connect with their children over common interests—say, how to write a classical novel—they're more than happy to answer in great detail.

Type Five parents are very cerebral. They give their children their knowledge and potentially their love of learning, and they know how to make things interesting. Because of this, they may find themselves connecting better with older children who are past the baby stage. But, Fives are nothing if not kind, so when they have very little children, it's important for them to use that kindness to engage early with them. Fives should take the time to play with young children and watch how quickly they stack blocks, how they try over and over again to walk, and how they develop their fine motor skills. Without looking at them as a research project (but also maybe just a little), they should try to enjoy the few years they have before their children will spar with them over a science experiment that just didn't add up.

In Love

The investigative, thoughtful, self-reliant Type Fives are not the most romantic numbers on the Enneagram, although they do want to love and be loved. Fives are thinkers—feelings are not their primary way of connection. They do have them, they just prefer not to focus on them. They need to be valued for their natural gifts of analysis, problem solving, and knowledge. What they don't need is someone clingy or dependent on them. They highly value their independence, and it can feel threatening if someone is prodding them into something they don't necessarily want to experience.

Type Fives bring loyalty, creativity, and improvement, and when their partner is struggling with anything, they are quick to come up with a solution to the problem. They truly want to make life easier for their partner, and enjoy sharing deep conversations and ideas.

A Type Five's privacy is top priority to them. Because they are not emotionally driven, Fives need their partners to be direct with them; emotional hints are annoying, and the Five will not receive them well. Rest assured, they do know that their partner would love to hear their feelings to help them connect but they also need reminding. What they might do more naturally is try to make sense of their partner's emotions (and their own toward their partner) in a direct manner, explaining them logically. Their focus is on being seen as capable and in their eyes, how could someone "capable" be blinded by emotions?

As natural observers, Fives have a more introverted disposition. They need a partner who won't try to get them out to places that they'd rather not go. No parties, no excruciatingly loud environments, and definitely no unnecessary gatherings where they'll have to socialize with their partner's long-lost Uncle Chad. If they go out in the first place, it'll have to be for a very specific reason, and only for something they really want to do.

Type Fives need someone who will actively listen to them on the same intellectual level—it takes a lot of work for them to articulate their thoughts cohesively, although they have no trouble writing things down clearly. If they seem out of it, it's likely because they're feeling uncomfortable. If they're feeling bored, at least they have their books, their mind palace. Their partner on the other hand, may or may not have their own proverbial "books." It's not that the Type Five doesn't care; they are preoccupied with thoughts in their own head. However, they deeply care that their partner has plenty of their own independence as well, supporting them as they need to be alone or out and about.

Fives are driven by their desire to make sense of the world around them. They are highly independent, fully functioning, and aware of their five senses and the observations they draw from them. Part of the reason they withdraw from feelings is due the fact that, while they may know what triggers them, emotions are an aspect of their inner world that they cannot entirely control, and that can terrify them. While a Five may feel emotions deeply, they try to explain them away or numb them, or even leave them unacknowledged to make them dissipate. While their partner may feel as if they are distancing themselves, a large part of why they do this is because they don't quite know how to express their emotions; they would rather spend the energy making tangible sense of what they're feeling and expressing it in practicalities, such as acts of service.

Fives are kind and generous with their partners, and they pay attention to the details that others miss. If you're in a relationship with a Type Five, give them the space they need, but remind them that they are safe and loved. Fives deeply value space with intentionality. Keep open lines of communication without forcing the conversation, bring dreams and big ideas, and bring problems. The Type Five loves coming up with solutions, and when they are introduced to a fixable problem it makes them feel like a hero.

In Work

As we have said, Fives are cerebral types whose strong points lie in understanding and knowledge; in a nutshell, Fives are driven by a need to thoroughly understand everything. Their perception and analytical recourse gives them the ability to easily detach from people and re-attach to another person's knowledge. Many of them can be brilliant. They are highly motivated by discovering a new idea or fact about the world. Learning a new skill can take a Five into a high-capacity, mentally challenging workplace. And in such a workplace, they thrive! On the other hand, feelings can be overwhelming and exhausting, even challenging to a Five, so they need their careers to make use of their full mental capacity.

As leaders, Fives are strategists who thrive in the creation of tools and techniques—the problem solvers who love finding solutions. Through their observations, Fives are system focused; they see a problem and figure out the best solution. This makes them well suited for the role of an engineer, scientist, author, scholar or researcher, or technician.

As natural innovators, Fives aren't content to remain on one idea or in a particular way of life unless it's been proven worthwhile through time and research—they aren't afraid to do things in a new way, and aren't at all interested in doing things the same way they've always been done.

Many Fives are considered pioneers or visionaries, relying on their ability to examine the world for themselves to keep safe. They want to see what's possible, challenging the status quo. Breaking into a system that appears to be working to make it better is an easy fix for a Five who is confident in their data and research skills. Fives aren't only curious, they really enjoy a problem, and if they need to learn a new skill set along the way, they'll do it. As long as the Five is feeling intellectually challenged, they're enjoying themselves immensely.

When Type Fives work alongside others who are more outgoing, they can offer advice; they feel energized and appreciated when others value their knowledge and insight, and when they are encouraged to express themselves in a logical way to explain their latest invention. If they're working with a fellow Five, it's important for there to be effective and concise communication between the two to make sure the work is done cohesively. As independents, Fives can easily distance themselves from others when feeling overwhelmed and struggling to connect with those who are overly emotional.

In the critically acclaimed show *Breaking Bad*, Walter White was a dormant Type Five (Wing Six) for most of his life. As a calculating, scientific, systematic man of few words, when confronted with conflict, he received it with ice in his voice and knowledge in his head. Luckily, dealing with a drug dealer is not the usual experience when confronting a Type Five.

Fives can make decisions based on logic, and they will weigh a well-researched list of pros and cons—without the input of other people, which is where they may hit obstacles. They make what they consider the correct decision based on logic but sometimes, the emotional decision is where the correct answer lies.

When resolving conflict and giving feedback to a Type Five, it's necessary to be honest about areas that need growth, and to stay in the realm of constructive criticism—they need the situation explained to them logically (remember the "why?" in childhood?). Encouraging the Five to look at both sides of the problem to find a compromise both motivates and energizes them. Communicate the facts before the feelings, ask about their thoughts and invite their response, and if they need privacy, respect it. To keep conflicts healthy, the Type Five needs to stay engaged instead of dismissed when communicating their thoughts and ideas. Allowing their emotions and feelings on a particular subject to be experienced as a process, instead of retreating per usual, allows the Type Five to receive a different kind of knowledge for self-exploration.

In Play

Fives aren't big on small talk. They'd much rather get to the heart of the matter, have their fun or discussion, and then get back to their business. For many Type Fives, family and friends are very important to connect with and navigate, but they still need plenty of time to pursue their current fascination and to reestablish themselves apart from their connection. Being with people teaches them to balance the tendency to withdraw by reaching *out*, even if it causes them uncomfortable sensations. Type Fives can get labeled as rebels, are happiest when venturing into some unknown territory, or when pioneering a new idea. Fives collect all the information and knowledge like some girls collect shoes ... or like I collect notebooks stuffed to the brim. It's just one of the reasons you want a Type Five on your trivia team.

Enneagram Fives are explorers who need their alone time respected. They can be caring and kind, but they're not overly demonstrative in their emotions; if a Five is taking time to be with you, that is the highest form of flattery. The people who respect the Type Five's time are the people who are highly valued and respected and loved by their Five. When the Type Five expresses themselves, listen carefully. Appreciate their intelligence, their humor, and never—ever, ever—put a Type Five on the spot. When bringing an idea or a problem, be objective and helpful when trying to come up with a solution. The Five will focus more on the facts and reason, but the objective solutions brought about will help to bring a different perspective and open both minds to new ideas.

Open-minded, calm, curious, insightful, and objective, Type Fives offer peace and commitment to sit beside you, happily in silence, to support whatever is needed.

To create rapport with a Type Five, providing lots of space is a necessity. Approaching them consistently, slowly, and with care gives them the space they require. A direct manner assures them that there is not likely to be an ulterior motivation. Fives pride themselves on being self-reliant, but can often isolate for days, cutting off all communication. Their challenge is merging the inside and outside worlds to create room for a relationship in the first place. Type Fives prefer to use isolation as a defense mechanism; they maintain their self-sufficient image, and they avoid their own emotions. They are stuck in their heads, and they think they are thriving there.

To resolve conflict in friendships, don't make assumptions about what's going on with a Type Five. Instead, emphasize the importance of the relationship. Approaching them with the logical list of facts regarding the scenario keeps them from controlling the situation by withdrawing. Challenging the Five through direct communication to be more generous with their time and opinion is seeking an invitation to be in their world *with them*. While the Five might not desire that (and this needs to be respected), there can still be a mutual camaraderie.

Type Fives bring a push and pull to all their friendships and relationships. They always want their space, but as soon as the other leaves, they want them to come back so they can share that intimacy. A lot of the Type Five feelings are below the surface, and as the observers, they think that others are observing them. Showing strong feelings or vulnerability contributes to the idea of being watched, but when they can release that vulnerability into health, they can trust that there will be enough for today, and for tomorrow.

Type Six

The Loyalist

"Don't give in to your fears. If you do,
you won't be able to talk to your heart."
—*Paulo Coelho,* The Alchemist

We once had a neighbor friend who was always *the* most prepared person you would ever meet. He looked up the rules before going to amusement parks and the menus before dining at a restaurant, and always found the exit doors at the cinema. It wasn't that he was paranoid, and he often felt hurt if he was laughed at, even by other adults. "I'm a dad! I have to take care of the group!" His family loved playing practical jokes on him; for good reason since his reactions were beyond hilarious. One time, this father went overboard and brought a fire extinguisher to a fireworks show on the 4th of July, even though there was a pool nearby. Although he insisted he did it as a joke, there was still a layer of caution underneath.

He was a Type Six stereotype—the kind that make most Type Sixes mad when they read a description of their type on social media. And Type Sixes are, of course, so much more than the typically portrayed pessimistic, challenging, doubtful, worst-case-scenario thinkers! They simply prefer to sit in the

Type Six at a Glance

Needs: To feel secure and protected from the world.

Fear: Lacking a strong support system and guidance, loss of safety and security, potential inability to care for loved ones.

Core Motivation: To have security and support from themselves and others, to have reassurance, to test others' feelings and attitude toward themselves, to win the fight against anxiety.

boat of caution and strategy, and assess the situation before they jump into a moving stream.

Passionate. Strategic. Intuitive. Devoted. Cautious. These are some of the traits that make up a Type Six. You'll hear them typed as The Skeptic, The Loyalist, and The Guardian, and they are, in their true form, aiming to be prepared for whatever might be thrown at them. In the cognitive triad, Sixes use their intuitive perception to understand the world and the people in it. Unlike the similar Type Five, Type Sixes are more concerned with the safety of the community, utilizing both relationships and intellect for the greater good. Their anticipatory nature allows an instinctive "first impression," where they can quickly discern and sniff out whether or not a situation or a person is friendly (or not), real and true (or not), potentially problematic (or not), and safe (or not).

The Type Six's forte is their strong and connective E.Q. The empathy that people would normally associate with a Type Nine Peacemaker or a Type Four or Two is very powerful in a Type Six. Because they so often tend to feel like an outsider, they are prepared and understanding toward someone who may feel the same. Their deep loyalty to their community is their driving point, and this is sometimes what puts them in their zone of caution and hesitation—but they can move from uncertainty to certainty at the drop of a hat. Deeply dedicated to protecting and remaining steadfast to their "people," they are considered reliable and trustworthy.

Clever, witty, and full of ideas, the Type Six is the strategist that everyone wants on their team—they empower everyone to solve the issue at hand, whether it's as simple as playing a game of Frisbee in the backyard, or dealing with a stock crash at the office.

You might say that their vice is fear and their virtue is courage—based upon ensuring *everyone's* security, loyalty, honesty, and physical health.

Being in the thinking triad, Sixes can struggle with fear that appears as doubt or concern over the public safety of others and themselves. Their ultimate fear is being defenseless or unequipped to cope with anything that could turn problematic. Type Sixes handle their fears in different ways. On the one hand, procrastination is the phobic Six's friend; it's how they stay safe and secure (think Marlin the clownfish father from the Pixar film, *Finding Nemo*). They don't necessarily have one or more phobias, rather a belief that everything could—and very well may—go wrong. On the other hand, the counterphobic Six prefers to deal with their fear by changing gears and rushing at their problem headfirst (think Rapunzel from the Disney film, *Tangled*). These Sixes often can mistype as Eights, with their collected attitude and stare-fear-in-the-face mindset. It's a heightened alertness directed toward any threat—and yes, sometimes the threats are magnified completely out of proportion. But, because Type Sixes often doubt themselves and the genuineness of others, they feel the need to be in control of the present and future. At the same time, they tend to constantly doubt their better judgment and question others' experience. It's their way of proving themselves and influencing others to appreciate them; and as they become more trusting of themselves and others, they can develop courage, and continue to protect and care for others.

Sixes are great at coming up with solutions to an anticipated problem long before it happens (knowing the rules helps with this). Their present self pushes them to be detail-oriented, while their visionary self pushes them to be strategic. They easily recognize and think carefully about others' perspectives, and have the ability to work through both logic and emotions due to their empathy patterns, offering help to others who need it, and spending time with those they love. They also are good at developing consistent and trusting relationships, and when healthy, have a good set of established values and personal morals. So long as they feel safe, supported, appreciated, and connected with, the Type Six will loyally and dutifully connect to a cause—person or idea—till the end.

Core Motivation: "If I Can't Fix It, No One Can"
We've all heard about the fight–flight–freeze method of dealing with fear. It's the body's natural reaction, responding to stress when there are any perceived threats. Your heart rate speeds up, increasing the oxygen to major muscles (to either prepare you to run or make someone else run), and your hearing heightens. During freeze, an attentive immobility takes place. Think about a scene in a film where two characters are in the midst of a fight,

but there's a good long minute or two (or at least it feels like it!) where they stare each other down. They know they're going to enter a confrontation, but they stand there and breathe through it, maybe saying something disparaging, maybe making some grunting noises. During freeze, the same changes take place in your body, but instead of moving to action quickly, your body gets ready for the next response.

A lot of what we deem as fear is conditioned based on a past situation or experience that was seen as "less than" we wanted: a perceived threat. Because of what your brain is conditioned to believe, it can see any situation as life threatening.

When I was a little one, my mum took me to Texas with her to visit my uncle, who happened to be having a cockroach infestation in his apartment building. If you've ever seen a Texas cockroach . . . well, maybe everything is bigger in Texas after all. I remember very little from that stage of life, but I do remember those massive insects all over the place, one even crawled up my leg. And being only two or three years old, I couldn't do anything about it. Guess what I'm deadly terrified of now? I'm fine with spiders and most other bugs, but the very (un)life-threatening, not-at-all-bigger-than-me cockroach . . . I don't want to fight; I want to flee or freeze when I see one on my floor.

Sometimes, our response to fear is overreactive. Traumatic events and anxiety are both natural causes that create a warranted response. But our response is our built-in mechanism that causes physical changes to enable us to protect ourselves. The key is testing if what we perceive as fear is truly something to be fearful of at all.

Highly motivated to achieve safety and security in their lives, Type Sixes work hard, are quick to take on responsibility, and are trustworthy. They can truly fix anything—if they see a problem, they fix it; if something is out of order, they find multiple solutions immediately; if they sense danger, they've already anticipated it and got it covered. It's part of their preparation interwoven with fear, but it's also part of their nature and wiring to see things that others may not notice.

While I was in college, a professor of ours shared his experience as he watched the terrorist attack in 2001 on the World Trade Center in New York. He had awoken in his home across the state line in New Jersey, made his coffee, opened his curtains that faced the city, started his laptop, and went to work. Not long afterward he glanced up to see smoke pouring from the buildings that were part of his normal view, and he had a feeling of helplessness come over him as he and his wife switched on the television. He was not only horrified at the destruction, damage, and loss of life, along with the rest of the American people—he was also petrified. As a phobic Type Six, this would have been enough to keep him inside for the rest of his life; but, also as a Type Six, he had prepared for this—thinking several steps ahead to prepare for the "just-in-case" scenarios that could come with living across from one of the world's biggest cities. From blackout curtains to food supplies, to extra postage stamps and a few spare tanks of gasoline in storage, my professor had taken time to expect the best, but still prepare for the worst.

His previous work on himself from his early twenties to his early forties had greatly benefitted his relationships with others, including his alertness toward *how* and *why* he brainstormed and thought the way he did. Coupling that with the balance between learning how to trust himself and see past the potential harms (of living in a highly populated area) and into the potential goods (of community, a good job, etc.) not only benefited his emotional state, but also his family. Actively working against the tide of his mental fear pushed him into the capacity of emotional confidence, courage, and security in his own decisions as a healthy Six.

Fighting against insecurity is part of the battle, but when the Type Six begins to recognize the changes to their resilience, something changes internally and they can become emboldened in their mannerisms. Type Sixes are not actually the pessimist, as much as they can seem that way. When they are off, questioning or challenging another person, they are most often playing devil's advocate to see if the other party has truly thought the situation through—and to test the other's true heart toward them.

One of Type Six's fears is betrayal, so they may choose to manipulate the situation through overwhelming warmth and kindness, even if they don't necessarily feel that way toward the other person. They are driven, motivated even, by the need to feel supported by others. However, they can still project their uncertainty about another person when feeling unhealthy or stressed. The interesting thing is that the Type Six's loyalty is intricately woven into their values, and shows up in conversations in which they choose to look past the fear, and speak up about the person or thing they care about, not because they feel they should or are expected to, but because they are loyal, and their community is more important than their fear. Their support system is what makes them feel safe, un-abandoned, and feeds into their basic fear. In fact, if they *don't* speak up about their uncertainties or verbalize their "Plan B in case of an emergency," the probability is that there will be more marked fear around losing their community because of their own actions or lack of communication.

Type Six Wings and Levels of Health

Sixes are very pragmatic. They deal with everything realistically, sensibly, and practically, instead of philosophically or emotionally (although they can be in touch with both).

With the Type Six as the central type of the thinking center, both of their wings extend into analytics and head-driven decisions, and also into fear. While this means that their decisions will primarily be logical, their wings differ greatly, with the Wing Five remaining on the generally introverted side, and the Wing Seven on the more outgoing, generally extroverted side. It follows therefore that it is important for the Type Six to find activities that get them out of their head, into the physical and emotional side of things. Type Sixes are wise and natural problem solvers, but they cannot build out of their regulated and calculated mental state of wisdom if they refuse to step into the experiential and somewhat spontaneous side of wisdom—booksmart versus streetsmart, if you will.

Learning to ask questions that put them on the side of positivity, "What if _____ and this (great thing!) happened instead?" instead of concern is a drastic game changer. Disqualifying the positive situations by crediting them only to luck is enough to keep the phobic Six locked at home forever—and the counterphobic Six exhausted for just as long

Sixes that wing Five are known as The Defender, and are very much in touch with their intellectual side. With more of an individualistic viewpoint, they have many different skill sets and things they have mastered. They can be quite interested in history, or the idea of a tradition or a past, using it as a tool to help predict into the future. While they are generally wary of people and take their time to let others in, they don't under- or overestimate other people as "projects," and once people have proved themselves as trustworthy, they are "in." The Defenders tend to be tip-of-the-iceberg kind of people; what you see is what you get, but others often have a feeling that there is much more to a Six than they can see.

However, when unhealthy, Sixes might exhibit a level of arrogance and pessimism when feeling fearful; leaning toward either being a lone wolf or a volcano when counterphobic, or diplomatic in their response when phobic. They can also frequently play detective, finding and building conspiracy theories and cases.

Sixes that wing Seven are called The Buddy, and are generally more outgoing. As opposed to Wing Five's more introverted tendencies, The Buddy is a natural charmer and can pull others in with their charisma and fun spirit. With a stronger connection to the Type Three Achiever, they are cheerful visionaries, curious, alert, and funny. Because of the connection to Three however, The Buddy can seem more confused and double-minded in their decisions, coming across as conflicted, although they have a more naturally upbeat tempo.

In disintegration, the primary defense mechanism of a Six is being demanding and hard to please, testing even their support system as the counterphobic becomes accusative. They choose to make plans without thinking them through in hopes of gaining material success (and hence security). They can be subject to mood swings and paranoia, inferiority complexes, and a deep need to be taken care of.

Childhood wounds that contribute to a Type Six are based on the idea that it's not okay to trust themselves, leading to a fear that they're unworthy of their own trust, evidenced through second-guessing, not because of people pleasing but because of lack of information and understanding to make a decision when they feel uninformed. Therefore, trusting others is a point where the Six feels particularly unworthy.

At home, the Type Six more than likely felt trusting of their guardian figures, even if their relationship wasn't always positive. At some point, the Type Six felt consistently unprotected and as if they could not depend on the very person who was designated to be their protector. It was only too easy that they conclude that the world must be the very same way— unpredictable, unreliable. The response to this was to be their own protector, constantly aware of the world and on the alert for anything that would try to shake their own personal security. All the while, The Loyalist longs for their own support system. In this early separation from their own inner voice, an unhealthy Six becomes uncertain and codependent to gain support from the ideal protective figure in their circle, by adopting their emotions and trying to figure out how others would feel about any decisions, before actually making them. As they mirror, their inner hope is that, with enough support and security, the Six will eventually be able to trust themselves and overcome their doubts and overthinking tendencies.

My Type Six friend, Liz, was looking for her second car, and had the opportunity to purchase a second-hand canary yellow convertible for about the same price as an early 2000s second-hand beige car with low mileage. Her father, who had passed away a few years earlier, was all about his cars, and for a brief time during her decision-making process, she almost went with what he would have wanted: the convertible. When she stepped back from the internal dialogue about what her father would have wanted, or what her friends expected from her, or even thinking logically about the price, and moved to thinking about what she wanted, she realized that the attributes of the no-nonsense camouflage beige car were exactly the things she appreciated about herself. She wasn't a threat to anyone, no one would "come after her" on the road if she happened to be speeding and she wouldn't have to worry about any extra insurance in case of an accident. She was creating her own security bubble based on the fact that no one would be looking unnecessarily at her. The car went on to serve Liz for many years, and she appreciated what it stood for, far more than she would have appreciated choosing the other car based on the opinions from other people.

Health and well-being are common values and motivations of a Type Six; but this can look different for each Six based on their personal context and their instincts (often referred to as a "subtype"). In their specific instincts of self-preservation, social, and intimate (the "three-legged stool" of instinctual reactions as discussed in the introduction), they reach past what we would perceive on the surface as a stereotype, and react to things based on their particular subtype. The self-preserving Type Six is much more family-oriented, and is driven to make connections through communication. They are more cautious with their opinions to avoid risking another's judgment or making mistakes, and thus losing their perceived sense of security. A social Six is more concerned with knowing the rules to avoid fear or risk of rejection. They connect more to social ideals, causes, and justice systems (and can often get confused with the Type One perfectionist). The intimate Type Six is more of a warrior—bolder, and more assertive and intimidating than the other two versions of

Loneliness does not equate to safety and neither does togetherness. Think about a human pyramid, where three or four people kneel and then two or three people clamber on top of them, and so on. It is all about the structure: if one person finds the weight too heavy, the other ones will fall. If the Six feels they have enough people and support to back them up, they can be confident in their decision-making and skill set. But if their support system begins to weigh them down, making them feel as though they are carrying life alone, or if trust falls apart even a little, their fear of being alone is reawakened. How interesting that a Type Six wants a social circle to support them but they want to show their loyalty by doing all their support tasks on their own.

A Type Six's disintegration zone leads them into the traits of a Type Three Achiever in the feelings triad where they can become overly competitive and zealous; while their integration leads them into the traits of a Type Nine Peacemaker in the instinctive triad, bringing out relaxation and more comfort in dealing with the flow of a situation. The three numbers act as a three-legged stool, tapping into both the growth and grace, heart and child zones. As they become more comfortable with their access to all three points of wisdom, there is just as much to be found in instincts and emotions as in their mental states.

When a Type Six is in disintegration mode, their general desire and draw to stability and loyalty begins to deteriorate, and they begin to behave like an unhealthy Type Three Achiever. They become driven by a desire to keep up with outward appearances and tasks, while coincidentally egging on their unhealthy connect-for-security mindset. Instead of the values of loyalty and relationship that they so treasure, they become more task-oriented. They care more so about the way they are perceived by others, building up their external image while (consciously or unconsciously) disconnecting from any empathy and emotions. The generally humble and caring Six becomes full of themselves, which stems from a fear of being unable to keep up with their appearance and to be all that they are pressuring themselves to become. To hide their self-doubt, they talk themselves up—not arrogantly per se, although it may come off as such—but because they feel the need to impress those around them.

For a Six to monitor stress, they must choose to trust others and themselves. Allowing others to help carry the many burdens they tend to take on (so that they can help others and not let anyone down) relieves the Type Six from overwhelming disintegration as they attempt to accomplish all they have set out to do. They care deeply about people, but by taking on everything to prove it, they can lose themselves in the doing (borrowing again from the Type Three's main core motivation). Instead of constantly feeling the need to be productive and a step ahead of everything, finding distractions and learning how to sit with oneself is vital to their well-being and consistent integration.

The character, Bilbo Baggins, in J. R. R. Tolkien's classic book, *The Hobbit*, is the embodiment of a Type Six: he does not desire any adventures; in fact, he'd much rather have a second breakfast and rest his feet on the hearth. His family (or Hobbit-folk, in general) are well-respected in their home, the Shire, because they never did anything unexpected and were predictable. When Gandalf presses an adventure on him, Bilbo is terrified for multiple reasons: "We are plain quiet folk, and I have no use for adventures. Nasty, disturbing, and uncomfortable things. Make you late for dinner!" Over the course of the book, Bilbo begins to accept help, realize he is a part of something much bigger, and recognize his capabilities lie far beyond his estimation. He has his adventure, and finds himself "doing and saying things altogether unexpected." Later in the book, Bilbo says, "This is a bitter adventure, if it must end so; and not a mountain of gold can amend it. Yet I am glad that I have shared in your perils— that has been more than any Baggins deserves."

A Type Six in integration moves to the Type Nine Peacemaker in the instinctive zone. This Type Six is more interested in a two-way conversation. Their focus homes in on serving others; as they express their own anxieties and concerns, they are also able to listen and recognize the value that they bring to the conversation. They can self-actualize as they begin to feel more at one with themselves as well as the world around them, allowing them to be more open and vulnerable. Their humility is genuine, and the guard walls come down as they become more accepting. Phobic Sixes need to learn to trust themselves. Counterphobic Sixes need to learn to trust others, but it's not as cut and dry as "let it go" and "stop worrying."

As the Type Six learns to trust themselves, they trust their ability to face problems and tap into their nature to fix them; they grow to trust their ability to anticipate the danger, but also any needs that arise; they also trust their ability to read and discern others, and their intentionality. They believe that their personal strength can help carry themselves over whatever comes their way. This is where they tap into peace and calmness—they are at peace with the insecurity of an ever-changing world, letting go of the idea of a primarily dangerous outside. Yes, it is dangerous. No, we don't need to let everything go. It's the belief that one can help contribute to a better world while still actively pursuing safety and the goodness of community. Perhaps things are not so "one way or the other."

My friend Brit was always caught up in fear of trusting herself. Following a string of bad relationships in her late high school and early college years, she was ready to declare herself "single forever." Going to counseling was where she first heard about gratitude journals and began one of her own. Her counselor gave her the idea to write down not only five things she was grateful for that day, but five decisions she made that day that were good. It could be something as simple as, "I chose to bring an umbrella because it looked like it might rain," or "I chose to compliment the saleslady on her hairstyle." The first two or three weeks that Brit incorporated this into her daily routine, she enjoyed it. Then her counselor recommended she start recording her response to those decisions, as well as any response that others may have had that validated her choice. For example, "I chose to wear yellow today to help brighten my own day," might result in "I chose to wear yellow today to help brighten my own day, and someone at work said it matched sunflowers. I feel _____."

Over time, this helped Brit not only look through the lens of what good decisions she was making (thus learning how to trust herself again), it helped her develop relationships with her support system while keeping her own head up without them. It also allowed her contact with her own feelings as she recognized gratitude and how her decisions made her tap into her emotions, garnering instinct. Later, her counselor began to incorporate going with her first instinct on decisions. It was that "first" instinct that led Brit to ask out a coworker—her now-husband. Instead of being struck with her initial doubt that he couldn't like her, she followed her first instinct, without wasting too much of her thought process worrying about what would or wouldn't happen.

Belief is difficult for the Type Six. The lonely boy, Billy, from the film *Polar Express*, wouldn't believe in Santa because he had never seen him. One of the brothers, John, from *Peter Pan*, refused to put his desire to fly in "faith, trust, and pixie dust." But Type Sixes want to hope. They cling to it. Once they find someone or something they can put their trust and hope into, they feel connected and validated, and they want to keep up that connection. It provides a sense of stability; gone is the self-doubt. But until the Type Six can understand and communicate with their own inner dialogue, and take their own guidance, they'll be stuck in their own mind-game of every voice's influence except their own.

So how do you develop that self-confidence in trusting yourself?

Type Six: If there are issues that need to be brought to the surface, give yourself a deadline, then bring them to the table—whether at a job, in a relationship, or in yourself. Fear of rejection is part of an ever-shifting world of uncertainty. But for abandonment to subside and growth to take place, self-acceptance must take root. Judging based solely on the result of one decision is an overgeneralization that doesn't help anyone. One cannot just build safety immediately; it's built over time—but it cannot be built at all if there is no personal emotional stability. Giving credit to good decisions allows for us to slowly peel off the mask of anxiety and low self-confidence, giving place to a strong inner dialogue that exudes loyalty not out of fear, but out of respect and mindfulness that we are all human, too. In the words of John Piper, "Whenever your heart starts to be anxious about the future, preach to your heart and say, 'Heart, who do you think you are to be afraid of the future and nullify the promise of God? No, heart, I will not exalt myself with anxiety.'"

Our thought-life should be our biggest ally, not our biggest hindrance. When we find someone or something worth doing the brave thing for, that is true loyalty. Practicing gratitude, making good decisions, and staying empathetic without becoming passive–aggressive is where trust lies. Staying tenderhearted is taking the power back from a world that says you need to be on your guard. Learning how to access and practice courage gives you a peace of mind. And when you are at peace, confident, and secure, you allow for gatherings where community is intertwined.

Life with a Type Six: The Consistent Carer

We've established that Type Sixes are loyal, understanding, empathetic, and a good friend to have on hand at all times, but especially during any kind of uncertainty as they *will* have a backup plan A, B, and C (just in case!). They are the problem solvers of the Enneagram; however, they tend to greet everything and everyone with a doubtful mind and a guilty-until-proven-innocent mindset. While they can be perceived as challenging, fake, or lazy (procrastinating!), it's all about being consistent and trustworthy toward them, appreciating their attention to detail and keen eye for potential problems, and being as unambiguous as possible.

Making up approximately 10 percent of the population, Sixes are logical, strategic, and committed. Think of the popular TV show *Survivor*. Chances are, some of the winners of the show have been Type Sixes: survivalists extraordinaire. Trust is important for a Six. So is thinking ten steps ahead in the game, and going over multiple hypothetical situations and outcomes. Tolerance and willingness to blend in help Sixes feel in control.

Psychologically, Sixes use their deep perception to understand the world around them, and their primary focus is on the safety of the group. Deeply rooted in truth and natural trouble-shooters, they recognize that the world is not always beautiful. Worst-case-scenario thinking is inevitable, and can throw the Type Six off from using their real gifts. It's not even anxiety itself that causes the issue—it's anxiety *about* the anxiety. But, as they learn to trust themselves, they can develop flexibility, and find their stretch and release points of becoming more courageous to act, even if they have some doubts or fears. The question that we need to answer is how do we help Sixes to truly grow at home, in love, in work, and in play? How do we help build consistency and strengthen the bond, without adding to our own concerns of an even thicker wall being built?

It all starts with a little thing called communication. Or rather, *how* we communicate. Communication style varies from type to type as we know, but there are certain trigger points that might cause a Type Six to go into a retreat zone (while the same might cause an Eight to roar). Sixes particularly need a lot of love, and a little acknowledgement goes a long way. The rhythm of home life can become overly comfortable to the point of never leaving. But trying new things, without fear, using their gift of intuition and awareness builds into strong decision-making skills and communication. Long story short: honor and acknowledge all the questions. Answer them with truth as much as you possibly can. An honest "I don't know" is more honored than a false answer.

At Home

At home, conflict resolution is not the Type Six's strong suit. While a healthy Type Six is generally aware of their projection tendencies, a lot of Sixes aren't at that place yet, and are unable to recognize the difference between projecting their feelings and fear, and communicating that their own feelings are their responsibility (without the other party having to read the Six's mind). It follows that the way one might give feedback to a Type Six would be straightforward; however, to allow a Type Six to feel confident and take the responsibility, it's important to keep conversations lighthearted and comfortable. Any kind of ambiguous questions such as a texted, "I have a question for you!" will immediately throw the Type Six into a flurry of self-doubt and worry, concern over their own actions, and a fear of both present circumstances and future propositions. It's just not fair, and can actually be manipulative.

Listen for key words that suggest insecurity and uncertainty, such as "maybe," or "possibly," or if they ask you multiple times if what they said "makes sense" or if they're "all right." It can feel as if they're insulting you or being passive–aggressive, but the Six is, in fact, undermining themselves—without even realizing it.

If there's a specific conflict that needs to be resolved, give them some time, and try to be patient if the Type Six becomes defensive or argumentative. You've tapped into their world, and trusting their own instincts is one of the hardest things for them to do. Type Sixes in general—but specifically children—feel safer when they've questioned things. Being reassuring, but not overtly protective, is part of growth; introduce them to new experiences early so they have time to adjust themselves and recognize that just because something is unexpected or uncertain, it doesn't mean it's always bad or scary.

When I was a little girl, my parents took me to Disneyland. I desperately wanted to go on the Indiana Jones ride, and was even tall enough, but as a Type Nine who was feeling my stretch point at Six, I just didn't have enough information. My mum flagged down a group of rowdy teenage girls coming off the ride and asked if they thought I would like it. My eight-year-old self was (so!) embarrassed, but the girls were enthusiastic about how much I'd love it, and also told me there was a massive snake and a few other surprises that I felt well informed enough to jump on with my dad (and after the first ride I insisted we go another three or four times that day). It's the same with trying a new food, going down the big slide at the playground, or making friends. Helping children to trust their good instincts without dishonoring their feelings is a big part of life. Type Six children deeply desire approval, and it's important for them to trust their conscience and instincts without them feeling like they need approval from everyone. Of course, parental authority is different, and should be treated as such (there's a reason we show babies the oven and teach them "HOT!" before they know how to talk).

Clarifying early on what Type Six children believe, and valuing those beliefs, helps them to home in on their own confidence levels in communicating what they believe. Dependability as a parent or guardian figure draws them back to their grounding as a member of the family, while encouraging their confidence and independence will help them tap into health at an early age when they are faced with their fears.

In Love

In romantic relationships, the Type Six is faithful and loyal to their partner—they have let them into their lives and are dedicated to working through any and all issues that may arise. However, they also have anxiety in general over past relationships that were unhealthy and didn't work out, and even though they might be over them, the Type Six's innate fear of abandonment requires their partner to be patient as they work their way through their fears, and learn how to let go and *not* project their worries about past experiences onto their current partner. While the Type Six may excel at making balanced decisions, they will still have trouble with facing decisions in the first place, and if they feel as though they are being attacked in any way, they are prone to explosion in the conversation rather than staying calm and talking things through.

Type Sixes aren't the most emotional people, and as task-oriented people their primary focus may be more on preparing for anything that may try to bombard their relationship. When their partner is idealistic and more easygoing and free at heart, Sixes can be a grounding force of peace, especially when in their healthy heart point. For a Loyalist, a key motivation is time spent with those they love—they will do anything for that. On the other hand, another energizing factor is advocating for their own beliefs and values. Remember, it's often very difficult for a Type Six to "believe" in anything that they haven't seen proof or evidence of. When the Type Six has let you into their world to the extent where they feel safe to share their values and beliefs with you (showing that they believe in *you*), make sure to validate and not feed into uncertainty or doubt around their personal values. Not only does this move the Type Six into a form of retreat, the stress can also trigger them into a stretch point of Three, where everything becomes appearance oriented, and they may feel as though they have to prove themselves to their partner.

On the opposite end of the spectrum, I had a Type Six friend named Amber who was dating County, a Type Three Achiever (Wing Four). Amber was constantly worried that she would become too much for him and eventually drive him away. She found herself testing his professed love for her to see if he really felt that way about her, even though she also knew his actions said that he did. Eighteen months into their relationship, County noted Amber would also go through phases every few months where she needed extra reassurance to make sure she shouldn't leave, overanalyzing every little thing from when he received a text message from a mate to when he was at school and away from her. Amber's mantra up to this point was, "Leave before I get left" (abandonment).

This would have been a manic relationship to handle at the best of times, but County's 3w4 of the relationship understood the key of communication and acknowledgement that was necessary to help his partner heal. Amber had communicated to him early on that she was an overthinker and a bit of a doubter. County's best and most honest contribution in acknowledging Amber's fears was his note that acknowledging the fear was not the same as saying the concern was true. Instead, he helped Amber acknowledge within herself—without gaslighting— that the fears she was prone to, the worries that she had, whether based on past experience and trauma or not, were what was shifting her perspective.

Think about the childhood wounds of a Type Six: based on the idea that they can't trust themselves, laced with abandonment.

For a while, County was hurt because he felt that Amber's approach was stemming from mistrust in *him*. Once they were able to get on the same page and County felt Amber withdrawing or pushing back, he was able to ask her, "What do you feel is going on right now?" and draw her out of her mental headspace and what would/could have been warped, to help create firmer ground in what was actually happening. This cleared up any projection, and helped her to find safety.

In Work

Type Sixes are great at making practical decisions that are logical and smart, although they do take the time to think about different perspectives. They also have the ability, when honed, to think both logically and emotionally. They are the administrators, the caregivers, the teachers and professors, the lawyers and law officers—feeling energetic and at high capacity when they can take care of others and feel confident in their roles, supported in their service, and appreciated in return. It's all about establishing trust within the business; but it could also just as much be about the hierarchy of fairness. Although the Six isn't necessarily known for being overly justice oriented, they are security oriented, so it follows that fairness out of security and loyalty contributes greatly to their trust orientation. They need to feel that they have earned the trust to be in the position they're working in, because they have devoted their time and loyalty to a specific area of expertise. When their environments place specific value on them as individuals, and where they are encouraged to build stability and positive relationships with their peers and colleagues, Type Sixes excel and move at a fast pace—work can effectively become one of their safe places, both practically and physically. Sometimes, however, a hard conversation will come up—or pressure from a new boss, or a conflict with coworkers—and this can create dissonance and instability in their workflow and support structure. That is when communication is important.

When communicating with a Type Six at your workplace, planning is key. Making decisions is not something the Type Six would gravitate toward or choose to do, and this can contribute to fatigue and lack of motivation. Taking time to think out a conversation with a Type Six in advance and guiding the conversation as it goes takes the pressure off of the Six, and moves the energy into a different sphere. Conscientiously drawing the Type Six's point of view to the positive and away from negative outcomes of a scenario will help them to avoid their fears and keep them from becoming too emotional or reacting very strongly as a counterphobic Six (similar to a Type Eight Challenger).

Developing new habits as a Type Six can be difficult. Type Sixes are not lacking in self-estimation, but more in self-confidence. They know they're good people—list-makers, volunteers—and have a likable persona that doubles as a good weapon of defense. However, they often place such high expectations on themselves as "good" people that they become easily overwhelmed when they don't feel up to the challenge, even if they are the only ones who have technically put that on themselves.

To help soothe their own fear and insecurity, Type Sixes may try to associate with authority or those who are surer of themselves and are confident, seeking out people who are nearly their opposite in strength to help balance out their weaknesses. It's a part of their support system and structure of protection, and they are deeply committed to these people. But with Type

Six dealing with their own abandonment, they don't often fully trust these individuals for years at least, without their proof of consistency.

To challenge the Type Six to take responsibility for their own actions is to refuse to take on whatever they have projected onto you. To take (a far-fetched) example, a Type Six employee may be triggered by something as simple as their employer suddenly drinking tea instead of coffee and immediately relate that to their horrible teacher from high school that bossed everyone around without any added tutoring or allowance for extra credit and—you guessed it—was an avid tea drinker. While that situation is a long shot, and most adults can recognize their thinking patterns, there may still be a projection that occurs in their habit of suspicion, which leads to either the withdrawal and cautious approach toward their boss (phobic) or a sudden aggressive attitude (counterphobic). As an employer or even a colleague, helping a Type Six take note of their patterns, look for the positives in what could be a stressful situation, and helping them find humor in everything helps strengthen their work ethic and responsible attitude. It's about creating an environment that allows them to feel they can ask for support, and allowance for enough safety to help them relax their mental walls and capacity that's focused on what could be, instead focusing on the job at hand.

In Play

In the comedy *Meet the Fockers*, the father of the family, Jack (Robert De Niro) establishes a "circle of trust," and shares it with his soon-to-be son-in-law, Greg (Ben Stiller), who he does not consider to be the ideal candidate to be marry his daughter, of course. Unfortunately, this circle of trust has a set of rules and guidelines that either make you trustworthy, or . . . not. As laughable as this scenario is, trust influences the interactions with everyone we interact with. Like Jack Focker, the Type Six has a circle of trust. The more trust exists, the better the relationship; it is earned, just like any relationship. But you don't necessarily get to choose your family or your boss. You *can* choose your friends, however.

Type Sixes have a nearly uncanny humor to connect to people in an endearing—sometimes quirky—way. If you have broken into the Type Six's circle of trust, you have broken into their support system. Consider it a great privilege; they are loyal to their loved ones beyond a shadow of doubt.

Communicating with a Type Six effectively means they will be checking in consistently, even if the questions seem misplaced or unnecessary—they are putting their mind to rest and ensuring they know *all* the facts. As the realists, sugarcoating anything to a Type Six automatically pulls you *out* of their circle of trust—if they have covered all their bases by asking questions, they expect you to do your part and give them the answers they are looking for so that they can mentally prepare or think ahead.

Type Sixes deeply desire authenticity in their friendships. To create rapport, it's all about appreciating their attention to detail and problems, and if they initiate, agreeing on any rules in advance. Most people wouldn't want to go on a long car ride through the Arizona desert without having a map of where to go; in the same vein, Type Sixes use their intellect and need to understand where their friends are going to end up to feel comfortable going along on the ride. It allows them to tap into their self-trust instincts, and become more comfortable, flexible, *and* courageous in the process, even if doubtful.

As The Loyalist, Type Sixes value their friendships dearly—and want to ensure that those in their friend group know they are valued. However, they also need to be verbally appreciated in turn; they often worry they've ruined a friendship after a mistake. In the series *Friends*, whenever Chandler and Monica have a bit of a spat, Chandler is always worried that the relationship is over. Sixes experience *fear* as one of their central emotions. Encouraging them to talk through their fears without downplaying anything and being understanding while still honest, allows them room to breathe and process while still building their trust and keeping rapport. Key questions like, "What would happen if your worst-case scenario actually happened?" allows them to keep things in perspective; even if the worst thing happened, it wouldn't be the end. Then, remind them to think of the best-case scenario.

Above all, encourage the Type Sixes in your life to trust their instincts and inner voice, rather than looking for approval and guidance from something or someone outside of their world. Remind them that action is better than being paralyzed by their decisions. Clearing the head through a physical activity like taking a walk, playing a musical instrument, or doing something creative allows them to shift their focus from what could be (in a negative way) to the present, to more clearly see what's really happening in front of them.

Type Seven

The Enthusiast

"I get up every morning determined to both change the world and have one hell of a good time. Sometimes, this makes planning my day difficult."
—E. B. White

Everyone has at least one or two Type Sevens in their lives: naturally enthusiastic, explorative, impulsive, adventurous, assertive, optimistic, creative, imaginative, glass-half-full kind of people. You never know quite where they'll show up next (they'll be at your house on a Monday night and then somehow randomly be in Paris on Tuesday); they'll always "pencil you in" to their schedule (and you'll stay there unless something slightly more exciting pops up); and sometimes you wonder how they ever get anything done (because they're literally planning the next big event while enjoying their latest event). They just know how to have fun in unique and creative ways. They're never just "out to dinner"; instead, it's a full-on seven-course meal with sparklers in the dessert. They're not superheroes, but they are wrapped up in finding the fun in life—and they're probably wondering why everyone else can't fill their schedule just as easily. They toe the line of freedom and anticipation about as carefully as Miley

Type Seven at a Glance

Needs: To be content, stimulated, and engaged with their environment as they seek consistent excitement.

Fear: Of being trapped without escape, necessary pain, deprivation.

Core Motivation: To feel freedom to explore all of life's opportunties in anticipation, to maintain happiness, stay busy, and avoid discomfort or hurt.

Cyrus (definitely a Type Seven) swung from her wrecking ball. It's just the nature of a Type Seven.

Not to sound biased or anything, but Type Sevens were some of my absolute favorite people growing up (without me even realizing what Type Sevens were). I often joke that the acronym FOMO (fear of missing out) was coined by a Seven. They literally explore and venture their way through life—and it's not a tiptoe, it's an, "I'm here, the life of the party! Everyone can truly start celebrating now! You're welcome!"

Known as The Enthusiast, The Adventurer, or The Epicure, Type Sevens truly love life and want to embrace everything it has to offer. They love telling stories about their insights and experiences, are great communicators, and their playfulness and knack for finding the silver lining in any situation make them resilient and positive people. In fact, the use of "The Epicure" stems from the philosophical practice of Epicureanism, founded in 307 BC from the teachings of the Greek philosopher Epicurus.

Epicurus viewed the goals of human life as based solely around seeking pleasure to avoid pain, freedom from fear and absence of physical ailment or bodily pain, and a state or sense of tranquility; a virtuous and peaceful life were one and the same, although centered around pursuit of pleasure (food, comfort, luxury). Translated to today, Type Sevens do a great job of embodying an Epicurean lifestyle. If they sense that things are about to get even the least bit boring, they are off to stir the pot and mix life up again. However, they can often feel that they are always on the move and overly impulsive, and yet are never doing exactly enough.

Spontaneity is a Type Seven's middle name; they thrive on stimulation, possibility, and keeping their options open. With a high-energy and easily distracted nature, they enjoy starting multiple creative projects and ideas, although they seldom finish them because that mentally equates to being constrained to one particular idea, and Type Sevens live to be free. They're creative and strategic visionaries, so they like to look for what's coming next and try everything because they don't want to miss out on anything. While this can lead to overextension, Type Sevens dwell in the thinking triad, which regulates fear; the coping mechanism for this stance is to avoid any kind of pain or emotions through focusing on opportunity and fun. While Type Threes are constantly working toward the ideal self, Type Sevens *need* to first visualize the ideal self. Although they tend to be indecisive, healthy Type Sevens not only spend time looking to the future, they envision how they want it to appear, and can sort through their opportunities well, ensuring that their decisions contribute to that future, rather than letting not-so-important "fun" take up valuable time in their already-busy lifestyle and schedule. Type Sevens desire simplicity in contentment; instead, they settle for an ongoing wheel of excitement in an effort to stay content.

Stepping out of their head emotion of fear (which causes minimization and creates mental filters toward people and opportunity) and finding alternative ways to both embrace the person/idea/opportunity in front of them—while still reining in and recognizing their emotions behind their choice—is a massive step toward integration and growth. To put it simply, minimizing emotions of pain and fear minimizes opportunity for true joy. Without realizing it, the ongoing round of fun creates a numbness toward any emotions.

Being in the thinking center, Type Sevens project their obstacle of fear through emotional avoidance. They have a habit of gluttony and lack sufficient empathy to drive a good path past borderline superficial relationships. It's simply not worth the effort to them to monitor and actively recognize the difference between love and instant gratification; it's easier to fill any void that would allow them too deep into their thought process and underlying fears of facing the more "negative" thoughts or ideas in their lives. Distraction through entertainment or work allows them to bring a certain charming joy to everything. Because they are triggered by the very idea of boredom, the leadership aspect of Type Seven is innovative and adaptable to the circumstance, and as they are incredible at generating excitement, can easily motivate those around them.

I have a Type Seven friend who has literally hundreds of connections from all of her travels and is a star networker. She calls these connections her friends, but doesn't actually talk to them until she needs something. It's not that she doesn't feel a personal connection with them; it's primarily that she's worried about forming emotional attachments to people and getting hurt in the process. When things go wrong or she senses hurt on the horizon, she can move straight along in her quest without being affected—no time for sadness, far easier to find the joyful or optimistic side of things. After all, if you're not truly connected, you can't feel bad.

As The Enthusiast, Type Sevens *thrive* in a culture of movement, momentum, and flexibility. They are confident, skilled multitaskers, and are productive and action oriented. Their active mind is a connector, not only among people in their networking circles, but also in the realm of ideas. This allows them to accumulate loads of knowledge across a broad range of topics, and contributes to their innovative and creative spirit; generating new information and integrating ideas while leaving others to do the finishing and fine-tuning is part of their leadership style. They are the true idealist and details don't matter because someone else will take care of that aspect of things. While some may see Sevens as scatterbrained, it is easy for them to make and maintain rapport because they are so charismatic.

Core Motivation: "Variety Is the Spice of Life!"

Remember how I talked about my dad being a Type One Reformer and sticking with his job for 28 years, despite absolutely despising everything about the last years leading to his retirement? My mum, as soon as they got married, said, "Now we can *do* things!" She's a hardcore Type Seven.

Type Sevens are driven by their desire to maintain their own happiness and freedom above all else. They also want to avoid lack of opportunity and experiences. They want to get excited and *stay* excited and busy to avoid their fear of pain, and if they begin to feel pain, they want to occupy more space and time to pretend it doesn't exist. Variety is the spice of life—the more options, the better! There's a future fixation on planning, and because Type Sevens are natural planners, they are always trying to fill their schedule up even in the middle of the event they're currently attending. But like The Individualist, they deeply desire an innate authenticity and *contentment*—there is barely any time to create that quiet time to bring contentment, because it is viewed as something to be achieved or sought. As Christopher Heuertz writes, "When Sevens practice resting in stillness, they can intentionally silence the mind."

Maintaining happiness and freedom at all costs is different from person to person, and for Seven it is an uncomfortable journey to begin to look past what they see in front of them to what they truly *need*. A few years ago, my Type Seven friend Jake, who is in his mid-thirties, experienced what he describes as "darkness" through migraines, chronic fatigue, and stress-related symptoms leading to bedrest. For a Type Seven, this was a massive swap from his day-to-day activities and life of exploration in Los Angeles, but being put on bedrest and without being able to actively speak to very many people, he took notes on what his body was doing and feeling. Instead of hiding behind podcasts and noise, Jake listened to what it felt like to not have freedom, and to *not* be physically and mentally happy. His body was stressing him out because it was tired. It couldn't handle the mine of ideas and opportunities all at the same time. In his body, he discovered he could actually sense his emotions and his feelings. Fear in the pit of his stomach. Anger and tension in his neck and shoulders. Sadness in his chest and fingers. When he began to listen to these feelings and sort through them from years of falsely maintained "happiness," he became his own sort of counselor through those several weeks.

Through that time, Jake was able to actively and effectively separate his thinking from his doing.

He spent a lot of time journaling, and learning how to soften and pay attention to specific things that his body was physically telling him. He changed his movement practices and worked on incorporating yoga (which literally stresses the body while still strengthening it) and changing his eating habits. Three years later, Jake is still a perky, happy, free-falling guy, but when he encounters an emotion or an opportunity that he recognizes, he stays with it. His biggest revelation was that *his true happiness and true joy can be self-contained just as much as his more painful emotions*. And if that's the case, why would he want to deprive himself of those emotions? Jake's authenticity with his emotions allowed him to realign properly with his cognitive center, and truly understand his logical and analytical side. A full social calendar does not equal a fully functioning emotional life. Knowing and being able to separate what activities energize and strain or demand unwanted pressure is what contributes to motivation and demotivation. In addition, Jake's active remembrance of his childhood wounds allowed him to access his fears and *why* they were fears to begin with. This solidified his freedom as it is presently, and integrated him into growth as he valued his present *and* his future, while still respecting his past, facing it head on and recognizing how it brought him to the place he is now.

The deep fear of a Type Seven lies in never feeling content, instead feeling emptiness and unhappiness. Learning how to ask not only, "What's next?" but "Why am I here?" is only an added door to looking past the "good" and into full purpose and contentment. These questions allow a Seven to go from a mindset of gluttony and consumerism ("How much can I get out of life?") to generosity ("How much can I bring to life's table?").

Getting people excited and *staying* excited themselves is part of the core motivation of the Type Seven. It's worth noting here that Type Sevens are *funny*. They *love* making people laugh and bringing lightheartedness to sometimes stark situations, or things that the average human being may just view as a way of life—think comedians like Robin Williams, Dick Van Dyke, Eddie Murphy, and Jack Black. Their lightheartedness is a piece of the childlike nature they choose to bring to every scenario, because when everyone around them is happy, they are also happy. Of course, they're happy even when everyone around them isn't, but it's much more fun and enjoyable when everyone around them is. Why not bring a joke or fun or laughter to the family table if you possibly can?

In contrast to the fear of confinement and self-inflicted chains as the defined barrier of the Type Seven, they rather look to the unknown with open arms and a "bring it on" mentality. It's just another aspect of maintaining their freedom (even if there should be some healthy fear involved). However, even when it comes to maintaining their freedom, Type Sevens are not fans of conflict (even those with a Wing Eight, although they are much more open to it). Conflict resolution to them can often turn to coping through minimization to mentally salvage the relationship if they feel it is going awry. For example, "I know they weren't kind today or yesterday or the last time I saw them, but maybe they're just having a bad day!" With healthy conflict, it's much easier for the Seven to counterculturally stay in the present and listen without self-referencing. It's almost as if the conflict brings them to their healthiest self because someone is engaging with them on a vulnerable topic; even if the discussion is more or less emotionally driven, there's a keen focus on whatever issues are brought to the surface, and they can be solved accordingly. Because they are in the thinking triad, Type Sevens need direct communication just as much as they need new ideas, new people, and new events. Telling them just *what* they need to do? Well, that's a different story. Living from their authentic self with a humble spirit and heart takes time and effort, and learning how to live in a mindset of "present" with themselves takes practice and patience.

Type Seven Wings and Levels of Health

While Type Sevens are rooted in the thinking or head triad, it's interesting to find fear at the base of their constant movement and need to be on the go. However, unlike Type Sixes, who are situated in the middle of the thinking triad, Type Sevens have a wing that allows them to tap into the instinctive triad to run and make decisions from that angle as well. In a fight-or-flight scenario, the Type Seven has access to both; their Wing Six will urge them to run, while their Wing Eight will dare them to fight. What they will do depends on the situation and scenario. Type Sevens winging Six (The Loyalist) are called The Entertainer. Those that wing Eight (The Challenger) in the instinctive triad are called The Realist. With both wings to fly, Sevens stay rooted more or less in their enthusiasm and zest for life, but there is an aspect of expansion and responsibility that comes with each wing's notable character traits.

The Entertainers (7w6) are responsible, loyal to a fault—and nervous. They tend to be more people and relationship oriented, and because they desire acceptance by other people, they can be far steadier and willing to stick with their commitments and ideas for the long haul, with a sense of longevity. They are usually very funny with a sarcastic wit and humor based on personal experiences (due to their communication style as Sevens), and are more openly vulnerable and sweet. They can have issues identifying and expressing anger, and avoiding authority while still very much being aware of it. The practical side of them is constantly looking for loopholes in the rules that allow them to experience more freedom; but the Six wing is constantly reining them in "just in case." They work hard for the cause, but hate to be told what to do and complain about the status quo when they feel they contribute just as much by their ideas. The Wing Six pulls them slightly to the more cautious side, but their main focus is bringing fun to others.

In disintegration, The Entertainers can often experience short bouts of insecurity based on hurt feelings and comparisons to anyone similar to them. This can contribute to an addictive need for people's approval and people in general, because they don't want to be alone; but, they struggle to uphold a strong relationship because they make themselves purposefully shallow, and fall in and out of "love" easily.

The Realists (7w8) are known to be generous and expansive, especially when it comes to their friendship circle, and they are best situated in a social instinct subtype (as opposed to a self-preservation and intimate subtype) where they are particularly desirous of relationships and ideas to help express their love for life. They are more aggressive than the Wing Six, and can be defenders in a boisterously obnoxious, self-centered way, although they don't mean to be so. Celebrations, travel, food are all very important central aspects of the pleasure-seeking Type

Seven. They are natural entrepreneurs, and have a strong sense of self-confidence for "worldly" matters that they believe no one else has any idea about—but they are happy to share their stories and experiences. Their wide range of ideas and interests, and their generosity means that they share with everyone alike, gathering their friends. The Wing Eight allows for more of a focus concerned toward goals, and less of a concern for any conflicts along the way.

When in a state of disintegration, The Realist's communication style can turn from charming and light-hearted to more demanding and narcissistic. They are quick to garner recognition and don't mind cutting the corners if it means achieving their goals quickly, acquiring money and the materials along the way. If reality doesn't meet their (high) expectations, they can become angry and need sugarcoating from others' opinions to calm down—they learn from doing, not from being told what to do.

As children, Type Sevens probably lived a very happy, comfortable life but they somehow felt a disconnection from whoever the "nurturer" was in their mind, leading to abandonment issues. Whether something as simple as not being able to go where their caretaker said they were going that day due to a misunderstanding, or as complex as abuse and not having their needs met as a child, Sevens learned to turn inward to focus on activities to fill the void and become self-reliant. They felt that, to protect themselves, they needed to self-nurture because no one else could do it adequately. Whatever they thought would make them happy became their own personal relief and form of nurturing.

A dear Type Seven (Wing Eight) friend of mine from years ago was always doing something. He was the life of the party: charismatic, charming, a traveler, a storyteller, loved by everyone. When we were younger, his parents went through a rough divorce and he became excruciatingly active: shark-cage diving, learning how to surf, turning up in New York to go couch surfing, skydiving. He turned up one night to a hangout and told me, "My parents just finished their divorce proceedings." After some chatting, we found it interesting that his parents' divorce (his mum's second in fifteen years) coincided with his burst of activity. For years as the oldest child, he felt he had to be the man of the house. When his mum remarried, he had to reestablish his identity as a young teenager. In his early twenties, during his mum's second divorce, something in him exploded to create an atmosphere of consistent movement so that he wouldn't have to feel the inner turmoil of the pain and emotional stress. It wasn't just a rejection by his parents—in some way, it stemmed from his childhood as a feeling of rejection of *him*, and a feeling that he caused the divorce. Taking time to face and understand negative emotions that night was one of the first steps toward his growth and unwinding of a very messy life that no child should have had to deal with.

Type Sevens have difficulty committing to plans in advance, and are often perceived as vain and self-centered. Part of that is because they equate commitment with the potential to get hurt—and Type Sevens will do anything to avoid that. Their armor is non-existent, but their defense mechanism is moving so quickly that no one will be able to touch them. Their justification of others' actions is simply for them to avoid being upset or disturbed; however, that can lead to an unintentional mental block of emotions and minimization of something that is, perhaps, a bigger deal than they want to admit.

The irony is that the search for freedom starts with acknowledging emotions, as temporary as they are. Ignoring feelings causes them to linger and almost "haunt" the person trying to mentally avoid them; however, accepting them for what they are and being present with pain allows for freedom in the journey onward. Grief and sorrow are emotions that are horrid to feel, but they also pass. Instability is not a feeling of "high" to chase at the expense of numbing. Type Sevens need to learn the difference between reflecting and understanding why, versus consuming to fill the void.

Stress and Security

Opposite of the Type Four Individualist whose stress point is in their own triad, the Type Seven's heart or security point lies within its own triad. While the Type Seven goes to the Type One Reformer in stress or disintegration, the Type Seven goes toward Type Five, taking on the healthy characteristics of The Investigator in integration and growth. Because the Type Seven stays in its own thinking triad for growth, much of their positivity and analytical mindset remains the same.

Integration for a Type Seven looks like a more research-driven (and slightly more intense) individual, with a stronger focus and attention span. For all types, but for Type Seven particularly, this means acceptance of who they are without taking on the false traits or mask of who they want to be (this leads to disintegration more frequently than we would imagine). They particularly grow by actively stretching themselves into their Type Five child center located in the thinking triad. Moving out of their futuristic and almost fantastical train of thought allows them to move into a sense of retreat with themselves, where they feel more liberated and capable of sitting with their own thoughts, and truly absorbing what's occurring around them. The aspect of Type Five allows them to become more grounded and focused on what's present, fascinated by the "why" of the world. Completion of the task becomes far more important, and they start to care about the deeper parts of life: meaning, contentment, justice. When this happens, their lust for life becomes more tempered and less intense, and it's replaced with the realization that their true contentment and identity *is* found in simplicity and authenticity—which is the true and original version of the epicure in the end.

Disintegration for a Type Seven can start with a sudden strong level of rigidity and intolerance to others' perspectives, believing them beneath themselves. With a sudden move to the instinctive triad, they can grow strongly critical of "the real world," and lose their child-like innocence chasing down what they think needs to be set right. They can turn melodramatic to show how little they care and how free they are, even turning to reckless and dangerous activities to avoid the boredom and "real world-ness" of reality. They become more perfectionist, task-oriented, and critical of everyone and everything around them as they partic-ipate; this changes their normally fully charged, happy-go-lucky demeanor to a more glass-half-full, I-don't-get-it-but-everyone-else-is-doing-it attitude. Stress confuses the Type Seven, and most of the time they recognize that they don't like who they've become in the process, although the situation is partially self-inflicted through their avoidance as they've deemed the initial stress-inducing responsibility "boring." Their Type One aspects make them feel that they have the right to become more critical toward their loved ones'; while they're normally laid back and conflict avoidant, they are suddenly frustrated and caught between their focus and fantasy—deeply wanting a distraction, but also not feeling "free" until they accomplish the task at hand.

On the flip side, this is also their growth point because they move out of the realm of what *could* be, and steady themselves with reality's norms and rules. While uncomfortable, it is still a point of growth and steadiness. Learning how to decipher and analyze the situation creates a cause-and-effect mindset for the future—uncovering whether they truly need to let things "pile up" or if their stress lies in their own doing, actions, or lack of empathy. What do they need to manage or address personally?

My friend Will, a twenty-four-year-old communications major and aspiring film and movie director, is all about the next latest–greatest thing. A natural entertainer, he almost sparkles when he talks about the next trip he's planning, adventure he's sorting, what he's making for dinner—all to shake up his everyday. In his zest for and romance of the dramatic, Will was ready to chase down any and every opportunity. Flying from Washington to Los Angeles for multiple potential roles in one year was enough for him to network his way into some very important rooms, but not enough for him to consistently keep in touch with his sought-after connections. When I met him, he was making the third and final try to move to Los Angeles to pursue his dreams, but without support or much experience, bouncing from job to job. The stress of moving to an expensive city with a nightlife to surpass any Type Sevens' dreams immediately tapped into his soul, but he began to lose bits and pieces of himself, and his mental state as he began to avoid his fear of not "making it."

When we first started talking through the possibility of him being an Enneagram Type Seven, he was honestly stoked to hear that he was a "glutton"; what a remarkable, marvelous thing! He immediately sought to understand the other types and began to communicate and type his friends back home before he realized that, perhaps, he needed to slow down. Freedom is the driven-home desire of a Type Seven, and in his move and his need to keep up appearances, his current hospitality job became his saving grace, as it offered consistency and money, but it was also his slave master. After helping him figure out some things, Will decided to go home to his parents' house for a bit—not to give up, but to center himself and be alone. In his integration to Type Five and during four weeks of alone time, he was able to tap into his innate nature and plan a solid plan of attack that included (1) a budget and precision, using his access to Type One, and (2) a research-driven plan of understanding with his access to Type Five. He spent the following two weeks calling his prior connections in the industry and setting up appointments.

Approximately two months after he left Los Angeles dejected, with a few weeks by himself, and then on his feet and chasing his personal contentment, Will came back a much more mentally and emotionally sturdy man. He was able to set up a three-month time frame during which all his planning and resources came together to get him a starter dream job, and within six months he began working constantly on one set to another.

Balance in contentment and hunger is crucial. Yes, the Type Seven strives to bring the future into present. The key is to understand that they have access to a built-in research center (Type Five) and access to the steadiness brought about by making time for the present normalcy.

Pain disguised as "bad habits" travels relentlessly through generations and family lines. If your grandparents didn't take time to heal, and your parents didn't take time to pray it away, who's going to stop it? Nothing, until someone decides it's time for them to break the chains and deal with it themselves. It's heart-wrenching work but by taking the time to heal, you no longer pass that same chain link onto your following generations.

So, Type Seven: What's important to you? One of the most complicated parts of identifying as a Type Seven is the mental separation and unraveling between identity and adventure—realizing that you have more to contribute and bring to your personal circles and communities than just the laughs and brilliance and ideas for adventures. After all, your identity doesn't eternally lie in how exciting you are, how much fun you are, and how shiny and distracting you may be. Your identity lies in being present in your current moment, listening to what someone is trusting you with, and connecting to the greater purpose to help realize and truly bring about your future.

"Waiting" is just as much of an action verb as "going"; we have just conditioned ourselves to be consider it "boring." Learning how to redefine action and pain can change everything. When the innate desire is to plow past in an "onward and upward" masked fashion, focusing on what's coming instead of dealing with what needs to be presently understood and dealt with, it's far easier to lose authenticity to bask in what others want you to do (and what you think others expect from you). Letting the decisions and active choices you make stem from a place of focused and raw authenticity with yourself allows for you to make guided decisions that bring your future into the present, instead of leaving you breathless from constantly chasing after it. Contentment is on the other end of recognizing your authenticity. It's worth getting to know you. It's worth the work of breaking the chains.

Life with a Type Seven: Playful and Spontaneous

Type Sevens are joyful, playful, and ready to enjoy all that life has to offer—an ideal match for just about any person, and the life of any party. They are the Peter Pans of the Enneagram, never wanting to grow up, embracing vision and creative thought, having their attention divided among their multiple talents . . . and avoiding any and all discomfort like a pro. The Enthusiasts like to try everything to fill the void because they just don't know exactly what they're looking for in life—or if they do know, they don't know if they can find it. It's like having Thanksgiving dinner every night of the week, and everyone still wants to pile their plate high with all the goodies just to try everything. Essentially, where variety is the spice of life, that is where the Sevens flock.

It's important to remember that Type Sevens primarily show their love through giving others a glimpse of their world, where everything is fun; or by reframing their negative experiences into a positive. "There's always a silver lining!" With Type Seven making up approximately 13.7 percent of the population, Sevens are charming, spontaneous, and enjoy the free fall and free will that life can bring. When healthy, they focus their multifaceted talents on attainable goals that allow them to journey to joy well.

Although they can be perceived as flaky or scattered, Type Sevens are generally more focused on the fun than an actual goal. However, they are very responsible about things that are "penned" (as opposed to penciled) in on their schedule. As long as no one depends on a Seven to fully organize or make their idea happen, you can just kick back and enjoy assisting in the brainstorming. If they can keep their mindset settled on "future fun," they'll be able to stay in touch with their end goals. I once heard a Type Seven friend state that the very last thing a Seven wants to do is get to retirement age, and have to skimp and avoid certain activities because they did "too much" as a younger person. So, if they can keep their goal at the forefront, they'll continue to work toward those goals with a vigor and excitement.

Communication with a Type Seven means verbally appreciating their positive outlook and ideas. Meeting them with a matched excitement and open-mindedness, while still maintaining your own stance is the ideal. Forcing a Type Seven into a steady, predictable routine is cause for a nightmare. Because they hate conflict, they are already always looking on the bright side; they appreciate lightheartedness and their infectious humor allows them to break the tension in a room. The ironic thing is that most of the conflict that the charmer Type Seven will encounter stems from wanting to do too much, all the time. Encourage the Type Sevens in your life to savor the present moment and take one thing at a time.

One last word to the wise: never, ever, ever try to control a Type Seven.

At Home

Type Seven's are known and loved for their "child-likeness." With their gift for communicating and storytelling, as parents they can relate to any and all children; and as children, they can easily tap into their own imagination, and embrace the world of make-believe. Parents can encourage taking risks and getting past fear; children can experience early independence and cultivate their love for variety.

As children, Type Sevens deeply anticipate the freedom they believe they will be entitled to as adults and it is resolved early on that freedom is to be uncompromised. In school, their lack of freedom may show up as they are instructed to sit in seats for an extended time; to push back, they cause distractions or become the class clown. This can also come from their developing desire for attention or excitement—if it's not already there, they'll initiate it, risking coming across as immature or labeled as a bad example. If they find that they're on the chopping block for punishment, it's easy for them to charm their way out of the "trap."

They find it much easier to avoid their feelings by distracting themselves, but that can lead to bouts of repressed anger (particularly for Wing Eights) or fear (more so for Wing Sixes). Instead of persevering their way through a frustrating situation, be it homework, basketball tryouts, learning a difficult dance move, making friends, they can develop patterns of quitting when they don't see an end in sight—and this is where parents need to encourage Sevens consistently to discuss why they think it's "hard," or "not worth it," and help them learn determination.

As children and adults, Type Sevens find it easy to make friends but can feel their friends only like them because they make things "fun," or that they can't be serious because people expect otherwise. Type Seven children can disconnect from their authenticity (while still holding fast to their individuality) to ensure that other people like them, although they may feel disconnected from their peers at school just as much due to their lack of vulnerability.

For Type Seven parents, children are in for their own adventures. Seven parents are often adept at coming up with plenty of creative ideas for their kids to do and enjoy, and try to spare no expense when it comes to having fun and keeping up with events. Bringing a lot of enthusiasm, love, excitement, and zest for life is *not* their problem. However, children with a Type Seven parent can sometimes feel that their parents are unavailable because they'll be caught up in a different pursuit—even if the parent *is* completely available. Allowing their child to feel settled may sometimes feel almost a punishment to the Type Seven parent as much as it may feel like a relief to the child to take a break from the exciting life they lead.

It's important for a Type Seven parent to realize that the "mundane" parts of life that they may not have chosen to lead in the past are absolutely necessary to the structure of a child—cooking, housework, etc.—so making time to teach children to both be and do as they occupy space and time is as important as making sure they have sufficient mental, physical, and emotional exercise. Sitting and coloring, turning a house-cleaning session into a vacuum dance-party, doing homework with a goal in mind—these are all things that allow children to remain steady and find grounding, while still bringing the element of fun that Sevens have perfected.

In Love

When it comes to romance, Type Sevens are already excited about new experiences. While seen as spontaneous and fun-loving, they still have an element of practicality. With their child-like wonder, they are just as enthusiastic about their love life and relationships as they are anything else. Just as they want to explore the world, they want to have fun and take time exploring their partner. Their curiosity and lust for life transfers to their partner, and they seek to understand who they are, connecting on a deeper level.

With their somewhat intense manner, they Type Seven needs someone who is reliable and can help ground them—the respect level goes up when they find someone who can rein them in, *without* them feeling as if they are tied down. Their ideal partner is someone who respects their desire to be independent, who doesn't have a need for control, and who isn't overtly clingy. If the Seven is flighty, they need someone to stay and fight; if they are intense, they need someone calm and collected; if they want to go too far, they need someone who is willing to go along . . . then help pull them in at the last possible second; and they need someone they can trust fully, and trust themselves fully to be with.

Dave is a Type Three Achiever who was in a long-term relationship with a Type Seven, Mina. She was hard to get close to because she was living her wonderfully active Type Seven (Wing Eight) life, creating adventure, running from pain, avoiding vulnerability, and only enjoying meaningful relationships with people she truly cared about. Once they began dating, things began to rise to the surface in Dave and Mina.

As an "image"-motivated Three, Dave's girlfriend made him look good—Mina was attractive, bright, and charming, a "cool girl." They both recognized that they gave unconditional love well, which Dave hesitated to give away, but Mina spotted right out of the gate; but they both also hid their darker sides well. As a Type Three and a Type Seven, they were both socially adept, high energy, and enjoyed all of their adventures. Dave loved taking Mina places, buying her things, helping fulfill what she wanted and needed; Mina loved the attention and experiences. But, they also had a very confrontational way of dealing with problems. Mina was very independent and felt that Dave could either lose his codependent tendencies or interact and engage more with her than he chose to. Dave would feel that he could only try so *hard* to make Mina happy without her acknowledging him or giving him the impossible standard to meet. They tried to sweep their issues under the rug, but they would often fail miserably. After several years, they called it quits. Both were simply not in a good grace zone and were constantly stressing each other out.

In relationships with Sevens, it's important for both parties to create a no-judgment zone. Type Sevens are genuinely curious, although they never necessarily "turn off" intellectually and prefer consistent stimulation, which can prove to be challenging for their partners at times. However, if the Seven feels that their relationship takes on any form of possession or idealism, they are likely to develop resentment toward their partner and feel entrapped. Remember, a stressed Type Seven moves to Type One, and this builds up an (initially internal) blatant defiance when they feel someone is being ungenuine or "trying too hard" to make them happy. After all, if the Type Seven feels loved unconditionally, you are giving them something they feel they lack from the rest of the world and their personal experiences—something they have chased after their entire lives. Pursuit of *them* may feel foreign.

Type Sevens have probably imagined their wedding day a thousand times as "the party of the century" (I've heard boys under ten tell their peers this), and know exactly what their dress, cake, and flowers will look like. They are romantic people and they deeply desire an emotional point of safety they can connect to.

In Work
Because they are in the thinking triad as a mental and analytical thinker, Type Sevens are naturally more forward thinking and

moving—they are highly, highly productive people. Positive, appreciative, and generally experienced in a wide range of subjects, they aren't necessarily going for a job that will keep them grounded and comfortable; but they're usually great communicators, and bring a lightness and warmth to every work atmosphere, so long as they don't get bored. Quick on their feet, enthusiastic about new ideas, visionaries that see the possibilities: it's all good. B ut, with an attention-shifting defense mechanism to ensure they stay out of "pain" and in the "pleasure" realm, it's important to help them learn how to understand "suffering" in the workplace, empathizing with others *and* themselves.

As artists, travel journalists and agents, designers, or even bartenders and tour guides, Sevens love the experience. When they work alongside others who are more consistent, they can be the innovator of thousands of ideas. The trick is to ensure that they don't have to follow through on every idea. Helping a Type Seven take responsibility for a good idea is easy—helping them separate the responsibility from the great idea, and following through on a plan to achieve it, is what brings the innovative and creative spirit in a Type Seven truly alive. While it may be uncomfortable and not necessarily in their ideal nature, it's a growth aspect that furthers their natural innovation. When Type Sevens are part of a working environment that is open to and appreciative of new ideas, creative, and full of energy, they thrive, and they love spending time with their colleagues outside of work. But they can become stressed by schedules, rules, boring routine, and lack of choice or development.

Encouraging a Type Seven employee to "get their hands dirty" is supporting them and challenging them at the same time. It helps force them to stay grounded, again getting their energy out of the rationalization/self-justification headspace, and balancing the physicality of the work with their vision of the outcome. When Type Sevens begin to justify themselves through their pain as "being okay," it's important to help them to stay *in* their physical state. Otherwise, I've heard the justification experience likened to floating up and out of their body, as if they're viewing the picture themselves from above.

As communicators, Sevens lean into the style of story-telling—everything they need to communicate is a story; and this can come across as being extremely self-absorbed or non-committal. If what they're doing doesn't contribute to their storyline, it's hard to get them to focus. Get the Type Seven to stop talking and listen to what you're trying to say and what you need from them. Framing it positively, while still framing it as *necessary*, challenges them to take responsibility. It keeps them in the moment and absorbed in in-depth work, either literal work, or work on themselves or relationships—all uncomfortable things. However, it brings them into a state of calm, where they can be present in the moment, take it all in effectively, and continue to communicate well.

In Play

We know that Sevens are all about the fun and how adventurous it can get, so they need a friend who can match them in their pursuit of spontaneity, fun, and adrenaline rush. They don't want someone who bores them, is less than genuine, and who tries to contain their burst of movement with schedules and advance plans. They are all about being the life of the party, but they don't want someone who is just like them. In fact, they loathe the person who has a similar life story, because it makes them feel put out in their own element. Instead, having a friend with a different mindset—perhaps someone more inquisitive, or emotionally in touch—helps to remind them that some problems, issues, or uncertainties need to bubble to the surface without being suppressed.

Ocean was a Type Seven girl whose adventure was travel, wherever, whenever, however she could. No worries if there were obstacles in the present, the future looked good, and she would purchase a plane ticket like some people would buy a pair of shoes to escape the day's realities. However, Ocean was also keen on having a long-term relationship, getting married, having a little camper van/tiny home, and working in cinematography. All these desires were within reach, but not one of her current decisions really contributed to them, outside of the video collected from her travels. Her many friends all loved her as she was, but were also worried about her because they knew that she had incredible calling and motivation. She just wouldn't stop long enough to gather the judgment and frame of mind to help her reach her goals. Her friend Ross came to the rescue one day as one of her oldest friends to help her pause in a busy moment before another trip to help her navigate that specific adventure as a time to reflect and get in touch with her emotions and feelings again. Even as an unhealthy Seven who didn't want anyone telling her what to do, avoiding the introspection and "weakness" of feelings, this was exactly what she needed; and it benefitted her in the long run. Ocean used her trip to figure out what goals she needed to attain (while still having fun along the way) to find her footing in cinematography, which eventually helped contribute to her other goals.

Communicating with a Type Seven looks different for everyone. It's important to be direct and upfront, but kind (Type Sevens are in the thinking triad and struggle with fear; if you're not honest with them, they don't want to trust you). While encouraging them to share their feelings, they often analyze before they share and may get overwhelmed. Oftentimes, they need to process these emotions on their own—or, if they are processing with someone else, it's helpful to have an activity planned while discussing. Taking a hike, going bowling, making pottery—something hands-on where you can be distracted, but still have opportunity for conversation and discussion is ideal.

Energetic and opportunity-driven, Type Sevens love the excitement of new opportunities, and can turn on the charm when their interest is piqued. Lighthearted and humorous, they bring optimism into every situation, but can be shy under the surface. Proving trustworthiness through consistency, not just appealing to their "fun" side, shows a Seven that you are in it for the long run. Hiding their real thoughts under a facade of life can take a toll on anyone. It takes a true friend to stick around, enjoy the good times, and love them as they are, honestly.

If you can encourage the Type Sevens in your life to be vulnerable with themselves and others, you are encouraging them into true freedom and positivity, unmasked. Supporting them in groundedness doesn't tie a Seven down, it brings them limitless possibilities as they realize how much they are capable of personally, outside of the doing. And that is something worth fighting for.

Type Eight

The Challenger

"If you're going through hell, keep going."
—Winston Churchill, Type Eight extraordinaire

Friends who have known me even briefly know that Winston Churchill and I have a solid relationship (or as much of a relationship as can be had between a writer in one time and a reader many years later). He said what he meant, wrote what he meant even more, and acted upon those sentiments; not only is that admirable, it's the sign of a healthy Eight. So many healthy Eights in our world have created change for the better or worse, and many have achieved historical prominence (whether honored or dishonored) by taking risks to achieve their vision. Think Rosa Parks, Franklin D. Roosevelt, Aretha Franklin, Fidel Castro, Indira Gandhi, Saddam Hussein, Donald Trump, Dr. Phil, Serena Williams, Mark Cuban, Christine Caine of A21—and of course, Winston Churchill.

And yet here we are, stereotyping anyone we don't prefer or get along with in our circles as a Type Eight. I've heard it enough times from enough people: "They're so stubborn! They must be a Type Eight." "Type Eights, man! How do you get along with them?" Or, my personal favorite, "Type Eights are just crazy and

Type Eight at a Glance

Needs: To be in control of their own lives and well-being, to protect themselves and others (regardless of whether the "others" want to be protected or not).

Fear: Someone else will try to control them.

Core Motivation: To prove their strength to others, to dominate their own environment, and to be in control over their (daylong, weeklong, lifelong) destiny.

mean. Period." We who have a brief understanding of the Enneagram and read the word "challenger" immediately assume that everyone we've had a bit of a run-in with is just that: a Challenger beyond reason. And while this can be partly true (I've had my own days where I just *want* to argue with everyone), their main core motivation is *not* to be in control. Their main core motivation instead, is to *not be controlled*.

Go back. Read that again. Understand it. There is a difference.

I have a friend, we'll call her Christine, who privately mourns the fact that she is a Type Eight simply because she hates the Eight stereotype and feels that people tend to shy away from her when they find out that she is a Challenger by nature. As a social sub-Type Eight, she prefers having people around, and often dislikes being in conflict, although she still feels the need to confront. Her entire life mission is a classic justice-oriented Eight: to be a lighthouse for other people so we are all free to sit at the same table. She is passionate about helping others and creating an environment of freedom, and loves leading her teams to do so effectively and with purpose. However, she often has trouble connecting with people she feels have a smaller capacity for growth and understanding the vision she has. This is the paradox of understanding and connecting intimately with the Type Eight. Connecting is achievable, but it takes time and work to move from their outer circle of potential threat to their inner circle of understanding and, finally, trust.

In Mark Twain's classic American novel *The Adventures of Tom Sawyer*, there is a famous scene in which Tom's Aunt Polly commissions him to whitewash their fence. Being a young boy growing up along the Mississippi River and prone to mischief in a town where there isn't much to do, Tom goes out, starts the project, and then devises a way to sell his friends into not only whitewashing the fence, but *paying dues* to do so. He ends up with quite a collection of treasures at the end of the day, and "had discovered a great law of human action, without knowing it—namely, that in order to make a man or a boy covet a thing, it is only necessary to make the thing difficult to obtain." This is the Eight leader. They never need to be the best at things (unlike the Type Three Achiever, which they can be mistaken for at times), but they can sell you on most things if they're feeling charismatic enough, and while they are charming, they are extremely self-sufficient.

The fact of the matter is, while yes, Hitler was probably an Eight, so was Martin Luther King, Jr. Opposite ends of the iceberg, both believing themselves utterly correct, but with different visions and beliefs, to the point that they were willing to die on their own respective hills. Self-confident, generally well spoken, natural leaders with the ability to thrive and survive the pressure points of life, Eights live the life of a Challenger with a will and a way, and aim to finish strong—if they choose to finish at all. The Type Eight drive stems from a need to protect themselves and others, with a strong sense of justice at their core. Although they have different subtypes that contribute to their differences and levels of health that keep them from wanting to kill everyone who has different ideals and instead channel that into being blunt and straightforward (with the odd kickboxing class to help with any added aggression).

Something to consider is that healthy and unhealthy Eights are polar opposites. The healthy Eight is protective of others, as well as themselves. They are led with justice and independence at the foreground of the mission. They are pragmatic and bring forth a can-do attitude in those around them when properly emphasizing culture in whatever business or institution or volunteer position they are working from. Results come from progress; progress is from results. Healthy Eights thrive on a good challenge that allows them to prove their strength and themselves in general, working from a sense of "I'm part of something bigger than myself" rather than their own egocentrism. The middling average Eight takes issue with their own emotions, where they may deny or let go of their feelings to keep their protective approach. Unhealthy Eights take everything that comes at them as an argument against their very existence, and as the victimized party, treat it as such. It's not pretty.

Core Motivation: "I'm Not Necessarily a Control Freak (I Just Want to Live Uncontrolled)"

You probably have people in your life who thrive in roles of docility. If someone tells them what to do, they do it well and competently, and eagerly await their next task. Not so with the Eights. At a job, they more than likely prefer having some say over their role. Healthy Eights don't care what you think, generally speaking. Healthy Eights don't care if they're the alpha, the boss, or even the supervisor. They just want to have some say over their role, whether that's creative or analytical. Control over themselves and their time is ideal. Control over others is optional.

According to the Enneagram Institute, the core motivation of the Eights is that they desire to be "self-reliant, to prove their strength and resist weakness, to be important in their world, to dominate the environment, and to stay in control of their situation."

As mentioned earlier, a type's core motivation stems from the formative years of ages one to four, and often levels of health are based around things as minimal as moving house, or as maximal as being bullied or seeing bullying occur within one's close circles. It is here where Eights develop their consistency in reaction, whether that's centralized in egocentrism and aggression, or in tenacity and with a steady zest for life. More consistently, they stand alone, the Challenger individuals of the Enneagram.

In addition, Eights are consistently wrestling with the underlying emotion of fear, whether it's only an idea in its earliest stages or an action verb ready to be let loose. Constituted by their personal history from their earliest childhood and triggered by injustice and anger, fear is often an issue that many Type Eights shove below the surface because they are all about showing strength and leadership. Their defense mechanism is to act as though fear doesn't exist, but coming from the instinctive triad as they do, that is often an unhealthy reaction because the initial reaction to anything is to show their strength and superiority. For an Eight to work with something or someone they've derived a sense of fear from/toward, they need to be of sound mind, and they need to *be* strong, not just "feel" strong or show strength as a cover up—which is a level of health they will consequently and ironically only get to by recognizing that they don't have to be the strong one all the time. Facing and working alongside fear is playing the pioneer in many circumstances because fear is such a personal and situational emotion. However, it is necessary to challenge denial, and open up helplessness and vulnerability, which paradoxically removes the denial that could occur from "living in fear."

During the early phases of the COVID-19 pandemic, I was a nanny for a five-year-old girl who was simply beyond me—not the usual occurrence, I might add. She would go from being a little angel to being an absolute terror at the drop of a hat. There were many days she would come home from school bubbly and chattering about her day, then turn to plotting her vengeance on a schoolmate who happened to cross her that day. We would often hear from her teacher regarding scenarios in which this little girl—who played the role of the victim—was actually the aggressor. I rarely "type" children, but six weeks into the job, I knew we were dealing with a hardcore Eight-in-training here. *How do we prevent this from escalating?* I had the answer when her mum left for work one morning and the little girl suddenly had mass hysteria and was terrified throughout the day that her mother would never come back. Her full-fledged tantrum lasted 45 minutes, and it dawned on me halfway through that she had abandonment issues, victimization fantasies, and consistent tantrums not due to my lack of nannying ability, but due to her first four years.

You see, I was the seventh in a long line of nannies throughout her young life, and every time one of them left, a detachment had to take place. Not only did this feel unjust to the little girl, but because she was so young, she couldn't comprehend that her parents would not go away and just leave her—hence the abandonment, hence the victimization and vying for attention with someone who had "done something to her," and hence the relatively drama-free days we had . . . until her parents got home. Then, it was a complete and utter attack on humanity to ensure that no one would or could ever leave her again. She wasn't psychopathic, and it wasn't a battle of who was controlling her, or that she "had" or "didn't have to" do things. It was a battle over her personal feelings of injustice—coupled with straight-up fear of abandonment.

Do you recognize how formative the first four years are? I'm not saying to never hire a nanny or a babysitter; I'm definitely not advocating for typing of children at such a young age, but I am saying that core motivation for all types stems from events in the first four years, and that they are particularly evident in Type Eights from an early age. Obviously (and hopefully) growth and development take place, but early scars run deep and can affect our response to *everything*.

No wonder the counselors and psychologists of this world will never go out of business.

Type Eight Wings and Levels of Health

We've talked about wings and learning how to healthily tap into them, and I pride myself on the fact that I wing Eight. Within the parameters of Type Eight, there are the two types known as The Nonconformist and The Bear.

The Nonconformist is the Type Eight that primarily wings Seven. I also refer to them as the free spirit or the original. They can hold their own as The Individualist 2.0 (second only to Type Four) of the Enneagram. In health, they are expansive in their capacity for people, tasks, and mentality. They are generous not only with their time, but with their energy and inner circle. Borrowing from aspects of the Type Seven Enthusiast, they can be on the more extroverted, sociable, "life of the party," laughing at themselves bandwagon; however, this type thrives in bringing vision to life, with an idealistic, entrepreneurial spirit wherein lies ambition and a materialist drive. They are driven creatures, with perhaps slightly more of an intellectual capacity and with more risk to the reward than The Bear (8w9), who can tend to be clouded by the "sleepy" influence of the Type Nine.

On the other hand, the most unhealthy Nonconformists can potentially be one of the most aggressive numbers on the Enneagram. While they are still willing to take risks, there is a drive of ulterior motivation; they can be fueled by addiction and are prone to more temperamental fits, whether stemming from depression, egocentrism, or anger. The unhealthy Nonconformist persona is fascinated by chaos, and can inflate themselves to more than they are to support their bursts of moodiness and ego. They bring people into their inner circle, and then use them up. Overreaction to most circumstances is not uncommon.

The Bear (not to be confused with the verb "carry;" more as in, Goldilocks and the three of, beastly kind of bear) lands paradoxically and almost with irony—a Type Eight Challenger stuck with a Type Nine wing whose direct and core motivation in life is to keep the peace. Healthy Type Eights that wing Nine have a natural sense of peaceful confidence, as if they've never experienced a self-doubt. They are naturally more nurturing than authoritative, and are gentle, patient, kind-hearted, and quieter than their Wing Seven counterparts. Extremely genuine, they are often more protective and friendly while remaining steady with their inner circle. Borrowing from the Wing Nine, their anger manifests itself similarly to an earthquake—you can't see it, but when provoked, the fault line is ready to erupt suddenly at any second.

An unhealthy Bear allows the Wing Nine to add to a numbness when hurt. They don't let anyone into their close circle, and truth be told, more people don't necessarily want nor choose to be there due to the insensitive and somewhat apathetic spirit they carry. Oblivious to their anger until it's too late, they can also stay in complete denial of their fear, and still blame the other person for instigating the blow-up in the first place. Unhealthy Eights can often dominate the room and energy as the leader that they are, but again have an almost angry aversion to weakness and emotions, probably causing more hurt to the party in question if they sense weakness just to spite. On the lowest end of the spectrum, they can simply be "mean," because they feel like it. Again bringing in the addiction aspect as noted in The Nonconformist, The Bear doesn't know when to quit. All they know is that they don't want to be seen as weak, and if they're the last man standing to plot out of paranoia, that's still better than losing the battle.

After reading through the two extremes, it begs the question: How do you move from "unhealthy" to "healthy?"

Is there no middle ground? The development between the two is based largely on our levels of capacity to be present; for example, what's particularly stopping an average Eight from becoming a healthy Eight is the difference between what suits them best and what suits the other person best.

Let's say a Type Eight is having a meeting with a colleague from the office, and they've penciled in a potential date/time for Tuesday afternoon. Suddenly, their counterpart realizes it's her turn to pick up the children from school, and asks if it's possible to reschedule to Tuesday morning, or perhaps Wednesday morning. "Ava, I already told you I could only do Tuesday afternoon this week. And now you want to know if I could make morning work?! I can't believe your audacity to even ask; and no, of course I can't make Tuesday morning," is a boss who will soon be out of employees—potentially in part because he feels like Ava is trying to manipulate or control his schedule. An alternative response of, "Hm, I think I can try to rearrange things; I will let you know," is already an improvement. If the Type Eight is willing to bend a bit to say, "Thanks, Ava! I think I can try to rearrange things; let me let you know," instead of taking it as a full-fledged attack on their schedule and psychological ideology that people are trying to control them, they're indeed a healthier version of themselves. Tone is everything. A well-functioning Type Eight recognizes that most people have not set out to manipulate them or to assert their dominance (remember, justice!). They can communicate with their own self-assurance and leadership skills in hopes of bringing out the best in others.

Another way to look at it is that if a Type Eight is present in themselves, and therefore based in humility and personal value of themselves *rather than their ego*, the results are more often a fully fledged, well-operating, unintimidating human being. Take it from my friends, Mona and Marc. They took the Enneagram test as part of a local church training, did some self-searching, and realized they were Eights by the core motivation only, although they wrestled with reading through the Type Eight descriptors because they recognized that version of themselves before they had done work on themselves. It was painful—both the reading of the description and the recognition that their instinctive need for control was hurting others around them. And yet, people in their lives who inquire into their type are blown away. "You're a Type Eight?! But . . . you're so kind!"

Because healthy Type Eights—well, they *are* kind. As we said back in the beginning, Type Eights are the leaders, the justice-oriented, the people whom others want to emulate for their strong leadership and communication skills.

For most my life, I cried every day. As a Type Nine, this was soothing to my emotions, and what some would deem as an outburst, I deemed a way to keep my own Zen and peace of mind. But in my early twenties, a large amount of stress followed by a rough breakup that I wasn't allowed time to grieve hit me, and I stopped crying. Looking back, I saw that my Wing Eight kicked in more strongly than it had ever before, and all my tension instead locked into my suddenly more physical gym sessions, where I went to run, lift weights, or practice high-intensity training. My hurt-turned-aggression was channeled into denial—I was fine, I didn't need to take a break. The thought of the exhaustion that grieving would cause was enough to make me live in fear of ever exploring that part of me. This wasn't my first time around the block with stress. So, what was the difference this time? I had learned that to put up a barrier was the best alternative to facing the multiple fears that were beginning to rear out of too much at once. Long story short, I acted like an exhausted and unhealthy Eight, and instead of grieving and dealing with the stress with something as "simple" to me as crying, it took me a lot longer to "get through it." Denial often results in hiding of true emotions and contributes to lack of empathy for others. The learning and high point of both a growing and healthy Eight is innocence, which means facing life with an open heart and without cynicism.

Expression is a necessity for anyone. How we express our emotions changes constantly with our levels of health and our interactions with a specific person or scenario, and can change how we speak and see ourselves, whether artistically or mentally or psychologically. Is it inward based, or outward based? A victim of circumstance, or a champion of my own and others? Learning how to "look inward" is essential to developing health and vulnerability as a Type Eight; learning how to "look outward" will help to develop empathy. As with most things, there is a true balance in each.

Stress and Security

In observing the Enneagram diagram, the Type Eight connects to both the Type Five (The Investigator) and Type Two (The Helper), taking on the unhealthy traits of Five during stress, and the healthy traits of Two during security.

In stress or disintegration, Type Eights borrow from the unhealthy Five by withdrawing and disconnecting with their emotional side (even more so than usual). They may seem more secretive and overly vigilant about betrayal; when they sense anything unsafe or out of their control, the stressed Eight withdraws and disconnects with themselves and their emotions. Again borrowing from the traits of an unhealthy Five, they want to analyze everything to keep themselves from making mistakes and creating more scenarios that would potentially spiral out of control. Although naturally assertive and confrontational, they take on too many things at once (people-pleasing), causing them to become overwhelmed when they don't ask for help (asking for help is showing vulnerability or weakness). No longer seeming perfectly in-tune with themselves, they become edgy and withdrawn into their mindset, analyzing by gathering data; at first believing that analysis is key to right decisions and choices. However, the detachment from their feelings and tendency to fall into analytics alone causes the stress to turn instead to muddled mentality, and loss of self and self-awareness.

To avoid this loss of self and self-awareness, it is key for the Eight to be conscious of what they say "yes" and "no" to—on the one hand ensuring that there is sufficient background and reasoning for their "yes" and "no" (outside of the control aspect); on the other hand, ensuring they have people in their lives and on their teams to back them up. The reason they handle things on their own as frequently as they do is what contributes to their stress rising to the surface. Learn to recognize when the Eight leader feels overwhelmed and on the verge of an explosion. While their emotions are not anyone else's responsibility, pushing down their emotions to numb them is the exact opposite of their nature and turns into stress. Stress turns into levels of health lost. Allowance and built trust in others and the art of delegation is an important—albeit unnatural—state for the Type Eight but it leads to growth and increased levels of health and personal learning.

In security or growth, Type Eights take on the healthy side of Type Two's incredible levels of communications—they allow others to take care of them, and stop with the constant insistence of their own personal correctness. There is more openness, tender-heartedness, and receptiveness to others and their opinions and ideas. Not only do they enjoy people more, they appreciate them for their added value and what others bring to the table. Not only does this keep them from sliding into the pit of Eight stressors, it allows them to grow their community and keep control out of the forefront of their minds.

I have a Type Eight friend, James, who is the kindest person, but in his spare time develops counterarguments to arguments that no one has brought to the surface yet. He has a list of responses to conversations should they arise, both for the fun of it, but also in classic Type Five fashion, to protect himself by simply knowing. He helped my flatmates and myself move house one day, not because he had to or because we were paying him, but because it's part of his ethical make-up. And yet, his entire framework and methodology is to leave before he gets rejected. Would he be considered healthy?

In her famous TED-X talk and later Netflix special *The Call to Courage*, career researcher Brené Brown (another hero of mine) digs deep into the true art of vulnerability. "To love is to be vulnerable, to give someone your heart and say, 'I know this could hurt so bad, but I'm willing to do it; I'm willing to be vulnerable and love you.'" In her book *Daring Greatly*, Brown originally defines vulnerability as "uncertainty, risk, and emotional exposure." Type Eights aren't born with this capacity for exposure. They suffer through years of not knowing how to let others in, feeling the insecurity of instability every time they step out of the boat to try to create a new comfort zone, or loosen the reins of control.

On the surface, we hear and see Eights as The Bears or the confrontational individualists of our circles. But Eights are also called The Protector. When we allow the mindset to shift from the Type Eight stereotype as The Challenger, confrontational and misunderstood, to instead recognize how beautiful their inner passion for justice and defending those in their world is, perhaps we can find it in ourselves to show vulnerability and allow others to feel safer as well. When the Type Eight in your life begins the need to feel defensive, defend *with* them, not *against* them.

When the Type Eight in your life begins to feel overwhelmed and disintegrated, learn how to best support them without making them feel weak. And when the Eight in your life has integrated you into their close circle, hold them accountable.

Life With a Type Eight: Confident and Assertive

The strong Type Eight Challengers make up 6.3 percent of the population.

Because they tend to be one of the most misread types of the Enneagram, I conducted a survey addressing our Type Eight friends, "What do you wish people would say to you?" The answers might surprise you; but on the other hand, they were also consistent enough with what we might assume, and makes one wonder why we don't say and support anyone with these statements. Out of 1,278 responses that blew me away, some of the most common (and most touching) were:

"You're not alone, and you are not too much—not your fire, not your passion, or your stubbornness."

"I see you, and I'm not afraid."

"I like having you around."

"I wish people knew that it's okay to argue with me since it's just how we process things—and I'll probably respect you more for it!"

"Thank you for your honesty."

"I'm committed to not misunderstanding you."

"I love you."

"'I'll handle that for you.' People assume we can do everything—which we totally can! But it's nice when you don't have to ask for help."

"I love that you are a strong leader."

"Your opinion is valued. Your voice matters.

"Thank you."

"My protective nature is appreciated and not just seen as aggression."

"I wish people would ask (and mean!), 'How are you really doing? What can I do to help?' Being tough all the time is hard."

"'It's okay to be rough around the edges' (instead of always saying we're not vulnerable enough)."

"I'll sit with you. I'm with you. I've got your back."

As we've noted, the difficulty for The Challenger is to understand and effectively combine assertion and personal control along with interdependence and teamwork. We ALL need people around us; but a lot of us connect, reach out, and reach back in multiple different ways. To help and connect with a Type Eight, there are a few things you need to do to build rapport. First, it's important that you make direct contact without beating around the bush. Be assertive and don't back down in the face of their strength. Your job is to use one of the responses just supplied to you above. "We don't have to talk about it. How else can I help?" is a good place to start. Second, connection is key. The old adage, "If you can't beat 'em, join 'em," absolutely rings true here. Establishing trust is necessary. (Remember the above? "My protective nature is appreciated and not just seen as aggression.")

If conflict is inevitable, you have two options: either (a) guide them away, or (b) confront the situation. Generally speaking, the impending anger is something that's not directed toward you, but rather at the situation. This is a very powerful place for you. Your answer will either challenge them to jump off the deep end or to stay collected. On the other hand, making sure to maintain your own control without being a doormat is your own challenge; being tough on threatening behavior and empathetic toward any hurt feelings at the same time creates a mutual feeling of respect when the Type Eight personality clicks into the realization that you're not weak, therefore you're not a doormat. Suddenly you're on the same playing field—in fact, you may even be on the same team.

Things tend to run very black and white in the Eight's mental justice system as opposed to other numbers who may find things tend to run a bit more on the gray or situational side, so when interacting with the Type Eight, it's imperative to keep the tension of balance in respect, otherwise you're deemed weak and therefore untrustworthy. ("I wish people knew that it's okay to argue with me since it's just how we process things—and I'll probably respect you more for it!") Because Eights are physically charged, lending themselves to the instinctive triad, having them "sit" or figure out how to control themselves would only lead to the Eight feeling patronized; the best bet is to retain respect on both ends. Assumption that all people need love and care even when they don't show it is a key in interacting well and effectively.

And when it feels like all else is failing? Well, a good dose of empathy ("I understand") never hurt anyone.

At Home

My two younger sisters are both self-typed Eights. There was a lot of head-butting between them and my parents growing up, because my father (probably rightfully) assumed he was in control of his children, especially when they were very young. Unfortunately, my sisters assumed that (again, probably rightfully) because they were their own people, they were also in control of themselves. It was all in the mindset. Within that context, what would normally be a fun-loving and great relationship had the potential to turn into a tumultuous one for years. Obviously as the girls developed into teenagers, then young adults, and could actually make rational decisions for themselves (as opposed to rejecting everything green as their proverbial hill to die on as a child of ten), things changed.

As children, Eights have a built-in drive to prove their independence, their ability, and their own course of action. They don't like to be held back, and have a lot of energy that contributes to their strength. If you tell an Eight child that they "can't do something," they'll quickly prove you wrong.

Peer pressure is not a problem—Eights don't care what anyone thinks of them. As natural protectors even from a young age, they stand up for justice and what they believe in. While they can sometimes lean to the side of being the bully, they are often more likely to keep the smallest, youngest, most picked-on person safe. With a strong sense of willpower, Eight children are sensitive and care for others. Their imagination makes them the hero, but if they are not encouraged in their vulnerability as a child, they tend to bury this side of them.

Eight children hate anything that may seem falsified or expected—from "silly" rules and regulations, to social norms and expectations. It's embarrassing to them to falsify something they may not truly believe in. When parenting, it's important to be straightforward about your feelings with an Eight child; anything wishy-washy or uncertain is a boundary for the Eight to push, and this will eventually irritate them and you. Don't expect them to respect authority just because you tell them to; proving competence is important to the Eight, and respect is something earned, not given. However, making sure that you are the parent and adult in the relationship keeps the boat afloat; they need to know they can count on you instead of feeling like you'll desert them.

Think back to the commanding traits of a Type Eight. In a child–parent scenario, it takes consistency on the part of a very understanding child before they decide you're just not going to let them in, and you're not worth it. Do you want to listen, or do you just want them to behave? Hit the pause button on your own personal pro-action versus reaction. Implementing active listening by changing your mindset toward the Eight teenager who just won't let you into their room can be difficult; taking time to acknowledge your four-year-old's emotions when she's in the middle of her sixth tantrum of the day is hard work. But active listening is where the Eight thrives and realizes that you are a safe place. Three of our statements from Eights above were specifically from teenagers:

"You're not alone and you are not too much—not your fire, not your passion, or your stubbornness."

"I see you, and I'm not afraid."

"I like having you around."

Being gentle with a Type Eight allows them to express more freely their own sensitivities and vulnerabilities.

Type Eight parents are the boss. They are protective of their children, and teach them to be strong in the face of challenges, relentless in the pursuit of their dreams. They want to see their loved ones succeed, and to anything/anyone getting in the way of that: beware! Because they are prone to sudden angry outbursts, their children may view them as more dominating and "mean" than they intend. Eight parents may also view sensitivity or vulnerability in their children as a weakness, and instead of teaching them that it is a strength, a more "survival of the fittest" mindset may be encouraged.

Eight parents must stay aware that others—specifically children—are often more sensitive than the parent would like them to be. It may be easier to see children as an extension of their Eight-ness, instead of individuals with their own softness or hardness, dreams, and coping. The Eight parent needs to ensure that the largeness of their personality doesn't make their child feel demeaned or unheard or intimidated. Encouraging the space for them to voice their feelings allows for vulnerability and connection, and builds a strong, lasting relationship.

In Love

Falling in love with a Type Eight is properly hard work for *both* parties involved. You could be the most attractive, intelligent, strong person on Earth—heck, you could be the very *last* person on Earth—but if a Type Eight doesn't trust or value you, then they won't fall in love with you. Type Eights themselves are very attractive people. They're naturally strong leaders, can be charming, intelligent, strategic, and perceptive, and they're great communicators. With all of this in mind, there's a reason why they remain the strong ones. They simply don't trust easily. Type Eights will not fall in love unless they've made themselves vulnerable, so it follows that *if* they've made themselves vulnerable, they are acknowledging the fact that you could hurt them, which would equal weakness on their part if they open up to, or trust, the wrong person. If you prove too vulnerable at first, they won't trust you at all, because vulnerability equals weakness in their eyes.

Dave and Elise could not be more opposite in all respects. Elise is a Type Two and amazing communicator; Dave is a

Type Eight with multiple degrees, who will debate you into the ground if he deems you worthwhile. When people meet them as a couple for the first time, I've heard many ask, "How do you two work so well together?" Eights usually say what they mean, and would prefer straight talk in return. But, in contrast to their strong demeanor and behavior, Eights truly do desire relationships and intimacy with someone they can depend upon, be afraid in front of, and not be called out by for their self-perceived weaknesses. In their few deep and personal relationships, they crave equality with someone who is truly worth it, someone who can stand up to them; and maybe of equal or perhaps more importance, strong enough to stand up for them, so they can release control and relax for a few minutes. Essentially, if they can control their partner, that partner is weak—and in the Eight's mind, no one who is weak is worth it because that means you can't count on them. When they manage to find a relationship with a worthy partner, they respond with much more grace; receive differently; and, like Dave, can express: "You care about me enough to understand me, and enough to tell me what you really think, even if it means telling me (kindly) I'm a horrible person today."

Trouble spots that hover very close to the Type Eight's surface are weak spots like learning *how* to be emotionally vulnerable (they may know they want to be vulnerable, they simply don't know exactly *how* to do so effectively and without hurting you), softening their overly dramatic approach when problem solving, and being the primary decision-maker for themselves. In their adult lives, it's difficult for the Type Eight to comprehend that they're now part of a new team and not just an individual. It takes some adjustment, frustration, and new balance on the Type

Eight's part, and patience, understanding, and realization on the part of their partner. If in a relationship with a stronger personality, this balance may take more time to achieve than with a more laid-back, altruistic, and secure partner (i.e., a Type Two or Type Nine).

While two stronger personalities (i.e., a Type Eight and a Type Three) take longer to develop to their fullest extent, they can become the ideal power couple, making waves in their local communities, businesses, churches, governments, etc. But to reach this stage, it is necessary for them to learn how to quickly de-escalate from tense situations, give their partner plenty of independence and freedom, and balance the power dynamic the two share by switching to a mindset of empowerment toward the other person as opposed to having an internal power struggle every time there is a disagreement. The less forceful personality types appreciate the Type Eight's mannerism of defense and protection toward the partner's softer nature. The Eight is dedicated to their partner's sense of happiness, and loves them far more than just for the emotional and physical aspect of the relationship.

At Work

In her book *Daring Greatly*, Brené Brown writes, "I think emotional accessibility is a shame trigger for researchers. . . . Early on in our training, we are taught that a cool distance and inaccessibility contribute to prestige, and that if you're too relatable, your credentials come into question." Beneath every Eight's tough, take-charge exterior is the need to be accepted and to stay relevant before people cast them off like last year's pair of well-worn shoes—easy to walk in, easier to exchange for the new pair. But to be truly accepted as they are, Type

Eight's struggle with vulnerability: how to connect, how to feel, how to *relate* when they already feel so un-relatable? In the workplace, this is even *more* prevalent. Although Type Eights are natural leaders of whatever team you put them in charge of, there is a percentage of Type Eights that contribute to a healthy atmosphere by not *just* taking charge of their entire organization, but incorporating themselves into the heartbeat of their coworkers' everyday experiences on the team (think Anne Hathaway's journey as the character of Jules Ostin in *The Intern* as she works alongside and incorporates her new intern, Robert De Niro's character, into the workplace).

Do you remember my friend Christine from the Type Eight overview? Her primary issue in her professional relationships is the fact that she has trouble connecting with people who she feels have a smaller capacity for leadership and vision toward the goal than she does. While she truly wants to create fun relationships within her teams, she struggles to find intimacy due to her consistent comparison of strength in her workplace (i.e., she is strong and extremely committed; others who are not as strong in leadership skills or capacity may or may not be not worth the developmental effort).

While many Type Eights would love to have close relationships, their primary relationship tends to be with their jobs, which they know without doubt certainly won't eventually harm them. With the (albeit unhealthy) mindset of, "leave before you get left," one can generally gather what the fear is within the workplace. Similar to their romantic relationships, when healthy Type Eights work alongside people who are more relaxed and comfortable, they can help with the decision-making process and be personal advocates. This helps place value on each person in their company or workplace, as well as the Eight feeling valued because their gift of defense is on display by making sure everyone is heard. They work well with people who respect their feelings and ideas, who stand up for themselves, pull their weight in the job, and can practice vision while remaining open to new ideologies and ways of thinking.

Working with other Type Eights is an altogether different story—although with the ideal job types that Type Eights tend to gravitate toward, it isn't an uncommon scenario. Two Eights together can be the making or breaking of a company. It is imperative that the two develop expectations to work together in advance to develop a balance of power and avoid consistent clashing of opinions.

Think back to our quotes: "I wish people knew that it's okay to argue with me since it's just how we process things—and I'll probably respect you more for it!"; "Thank you for your honesty"; and "I'm committed to not misunderstanding you."

Classic Type Eight jobs include those that are geared toward the social justice and leadership ideology. Type Eights are the activists and philanthropists, program managers, executives, professional athletes, and governors. They are not usually secretaries (too boring), assistants (too much critical feedback from people they believe could hardly do a better job), nurses (requiring too much sympathy that they just don't have), or co-hosts (because let's face it, they are the *only* host in their world).

Mark Cuban, owner of the Dallas Mavericks, *Shark Tank* investor, and business mogul extraordinaire, is a prime example of an Eight. If you've ever seen an episode of *Shark Tank*, he is arguably the most charismatic investor of the bunch. Assertive, powerful, confident, it seems he thrives on intense debates, tougher decisions, and pressuring the less-than-confident into either *being* confident or taking another deal due to his evident anxiety when others are trying to make decisions on his behalf. The encouragement he provides others on his teams is evident, and he works consistently to make deadlines. This is a healthy Type Eight fulfilling their utmost potential, and it shows in how they handle themselves—and others—without it seeming as if they're manipulating the entire room.

At Play

There is an intense compulsion to be self-reliant in the Type Eight mindset. That remains just as true for friendships as it does in their romantic relationships, work relationships, and family boundaries. Trustworthy friendships are what is truly needed, and although the Type Eight avoids vulnerability, they are still desperate (albeit internally) for intimate friendships in which they can open up and truly communicate.

Their friends need to realize and understand that Eights are naturally angry, instinctive people. They must physically release the anger before it becomes rage, whether that's through externalized exercise such as kickboxing, CrossFit, or playing an instrument, or through mental practices like debating a hot topic within the confines of a safe space. Through this, the Type Eight can make room for vulnerability. Whether you are worth being vulnerable with is based solely on whether they deem you worth respecting—harsh, but also aligned with their devil-may-care attitude toward life and others. You are not the only person in their world, and they would far rather be friends with someone who respects them enough to care about their individualism and challenging persona anyway.

Type Eights already know they can get intense and blustery very quickly if they sense something underhanded or unjust in the wind. Once their friends realize they may be the recipient of this frustration, it's important to back off a bit, and then *afterward* (I cannot stress this enough), confront them (showing your own personal vulnerability). Oftentimes, Eights are unaware of how their words have affected someone else. Your vulnerability with them affects their trust with you. Remember: "Your opinion is valued. Your voice matters"; "I'll sit with you. I'm with you. I've got your back."

Two Type Eight strengths are their obvious ability to generally express themselves with clarity in every scenario, and their uncanny ability to effortlessly—but effectively—lead those around them toward success. Acknowledging that their assertiveness doesn't equate to a personal attack on you, but matching it with your own sense of intensity and ideals *without* being overly flattering (because flattering means you potentially have a reason behind it) means an enjoyable relationship for the both of you. Avoiding passive–aggressive remarks entirely will deepen the friendship. Some sarcasm is banter, and that boundary line will be clarified in each friendship.

Affirmation is what a Type Eight deeply needs from their inner circle. Because Eights oftentimes feel like the loner in many situations (the secondary Individualist of the Enneagram) and tend to reject people before being rejected, they *need* to feel understood to feel respected. While other number types may not receive criticism so well, when relationship and rapport is built with the Type Eight, they respect your opinion as something that truly means something. *To be intimate is to become vulnerable.* When the Type Eight has given away their power, they feel they have given away at least part of their strength. The two go hand in hand.

Type Eights at health are tough, confident, loyal, supportive, energetic, confident, protective, unpretentious, and generous people. While they may seem tactless at times in their communication style, this is part of their nature, and it doesn't mean dislike or disrespect. Although known for their intensity, they are willing to go down with a fight for those they love and value. If you have an Eight that you would call close, understand that they have opened themselves up to you, and must value your trust and opinion—and therefore, they have empowered you. Knowing them for who they are truly, we can allow our first impression of Type Eights as purely crazy, purely intense, and purely overconfident to become one of empathy, value, and empowerment of close friends. Showing them you're a safe person to be with allows for growth, beauty, and deep vulnerability and comfort to take place.

Type Nine

The Peacemaker

"Most people think of peace as a state of 'Nothing Bad Happening,' or 'Nothing Much Happening.' Yet if peace is to overtake us and make us the gift of serenity and well-being, it will have to be the state of 'Something Good Happening.'"
—*E. B. White*

Type Nines: aka, The Peacemakers; aka The Diplomats; aka The Mergers and Mediators. Their best stereotypes find them on a yoga mat in a child's pose, or curled up with a favorite novel and a cup of tea. Less-than-creative Instagram memes suggest giving them massages or fuzzy socks for birthday gifts. Their favorite song is John Mayer's "Waiting On the World to Change." And yes, they've heard once or twice before that they are the true hippies or chameleons of the world. One thing out of the above clichés that does hold true? The old adage: what you see is most definitely what you get.

Type Nines live to bring people together and to heal the conflicts of the world. They are attracted to peaceful and harmonious environments where there is an atmosphere of stability and comfort. They thrive when they feel connected to another person, and seek to truly understand others. And yet,

Type Nine at a Glance

Needs: To have inner stability reflected in their outer relationships—peace and harmony.

Fear: Lack of harmony, high conflict/stressful situations, loss of deep community with their loved ones.

Core Motivation: To resist the disturbing or upsetting things in life by creating a peace-filled environment and preserving the past and things as they are, and healing conflict in others and themselves along the way.

Nines are in the deepest state of metaphorical sleep—the sleepwalkers, if you will. They prefer to be at peace with the world, and if that means closing their eyes to anything that disrupts that—from turning off the news to keep the world's intensity at bay for a while longer, to turning off their own emotions to create harmony with family and friends—they will. The opening quote from E.B. White describes the peace that Type Nine prefers: peace as a state of "nothing bad happening" or "nothing much happening." However, the Type Nine needs to understand that they are part of the solution; and as much as they'd *love* to spend their life on an island pretending that everything is beautiful, it would disturb the inner Zen just as much, because Type Nines are also intelligent and *know* that the world is not at peace. It's just that much easier for a Nine to fall asleep on their own emotions and needs, and instead help others heal.

The reality is, most Nines are actually quite high-capacity people. They have to be. The Type Nine sits at the very top of the Enneagram, and justify the position there by seeing everything from everybody's point of view. Nines are accepting, stable, trusting and trustworthy, and more than willing to go with the flow at risk of sublimating their own opinions, wants, desires, and needs. Lack of conflict is their biggest strength and weakness all in one go, because they can overly simplify the problem by chalking it up to a lack of trust in themselves, and minimizing their feelings to avoid of anything upsetting or frustrating.

"What do you want?" I had a dear friend ask me once on a late-night drive through Los Angeles; and to be honest, I burst into tears because, at the precious age of twenty-two, I had no idea how to verbalize what I knew internally was my calling, my strength, my deepest desire ... because it was too much work, too emotionally exhausting, maybe even too radical—to let it out. I still don't remember what I answered that question with, besides potentially a very teary, "I don't know," but I do remember the emotions and thought-provoking journal entries that followed, punctuated by a learning curve that lasted for the next six months, and into my decision to move to Australia.

Although the Type Nine desires deeply to create harmony in their environment and atmosphere, and takes a bit of pride in their empathy and understanding of people's emotions and mentalities, they often fail to speak up about any personal emotions, and thus often feel misheard and create their own inner disharmony—or simply become dismissive of themselves when they feel as if what they have to say isn't that important after all. Generally, borrowing from their Eight and One wings, they can be excruciatingly internally stubborn. Part of their structure is not forcing action, and seeing what they choose to see is an attempt to hold their own control. The more you bring something up, the less likely the Nine is to listen to you or do what you're asking. But while they rarely choose to rock the boat, the most common strong-arm push-back looks like an almost shocking passive–aggressiveness that very few recognize as such. It's their way of drawing the line in the sand before they collapse.

Speaking of emotionally, physically, and mentally exhausting days or situations: with a Type Nine, everything is relative. I once heard that what others would consider a relaxed debate can feel like World War II to an unhealthy Nine. If the type wings Eight, chances are it's a bit less impactful; so while the 9w8 may decide to start something in an effort to assert themselves, they seldom choose to finish it. Because Nines tend to naturally take on the weight of the world for anyone who talks to them about their personal lives and issues, emotional exhaustion can kick in after two or three conversations, creating an unspoken passive–aggressive boundary that can manifest in the moodiness of a very unhealthy Nine. Remember, Nines would much rather fall asleep on the world's problems.

While they pride themselves on understanding everyone, unless they are in a relatively to very healthy state and ensuring that they are only drawing from a full cup, they're automatically setting themselves up for an unhealthy withdrawn stance. Asking questions like, "Why am I withdrawing right now?" or, "Why am I leaving this conversation?" will set them up for success not only mentally, but in a relationship. And simple things like making sure they have boundaries in the first place will contribute to their initial health and well-being to make sure they are the best they can be.

My friend, Elizabeth, once had disagreement with her partner, and took it to another friend of ours, a Type Nine named Jade, to help chat it through. Elizabeth left feeling understood, well heard, and that she was completely justified in her thought process toward her partner—and equally justified by encouragement from Jade to bring the scenario up again. Peace restored! All was well and good until Elizabeth (being a Type One perfectionist) decided to bring up the disagreement with her partner a few days later just to show that she was right after all . . . and discovered that he had, of his own accord, had a very similar conversation with Jade—and left the conversation feeling equally understood, sided with, and comforted through the situation, as well as convinced that it was better for him to not bring it up. What a turn of events! The story got back to me eventually, and my fellow Type Nine and I shared a laugh. Some may call this manipulative—and for an unhealthy Nine with the wrong reasons, it could be. On the other hand, seeing multiple sides to a disagreement also creates a harmonious environment in which neither party was "meddled with." Both felt seen, heard, and understood, and the problem was quietly addressed. Isn't that what both of them wanted to begin with? Let the Type Nines emerge here and now to declare, "We are not as boring as you think we are!"

Core Motivation: "Keep the Peace"

"Emotionally stable as an Ikea table." My sister texted me a photo of the sign she found in front of a little beachside boutique. "This is you, in denial of your own emotions while still helping others figure out theirs, living your best #typeninelife."

I laughed. Then, I almost cried. Then we had a healthy conversation about how I felt about it.

With a typically withdrawn stance that moves away from others to meet their own needs (and only after a very emotionally/physically/mentally exhausting experience), Type Nines constantly turn away from conflict and dissonance to fulfill their own basic need for harmonious environment; this contributes greatly to why Nine's can tend to be the friend and comforter of all, but still the loner who hates detaching from people while also accepting it as an (albeit unfortunate) way of life. They know internally that as long as they're by themselves and in their own space, they can control their environment (Type Eight wing kicking in). However, the more passive stance when moving away from others also reduces the desire for connection and can create a deeply rooted resentment as they struggle to create *and* stay firm in their boundaries and personal emotions and stance toward anything.

Type Nines not only merge with people, they can tend to merge with their environment because they don't know their own inner world, resulting in a diverse focus in which, because they're not 100 percent in touch with their internal desires and choices, they do everything. Slightly counterproductive, don't you think? Most Nines think so, too; but by a certain point it has become such a cycle of "jack of all trades, master of none," that learning to pick and choose is simply too much (causing the Nine to fall asleep to their own desires again).

The main core motivation of a Type Nine is actually simple on the surface: to maintain healthy relationships, to avoid conflict and uncomfortable situations, and to have inner peace of mind. They dislike change, and generally prefer tradition and preservation of things as they are now to keep an uninterrupted consistency to their lives. Mixing it up isn't bad per se, it just disrupts the routine of daily existential merging with their environment . . . and Nines *love* to merge. However, it can be detrimental to their own growth as they can lose exactly who they are in the quest for relationship with others and their environment. Nines know this about themselves! But with a fear of the loss of relationship, creating stress, and the feeling that they don't really matter, it's just that much easier to keep merging so that nothing is their fault.

Clear conscience? Yes. Unhealthy? Also yes.

So what in their formative years contributes to the Nine's insatiable need for harmony? Potentially, it's the lack of their own sense of identity that contributes to the need for peace and being what others need them to be. Growing up, this could have come from something as simple as being smaller than their friends, and so subconsciously overcompensating by being "the good one" or everyone's best friend, or as complex as having a set of argumentative parents (or even lacking a parent, which would create the subconscious burden of being the "other" mum or dad). From a very young age, the mediator would be cultivated in all arenas. With a usually recognized, "peaceful presence," the recognition is received and taken in, and the merging nature and people-pleasing tendencies root deep.

Even as children, Nines are natural comforters and slightly less independent than the average child, coming to voluntarily sit on laps for a cuddle, or even becoming the goofball during what they perceive as a tense conversation. They usually don't have difficulty sharing with their friends or playing with the underdog on the playground, and have an evident emotional maturity as children. As children, they were often told that their anger was a negative emotion, leading to the "stuffing" of it. Many adult Type Nines that I've interviewed laugh when they recall their affinity for naps as children; then they cry when they realize or verbally acknowledge their internal need to mature quickly so that others could depend on them even more—even if they weren't ready. "I grew up too fast!" is a common statement from a Nine. Type Nines need to take care of people; but unlike Type Twos, they don't do it to feel loved and accepted, they do it to make sure everyone can also attain their inner peace. Which, while a noble goal and calling, isn't necessarily attainable for them in all seasons of their lives, especially while still growing and maturing themselves as children.

Having an internal anger (as opposed to the Type Eight's externalized anger and the Type One's suppressed anger) generally means anger toward themselves. Type Nines would much prefer being invited and saying, "no thanks," than to moving outside their comfort zone by asserting what would be their natural inclusion. When they say "yes" to too many things, a fear of the unwanted obligation to please is triggered, resulting in anger because saying no and asserting oneself is just not worth the outward turmoil that could occur.

And yet, after all that, the common question still begs to be asked: why are Enneagram Nines *so tired all the time?* As the mediators of the Enneagram, Type Nines are massively busy with trying to, well, mediate. Without strong boundaries, it can easily become an overwhelming balancing act, creating a stable environment for others at the cost of their own emotional environment. It causes the Nine to turn inward, *away* from people and communication, and fester feelings of disconnection or even resentment (merging with their Eight and One wings well). Fluid boundaries are *so* much easier, and much more naturally accessible. No wonder Nines have the potential to spend a good portion of their lives exhausted.

Okay, so there *are* many Type Nines who don't offhandedly relate to the idea of complacency and falling asleep, arguing that their goals and work keep them very much awake and active. However, they still fall asleep to their own daily lifestyle regardless of how stimulating the activity is. It could be cleaning toilets while listening to a podcast or running a full-fledged church service; the unhealthy hyperactivity isn't accomplishing a mindset of full attention or presence in their everyday; it's staying active to constitute a merging mindset of what will keep things in harmony in their world. Staying busy is just another way to ensure there is no extra space for anxiety coming from existence in a not-at-all-harmonious world. Regrouping through inaction is often justified—whether that's after the day's to-do list, or accomplishing a massive project. Enter the paradoxical idea that they were already sleeping the entire day through their project, their to-do list, etc. By checking out, they avoided checking *into* themselves.

Type Nine Wings and Levels of Health

Being Peacemakers, Nines are also considered the spiritually driven beings of the Enneagram. Often they thrive on creating peace not only within, but with God, and seek that relationship to center themselves even more. As the central type of the instinctive triad (surrounded by Type Eight and Type One), Type Nine should be the most well rooted both in the physical world with their own actions and stance, and in the spiritual world as they outwork that connection in a tangible way. However, there can be a massive contradiction between knowing exactly who they are as opposed to who they can be, who they want to be, and/or who others around them prefer them to be. This is resolved only when the Type Nine is in touch with their personal instinctive qualities and influence, and knows their power and individual magnetism (healthy). On the other hand, an unresolved Type Nine in this contradiction is so merged with another that they have cut off their instinctive strength and power of influence through disengagement with others and their spiritual connection with God. They become remote, unconcerned, and unemotional, although appearing to be cool, calm, and collected as ever on the surface.

Nines must self-identify to keep from merging with everyone else's views of them. We've said that wings "borrow" from the personality type next door but with the Type Nine, this is where things get tricky and often misunderstood. When looking at the broad overview of the Enneagram, Nines may relate with the moodiness of Type Four, the intellect of Type Five, and the zest of the Seven; they take on the idealism of the Type One, the desire to be seen from the Type Three, and the authority of the Eight. Truly, the Type Nine sees from everyone's point of view, and relates to everyone's hopes, goals, and dreams. Again, this is where boundaries come helpfully into play. Within the parameters of the Type Nine, we introduce wings The Referee (9w8) and The Dreamer (9w1).

Nines that wing Eight are called The Referee for a reason, and are considered one of the most paradoxical numbers of the Enneagram because they have the Nine's innate need for peace coupled with the Wing Eight's innate desire to challenge. At health, there's a modest and comfortable reception to everyone. They're comfortable in their own skin, and, charged with the Eight dynamic, goals give them a great force of will. They're get-it-done, leadership-driven, magnetically attractive people with a solid sense of internal direction. Although praised, they are unimpressed with themselves. Although highly intuitive, they are often deflectors of praise: If they can't see themselves, how can others truly see them? On the flip side, an unhealthy Referee can switch on and off from a relatively collected, happy-go-lucky Nine to a terrifyingly blunt Eight, and from supportive and genuine to opinionated and gratingly stubborn. They still hold their anger, but the likelihood to explode when not feeling heard or seen (even though they struggle to hear and see themselves) is much more constituted. For a 9w8, assertiveness can often come across as rude and tactless as they continue to numb their primary emotions.

The Nine Wing One is rightfully called The Dreamer. True to their Wing One, there is a connection from when they were young to being the model child, working instinctively to put aside their own needs to please their parents or those around them by being "good": virtuous, orderly, and as little trouble as possible. When healthy and "awakened," there is a sense of moral authority, plus healthy peacemaking tendencies of being aware of their own needs and the needs of others, but balancing them accordingly. They have a public or private mission orientation, with a distinct and committed sense of right and wrong. They love people on principle and at times get out of their own box by being spontaneous. However, when unhealthy, they are often self-neglecting and can be emotionally dead, doing right only for the sake of doing right with the incentive to not feel guilty about it later. Regardless of the scenario, the unhealthy 9w1 becomes dutiful about what they should be and passive–aggressive toward what they shouldn't, eventually allowing themselves to disappear into contexts that aren't necessarily healthy. They become tolerant of self-damaging situations and one-sided relationships that could turn abusive through rationalization, minimization, and pep talks that everything is "fine," until they can't even tolerate their own feelings.

With such stark and terribly self-damaging differences between healthy Nines and unhealthy Nines (not to mention the diversity that are the wings), this is precisely why writing out personal goals, to-do lists, or even affirmations is crucial for the Type Nine. Saying "yes" to one thing only as an act of pleasing the other person means saying "no" to the things you've set out to accomplish for yourself; but with proper boundaries Nine doesn't have to be this way. Not all Nines enact their view of harmony with the same basic route or ideology. Based on their subtype, they may have a self-righteous image of empathy and being helpful. The 9w8 finds it much easier being strict about their boundaries and sticking to them; the 9w1 can be much more fluid because they're basing things on a black-and-white clarity. On the other hand, a self-preservation Type Nine practices actively saying no to people to avoid the merge, and remain in control of the access to their own impulse and anger in the instinctive triad.

My good friend Zach is a Type Nine who misidentified as a Type One for years (things are very right or wrong for him). As a child, he was constantly told that his anger wasn't a necessary emotion; so, he learned to stuff his anger because it was "wrong." As he grew older and into his adult skin, he realized that he wasn't as "kind" as people thought he was and as he began his journey into the Enneagram he found even more evidence that brought up long-dormant emotions. Things that he strongly disliked but that he had made important (such as vacuuming every night like his life depended upon it) were no longer important. One thing that he continuously came back to when self-examining though was the definition of "heedlessness" that is thrust upon Type Nines. "Heedless" according to the Cambridge Dictionary is: "not giving attention to a risk or possible difficulty."[1] While on the surface Type Nines may shy away from the idea of "heedlessness" as a degrading thing, this was Zach's turning point into realizing he was, in fact, a 9w1.

Why? Zach is constantly taking care of people (like a Type Two) in projects that appear to be simple enough at the start . . . but then, because of his own ideas and effort and responsibility, the project begins to manage him. This becomes overwhelming, and eventually oppressing, landing him in a place where he begins to deeply resent those who first began the project with him while not eventually picking up their own share. The ironic thing is, those helpers never verbally took on the weight of the project as he developed it to be much bigger than the original concept. Once Zach began to realize that this was of his own accord and initiative, he began to take pride in his influence and stepped into his own as a much healthier Nine-turned-volunteer-project-manager, tapping into both Wing Eight and Wing One. The initially exhausting task of waking up is the thing that will eventually make you less tired—and will create more space in a busy life to say your best wholehearted "yes."

Stress and Security

The primary issues relating to stress versus security in the Type Nine are mostly fundamental to the spiritual, mental, and emotional work of being and living well. On the one hand, it's

---

1 "Heedless," Cambridge Dictionary, dictionary.cambridge.org/dictionary/english/heedless.

working to stay awake (creating extra effort for a "tired" Type Nine) as opposed to falling asleep on their true nature and feelings, manifesting itself in an openness to spontaneity or a difficulty finding rest. It could also be remaining present in the daily, before falling hypnotized into the routine of busywork.

Let's reference the Enneagram diagram again to observe the arrows. In stress, the Type Nine arrow points toward Six (The Loyalist), and is pointed to by the Three (The Achiever). The Nine takes on the unhealthy traits of Six during stress or disintegration, and healthy traits of Three during upmost security and growth. And just as a note—although stress and security are different than levels of health and unhealthy zones, you can still navigate what triggers disintegration and actively find your way into growth. Remember, living to help others is not a terrible thing, it's beautiful; it is the living *through* others that creates a further divide from your true personality that is negative. You are *you*, after all and staying in charge of your reactions, while understanding that reactions aren't a "bad" thing, is part of the growth process.

In security or growth, Type Nines take on the healthy side of Type Three's achieving mindset. This means there's room for energy and productivity, focus, stronger confidence about reaching their goals, and more time from establishing firm boundaries. They stop believing that their voice and feelings are unnecessary to the conversation, and instead believe that they are integral to contributing to the move forward into the "something good." They recapture the playfully imaginative spirit, putting their pursuits into action with inspirational communication and confident team building, bringing others into the mission. They vocalize their concerns, but tactfully, without numbing, coming into their own with a patient authenticity that allows others to unburden themselves in their peaceful presence and emotional stability.

While Type Three is a direction toward positive growth, it can also be a stretching point for the people-pleasing aspect of the Type Nine. They might unwittingly take on too much, and like the Three, seek appreciation and validation from others (enter the people pleaser) instead of actually doing things for themselves because they like to do them.

In stress or disintegration, Type Nines borrow many of the negative key traits of Type Six—self-doubt, anxiety, and thinking too far in advance, which is paralysis waiting to happen. On the other hand, Type Nines do become much more direct about their thoughts, contributing to a realistic viewpoint that isn't necessarily consistent with their everyday lives. Under extreme stress and disintegration, the Nine shifts from their generally positive nature to a pessimistic and reactive stance, sometimes becoming angry and erupting, but feeling right in their eruption (which may also be rooted in a strong Eight wing). Instead of seeing the silver lining, they begin to verbally vent about what's going on in the world, how things are all wrong, how people are all hurting each other or a group, and become very focused on the negative aspects of people (remember, fear is a recurring theme of an unhealthy Type Six and may also be a controlling factor based on the Nine's health). Finally, a sign of true Six stress is having a backup plan to help control anything that may go wrong, ensuring that *when* (not if) things go wrong, they'll be able to handle it and protect themselves. Gone is the easygoing Type Nine, replaced with a devil-may-care, nervous wreck . . . and it's a hard clamber back to the surface.

In our first example, my Type Nine friend Jade was the go-to built-in friend–therapist to multiple people for years—it was simply the role she took on, and she truly didn't mind doing it. However, over the past six months, she has made it a point to have very linear friendships in addition to having non-linear friendships that treated her more as a therapist and called when they needed advice. She is acutely supportive of everyone's agenda and always has been, but has become more aware of her own agenda and plan of action. To move forward with her own ideology, tasks, and long-term goals, she had to create an action plan . . . and she *hated* doing that, because it required action as opposed to letting things go and becoming a victim of circumstance! It meant that she had to take responsibility for the fact that she technically could do what she wanted to easily—and just as easily face the idea that people wouldn't love her as much if she focused on her own needs and goals.

Jade has an online teaching business that has grown over the past six months. To become successful, she had to make several changes. In the first week of her business, she turned down a friend's request for a coffee date to discuss her impending move (saying "yes" means that you say "no" to something else). The first step was to counteract the negative feelings she immediately took on toward herself for saying no. Next, she calmed herself down—the part of her heart that was consuming her with internal suppressed anger (toward her friend for asking for advice even though she hadn't asked "How are you?" for several months), her fear that her friend wouldn't love her anymore, and the personal frustration with her lack of action. Next, she challenged herself to instead focus those emotions and her attention toward them, and take action. Working from a quiet café was what did the trick; instead of looking out the window, flicking on a documentary, or keeping her brain static and numb by getting caught up in the autonomy of the task, she picked up the phone, wrote the emails, and supported her routine with active planning and consistent gym sessions.

Jade had figured out how to properly direct her previously lapsed energy to the self-motivation of the healthy Three. Instead of staying complacent and allowing resentment to grow like she could well have done, she implemented key steps into her daily life that allowed for her lapsed energy to be turned around, simply by taking the time to figure out what she needed for herself and to help guide her. Instead of disintegrating, she understood what she needed to do personally to jump into a healthy situation. Now, rather than feeling spent after having just three conversations in a day, she's "wide awake."

Stuffing feelings feels like a good thing because it's an active avoidance of the discord that may occur when voicing opinions, but it is something that contributes to the disintegration process. Hence, it is *imperative* to have some form of release, and to find your true emotions while not letting them become the central piece in your life. Whether it's writing in one of the five hundred journals you've been gifted over the years; talking to a trusted mentor, friend, or counselor; or even having a musical or analytical outlet, keeping something personal that is not busywork or a means of shutting down thoughts or emotions is the best way to release.

Remember my friend Zach's struggle with the description of "heedlessness?" I would personally argue that the world does indeed need the heedless people. Even if it feels as though heedlessness lands on the list of negatives of a Type Nine; it is one of the things that make them Type Nines—jumping in where needed, understanding all viewpoints, and being among the people getting 90 percent of the work done (even if only because no one else stepped in). Nines are *powerful* people. They have massive influence. But they also have the potential to be the world's doormats. Don't leave them with a less-than circumstance. To the Nine: don't get comfortable. Don't be someone so deprived that being comfortable is a guiding force in your everyday existence. You are worth so much more than that; and you do have the power to create something good.

Type Nines find it difficult to make decisions. It's difficult to minimize what others want and listen to what you have to say. It's difficult to take time to understand yourself. And yes, it's *really hard to get started*. Knowing and acknowledging that it is hard work is on the other side of the fuzzy socks, the yoga mat, a little bit of self-care, and that kickboxing class you always wanted to take but were too afraid of because anger is just too much to feel. It's acknowledging that life is about doing something, even if that something *is* nothing some days—it's about making a mess, moving your hands, leaving a mark, creating. It is about ideas. The point is the mess despite the desire to *let it all go* and *let it all be*.

Maybe you'll let something beautiful out to breathe. Maybe it will be the beginning of creating a state and stance of "something good happening."

Life with a Type Nine: Empathetic and Magnetic

Type Nines are the magnets of the Enneagram. People are naturally drawn to them because they are genuine, warm, and consistent; if they are joined by people who are also positive, open-minded, and comfortable in their own skin, they thrive! If they are joined with people who cause conflict, refuse to see all sides of the story, and are constantly interrupting their thought process, they can feel unheard and withdraw.

Type Nines make up approximately 16.2 percent of the population. The dominant Eight wing only comes in at 23 percent, while the dominant One wing racks up 77 percent.[2] This is an astounding difference in percentages, but it's definitely worth noting because while most wings are fairly evenly balanced out for each number, the Type Nine would more generally gravitate toward the characteristics that wing to a Type One perfectionist—partially because it sits more easily with The Peacemaker personality than the option to wing toward the Type Eight Challenger mode. Think about the balancing work that it takes for a Type Nine to wing Type Eight: a person who is motivated by ensuring everyone is happy and at harmony with themselves and others, coupled with a wing on a challenging streak and concerned with justice. The Eight and Nine combination would constantly be at odds, hence the heavily uneven percentages.

Nines are calm, cool, and collected (or are perceived as complete pushovers, depending on how you look at them)—or are a passionate force for justice (with slightly less temper than you'd expect). It's important to note that Wing Eights communicate differently than Wing Ones. That being said, Nines can see all sides of a conversation, a discussion, a controversy, or—God forbid—an argument and thus can often empathize deeply with each party. Earlier in this chapter we had a little laugh about my friend Jade and how a couple both brought their frustrations to her—and both left feeling justified and encouraged that they were in the right.

The Nine's superpower, however, can also be their downfall—with indecision showing up as their biggest conflict, and following them everywhere they look. Another's communication style (passive–aggressive, harsh, or overly emotional) can easily cause conflict within the empathetic Nine, but their frustration is not often verbally expressed until a pent-up anger boils over. Their more conflict-avoidant nature of absorbing can actually *cause* stress when it comes to confrontation and lead to even more indecisiveness and frustration.

Type Nines can appear complacent and weak because of their desire to create harmony and peace, and others can interpret this as the Nine being incapable of standing up for themselves or others. Nines want to be supportive, but they can merge and lose themselves quickly as they go with the flow to avoid an argument—and that's not conducive to a genuine, lasting relationship; rather it creates a relationship featuring long-term internal struggle (leading to external conflict). Encouraging Nines to engage with their frustrations is one of the best things anyone who knows a Nine can do; making sure they're heard, genuinely acknowledged, and appreciated for their sense of justice and peace.

Nines need to know that the world values their effort to contribute harmony; they are undemanding, contain their own energy, and believe that anger disconnects them from their relationships. But, in health, they are fully alive and awake to everyone; strong, resilient, and fully present. They are ultimately connectors, bringing people together to heal the world. They show their love by accepting everyone as they are, because they are naturally non-judgmental; and they are receptive to environments that are just and open to multiple perspectives as well.

At Home

Even as children, Type Nines desire harmony and peace and are the most conflict-avoidant type. Their ability as adults to see and understand all sides to a situation was not honed over time; this is something the Type Nine child excels in even as a toddler. Their imagination allows them to empathize with others and where they're coming from, and their innocent acceptance of peers and adults "as they are" helps them make many friends. Easily "at one" with the harmony and peace of nature, Type Nines thrive in outdoor experiences. They generally want to improve everything around them—the environment, their own world, relationships with others—their desire is a world at harmony, and they feel that their voice can make a difference if encouraged by their parents to speak up and embrace their true thoughts and ideas.

Conflict for Nines takes its form in indecision. Their childhood wound was a feeling that their voice was rejected, and they have trouble letting go of others' feelings after they have merged and adopted those feelings as their own. With initial connection to their parents as a form of identity, they can feel as though their own emotional, mental, and physical participation isn't necessary. The Type Nine child can create a safe, no-judgment space for their friends and family; when they have siblings this is only enhanced as their nurturing empathy makes them an anchoring point of security in their family. Their calming nature in a chaotic world, whether at home or at school, can bring much comfort to their families and those around them. But, they need to be reminded that the feelings of others are not *their* fault, otherwise with their caring and sensitive nature the Nine can take on the burdens and conflicts of those around them.

Making sure that the Type Nine child in your life feels that they have a voice by asking open-ended questions (that is, questions that won't end in, "Great, thank you; how was yours?") allows them to reflect on their day. If they feel angry, let them feel that anger, and understand that there might be six months' worth of frustrations leading to this energy. Keep a solid routine and praise the Nine's uniqueness by keeping an eye out for situations in which they are truly themselves. As they are encouraged toward their own mindset and gifts as an individual, as a child, this in turn gives them an outlet for their imaginations.

Type Nine parents typically have a laid-back attitude to life— and parenting is no different. With a warm and caring tone, creativity, and a great sense of wit and humor, they easily make their children (or children around them) feel loved and protected, and that the parent is "on their side." Type Nine parents and teachers alike often have an uncanny ability to connect with their students, because they have genuine acceptance and love. They desire peace, and that can be overwhelming for any parent who has a strong-willed child. When it comes to discipline that they don't want to give, if they feel their partner is not participating or is avoiding the situation, their passive–aggressive nature can rise, and their indecisiveness can create inner turmoil.

Type Nines can easily help others through their issues without personally acknowledging their own frustrations, or even knowing that they "need help." Acknowledging that they *need* help while remaining accepting of themselves is where the

Type Nine will feel as if they've shown up for themselves and their family. The challenge is to remain consistent with their direction and choice of discipline, instead of giving in to their inner desire to flee or to feel that they are not measuring up to the expected parenting style around them. Avoiding behavior that needs addressing or tuning out the noise that chaos brings can block the necessary emotional needs and tendencies of children. Having awareness of their tendencies helps to bring the focus back on their understanding and empathy.

In Love

Type Nines are naturally loving people. Before they even begin a relationship, they've probably told their potential or eventual partner either literally or through their actions, "I love you!" Warm, patient, and supportive, they want their partner to feel loved, accepted, and safe with them. Their peaceful nature extends past their personal world, and they now want to create that same peaceful atmosphere for their partner's world; if their partner feels uncomfortable in any way, the Type Nine can take it personally as they spend a good deal of effort to make their partner at ease. A childhood wound of rejection carries over to their relationships, and they can err on the side of codependence when they sense something is even slightly off, and will do whatever their partner needs to help support them—mentally, physically, or emotionally.

Type Nines are about bringing harmony and peace, but they also seek to be fulfilled, be fulfilling, and be rewarding to the world—their relationship is no different. It's a big part of their lives, and they don't necessarily get into relationships until they feel ready to enter with commitment so they can put the adequate amount of focus and prioritization on their partner. But, they want this to be a two-way street, and when it's not, they can struggle deeply with wanting to be cherished but still feeling like they're not loving the other person well enough.

The Type Nine needs someone who is confident at making decisions, and patient with them as they allow their inner voice and assertiveness to rise up through their discomfort. Nines want someone willing to get them out of the comfort zone and into unusual activities—all while seeing, hearing, and acknowledging them in their uncertainty. On the other hand, Nines are all about "taking things slow," and "going with the flow." They are extremely low-pressure people, sometimes to their detriment.

My friend Renee is a strong 9w1 who completely idealized her partner, Tom, in their early stages of dating. Tom was a strong 7w8 and was happy to assist Renee in the "getting out of her comfort zone," early on. They went skydiving, sailing, hiking, bird watching; Tom tapped into her appreciation of nature, and she loved him for it. However, whenever Renee suggested "a quiet night in," meaning a movie and maybe some Chinese take-away, Tom took that to mean a banquet, and turned it into a seven-course house party. It wasn't that he didn't care what she said, it's just that *she didn't say it*. After six or seven months, Renee began to feel unheard and unseen; driven by her strong inner desire to avoid conflict and maintain peace, and to make sure Tom felt he was in a safe space, Renee began to develop feelings of resentment and bitterness, and thoughts that Tom was not doing "the correct thing." When Tom sensed this, his immediate reaction was disintegration, feeling that his freedom was being stifled, and (as a fellow conflict-avoider) began to minimize their present scenario to look for better days ahead.

When Renee and Tom finally decided to make some changes, both were able to tap into their shared Eight wing; get to the heart of the matter quickly; and while remaining sensitive, were able to reconcile their differences. Tom didn't feel that Renee was communicating what she wanted—when Renee said, "Whatever you're in the mood for," she was merging her feelings with Tom's. Renee felt Tom didn't see or understand what she needed; Tom had to learn to tap into his empathetic Six wing to make sure there was enough consistent quiet time for Renee to be both heard and acknowledged. Implementing these few "simple" communication skills was enough for them to salvage their relationship and transform it into a stronger partnership.

Coming from an instinctive thought triad, the Type Nine's independence is just as important as their connection to someone—not because they don't care, but because they do. If they feel something is off or that they need to regain their footing, they withdraw. Although they prefer to avoid conflict at all costs, they need their set and protected personal time and to feel prioritized by their loved ones. If their partner is meeting these needs, and giving them clear options in a safe space, giving them room to speak and valuing their opinions, the Type Nine thrives. Type Nines want to love unconditionally and be loved well (and swept off their feet!)—and if they feel that their partner is neglecting an aspect within those perimeters, they'll retreat.

In Work
Being in the instinctive triad and situated at the top of the Enneagram, Type Nines are the life of the community (not to be confused with the life of the party!). While they create harmony and establish themselves early on as the connector of a group,

they have a commonality with other Type Nines in their circles, particularly in the sense that there is common ground—such as taking issue with having their own priorities and to-do lists. It's not that Nines are lazy, underwhelming, or avoidant; it's just that their primary strength is supporting people with empathy and understanding, and creating a safe space for others. Drawing the Type Nine partner into the willingness to *do* what needs to be done is a key changer in any working relationship. They are balanced, and an ideal person for all workplaces, because they can see all points of view almost instantaneously.

A lot of Type Nines get a bit of flack for being considered a "lazy" number. While this may be true for some Nines, most of them are quick thinkers, and many of them can be "on the move" almost constantly throughout their day. As the counselors, human resources professionals, social workers, librarians or government workers, editors, psychiatrists, and writers, many of their jobs are highly emotionally taxing for an average human being. For a Type Nine with high empathy, this could be detrimental if they *don't* have strong boundaries. When they work alongside colleagues that are more driven and task-oriented, they can bring that sense of community and harmony to the team: encouraging, breathing life back into tired or overworked ideas, and cultivating camaraderie and harmony. If, however, they work alongside someone who is just as laid back and relaxed, routines will be their best friend and saving grace of the more hectic and less flexible time schedule and will do well to create boundaries with their colleagues.

If Type Nines feel unacknowledged at work, or feel that someone in their life is responsible for adding conflict or drama, they may experience some mental roadblock that results in a standoff or standstill. While their adaptability to the unexpected is to be envied, their adaptability to conflict will often make them feel overwhelmed or disregarded. If the Type Nine employee begins to feel stress, it's important to (first) sit down and establish more rapport with them through finding common ground using strong listening skills. Creating a relationship ahead of bringing in immediate and intense pressure will allow the Nine to be receptive to constructive criticism without feeling the shake of conflict. "Hey, would you like to grab lunch? Go for a walk? Grab a coffee?"

Second, get to the heart of the matter, ask good questions, and pause to listen. "So, how's it all been going? Do you feel as if you're well supported?" Encouraging the Type Nine's action through creation of structure, routine, and schedule will help them keep on top of their priorities. Telling them what is *needed* from them is far more motivating than telling them what you *want* from them. If they're a team leader, encourage delegation. "What are your thoughts on _____? Would you do anything differently?" "Let's set an achievable deadline for this goal, and then that way you can have Samantha take over that responsibility while you work on this project." Nines are excellent team builders but struggle to lead their peers.

Third, challenge them kindly, help them to take risks and think outside of the box, and accept them. Lead with encouragement. "What do you think that you're saying that other people are having trouble taking on board? How do you think you can communicate that differently?" "I like that you've added value to the people on our team; the community enjoys you a lot! How can we work on incorporating more task-orientation into community projects?" The message the Type Nine needs to hear is, "Your presence *matters!*" They need to know they are heard and seen, that they do indeed bring value to the table. There's a reason they were hired; remind them to set their boundaries and be fair to themselves and others.

In Play

As a gentle, agreeable, comfortable friend, Type Nines are easygoing, and know how to get along with *everyone*, creating a safe space where others can rest, not be judged, and are allowed to go with the flow with no dramatics. The healthy Type Nine is open-minded and is often the sounding board for friends' deep secrets and stories because they do not judge. Their natural ability to understand many perspectives makes them a magnet for everyone—they have an attractive spirit and seem to carry themselves with a grace and ease. The unhealthy Type Nine is overly accommodating and checked out, so while they listen, they don't necessarily seek to understand.

While Type Nines are great connectors and potentially have many acquaintances, they have very few kindred-spirit friends that they allow into *their* world of opinions, secrets, and stories.

Type Nines are not usually the type to fight to make their voice heard. At the same time, they're generally fine going with the majority vote, although they are desperate for this to not be taken as a sign that you can boss them around in any way, shape, or form. In fact, if they feel this way about you, they'll probably respond with a stubborn pushback in the form of passive–aggressiveness. Nines assert themselves through inertia, and they can make conflict avoidance an art form. The thing with many Type Nines is that if they truly care about something they deem minimal (i.e., where to walk this afternoon), they'll speak up about it. But if they truly don't have a strong opinion, it can feel intrusive at times when someone insists they make a decision, and this leads to a Nine's stubbornness and self-doubt if/when the other is not as enthusiastic about the Nine's choice. It can be difficult to be an empathic people pleaser, because Type Nines can often feel judged for being indecisive.

I once had a friend tell me it seemed like I never really cared about things, to which, "I don't!" was not a good enough answer (oops). I didn't realize she was hurt by the belief that I didn't care enough about *her* to give her an opinion about what movie we should watch, or where we went for dinner. The fact of the matter was that I genuinely didn't mind and was exhausted by the idea of figuring out those simple details after we'd already had a long conversation working through a problem she had. But, to care for my friend (a Type Four Individualist), it was important to her that I tell her, "*The Chronicles of Narnia*" or, "Anything but pizza!" While it made me have to leave my comfortable, go-with-the-flow zone, it was well-meant on her end, and I realized that she was trying to show me that she cared by helping me recognize what I was interested in, and then verbalize it.

To show love and encouragement to a Type Nine friend, give them simple options so they can utilize their voice, without feeling they are treading on anyone's toes: "Would you like to grab a coffee at BTB or Starbucks?" "I either want to go to the mountains or the ocean; what do you prefer?" And then, affirm it. "Agree, BTB has *amazing* batch brew! And that'll be perfect to prep us for our drive to the beach!" This doesn't need to be over the top (Nines are driven by authenticity and can sniff out another's fake reply in an instant); but if they are encouraged and affirmed in their choices and appreciated for their contributions both in decisions and in personal matters, they know you care. Being sensitive and patient when giving a Nine feedback allows for reception instead of conflict. "Hey, I know you didn't mean it, but that felt passive–aggressive. Can I help with anything?" and then being open to listening to what they have to say will help keep the environment as peaceful and open as possible.

Type Nines need to know you can love them and meet them where they are, because they strive to keep the atmosphere harmonious for everyone. If you put them in the middle of a circle of conflict or drama, they'll mediate, but they'll probably withdraw afterward. Supporting them on their journey allows them to be verbally expressive, imaginative, and kind—and honest, nonjudgmental, and supportive in their feedback. That in turn allows them to feel as if they can conquer the world—which means you can, too.

Conclusion

You made it to the end of this introduction to the Enneagram types: congratulations! Hopefully you have formed some ideas along the way regarding information, emotions, and how to reveal and befriend your inner child once more. Some may say that this is where the hard part starts. How *can* we make space to recognize and offer a seat at the table to the parts of ourselves that we see as damaged and flawed?

This is the part that's all about application. I have watched the Enneagram system build teams, repair friendships, and bring a strengthened commitment to learning and growing in community. I have heard communication change between parents and children, and seen families learn how to live together again. I have seen the Enneagram allow businesses to thrive; promote healthy workplaces; and teach deeply hurt individuals how to unwrap and unravel years of time to find reconnection with their inner child, releasing themselves from a self-prescribed bondage.

It is truly beautiful.

But none of those results were because of this system itself. It was because of the people, like you are now, taking time to put in the work on themselves, learning how to best love and communicate with others in their world to bring out the best in them, and chosing to make that courageous difference and step toward a healthy atmosphere rather than accepting a just-"okay" atmosphere. Learning how to love yourself genuinely isn't easy, but it allows for freedom to love others as they are, and *your* freedom means that others can feel free to be their true self around you. What you've been given has simply been the tool of knowledge. The important part is learning how to live out what you've taken in with integrity, and applying the knowledge to your everyday lives and relationships.

Your Enneagram is not what defines you. It's not your identity. In fact, when I ask people about it, I change the language to ask, "What Enneagram number do you identify with?" rather than, "What Enneagram number *are* you?" Removing the identity from the number keeps things real and down to earth. Anyone who ever attempts to limit you through your type is silencing your voice. The Enneagram is designed to help you work your way around the entire set of types, and to reveal those voices should you allow them out to play.

We're not all Fives, we're not all Ones, and we're definitely going to run into our fair few people that have absolutely no idea what you're talking about when you mention the Enneagram. You can't just go out and type your friends and your family, and then think you have them all figured out (that would be manipulative at best, and hopefully you've picked up on that by now). It's easy to get so caught up in the typing of others and how they can be healthy and change that we forget to look at our own lives and where we need to change. We go about our lives putting everyone into a category (right and wrong, good and bad, true and false; friend/best friend/colleague/acquaintance/manager). However, when given this information, it's also ideal to share— it's exciting! In the words of Bob Goff, "We need to replace what we've settled for with what we've been longing for."

The interconnected nature of the primary type, merged with the dominant wing, coupled with the child-heart and growth– stress points, make up a lot of your personality. Adding our specific order of subtypes creates even more depth. The Enneagram is a form of love language, and everyone speaks theirs a little differently: if you are speaking from your feelings triad, and someone is speaking from their thinking triad, too much will become lost in translation. Communication is utilized effectively when each center is spotlighted correctly, and we learn to speak the other's language. Spending time learning how to "find each other out" makes for a wholehearted journey based on two people's choice to fight for each other to have a say. It says, "You're important to me. Let's empower each other."

As you begin to learn more and ask questions in each situation, you are practicing self-discovery and learning how to actively trust yourself again, and this is a never-ending journey.

Empowering yourself by knowing your identity and being self-aware is one of the most important things you can do personally on your life's journey. Starting a colloquium, joining Enneagram-based seminars, or meeting with a coach will greatly enrich your personal Enneagram journey. Looking at your patterns, your wounds, your backgrounds and triggers honestly, and learning how to backpedal on those compulsions will give you more clarity and navigational skills. This knowledge heightens your compassion and empathy as you learn to put yourself in the shoes of others. And it allows you to impact the world around you on a minuscule to massive scale as you contribute and share as only you can. Your ego may fight to consistently rise to the surface, but your authentic sense of personal freedom is growing all the time.

So I ask, again: How will you continue your journey? Fight the hard fights, find your triggers and defaults, and above all else, remember your original purpose and destination, and go well. Believe me, *you* are worth it.

Resources

Daniels, David N. "What Is the Enneagram." David N. Daniels (blog). n.d. https://drdaviddaniels.com/the-Enneagram-of-personality/.

Gadd, Ann. "Enneagram Parenting Styles." Ann Gad (blog). October 25, 2015. https://www.anngadd.co.za/2015/10/Enneagram-parenting-styles/.

Goff, Bob. *Dream Big: Know What You Want, Why You Want It, and What You're Going to Do about It.* Nashville, TN: Nelson Books, an Imprint of Thomas Nelson, 2020.

Hall, Steph Barron. "Communication Styles by Enneagram Type." Nine Types Co (blog). May 1, 2020. https://ninetypes.co/blog/communication-styles-by-Enneagram-type.

Miltenberger, Laura. *Enneagram Empowerment: Discover Your Personality Type and Unlock Your Potential.* New York: DK Publishing, 2021.

O'Hanrahan, Peter. "Enneagram Type 9—The Mediator." The Enneagram at Work (blog). n.d. https://theEnneagramatwork.com/type-9-mediator.

Owens, Molly. "Enneagram Type 6: The Skeptic." Truity (blog). n.d. https://www.truity.com/Enneagram/personality-type-6-skeptic.

Riso, Don Richard, and Russ Hudson. *The Wisdom of The Enneagram: The Complete Guide to Psychological and Spiritual Growth for the Nine Personality Types.* New York: Bantam Books, 1999.

Robinson, Ashley. "Enneagram Type 5: The Investigator." PrepScholar (blog). December 15, 2020. https://blog.prepscholar.com/Enneagram-type-5-careers-relationships.

Roh, HyeRin, et al. "Understanding Medical Students' Empathy Based on Enneagram Personality Types." *Korean Journal of Medical Education,* Korean Society of Medical Education, Mar. 2019. https://www.ncbi.nlm.nih.gov/pmc/articles/PMC6589630.

Rowles, Kristi. "How to Love Each Enneagram Type." Full & Free Enneagram Coaching (blog). n.d. https://kristirowles.com/how-to-love-each-Enneagram-type/.

Sikorski, Ashlee. "How to Handle Conflict Based on Your Enneagram Type." yellow co. (blog). January 29, 2020. https://yellowco.co/articles/how-to-handle-conflict-based-on-your-Enneagram-type.

Stafford, Scott. "Enneagram Type 4 Love: How Enneagram Type Four Falls in Love." Personality Growth (blog). June 25, 2020. https://personalitygrowth.com/Enneagram-type-4-love-how-Enneagram-type-four-falls-in-love/.

Storm, Susan. "Here's What You Need in a Friendship, Based on Your Enneagram Type." Psychology Junkie (blog). September 9, 2020. https://www.psychologyjunkie.com/2020/09/09/heres-what-you-need-in-a-friendship-based-on-your-Enneagram-type/.

Storm, Susan. "How Each Enneagram Type Makes an Amazing Friend." Psychology Junkie (blog). July 1, 2020. https://www.psychologyjunkie.com/2020/07/01/how-each-Enneagram-type-makes-an-amazing-friend/.

Storm, Susan. "The Childhood Wounds of Every Enneagram Type." Psychology Junkie (blog). March 10, 2020. https://www.psychologyjunkie.com/2020/03/10/the-childhood-wounds-of-every-Enneagram-type/.

Storm, Susan. "The Enneagram Six Child." Psychology Junkie (blog). January 2, 2021. https:/www.psychologyjunkie.com/2021/01/02/the-Enneagram-six-child/h-tips-for-parenting-an-Enneagram-six-child.

Storm, Susan. "The Relationship Fear of Every Enneagram Type." Psychology Junkie (blog). April 1, 2020. https://www.psychologyjunkie.com/2021/04/01/Enneagram-relationship-fears/.

Southard, Ashley. "How to Communicate Most Effectively with Each Enneagram Type." Thought Catalog (blog). January 9, 2020. https://thoughtcatalog.com/ashley-southard/2020/01/how-to-communicate-most-effectively-with-each-Enneagram-type/.

Tato, Dani. "About the Enneagram." Corporate Consciousness (blog). n.d. https://www.corpconsciousness.com/about-the-Enneagram/.

The Enneagram Institute. "How the System Works." n.d. https://www.enneagraminstitute.com/how-the-enneagram-system-works/

The Enneagram Institute. "Type 4." n.d. https://www.Enneagraminstitute.com/type-4.

Acknowledgments

Writing a book is profoundly more difficult than I had ever imagined, but I had only ever *imagined* publishing a book before, and the reality that we are here is beyond comprehension. I am ever grateful to my mum, Phyllis, for spurring me on in self-education and openness to ideas, reminding me that I am capable even when I felt I was not, loving me unconditionally, and helping hone my Eight wing. Mum, your patience, understanding, and exuberant expectation inspire me. Thank you.

To my family: my sisters, Alexandrea and Grace-Hope, who push me out of my comfort zone simply by breathing, I am constantly catching up with your unspoken but well-actioned challenge to live a life worth living. For Dad, who challenges my mentality in nearly every aspect I could possibly imagine (thank you anyway), and who always says, "I'm proud of you," even when there's some questionable aspect to most things; I'm ever-grateful for your provision and love. Thank you to my Aunty Eunice and Uncle Wade, who introduced me to the Enneagram in the first place. You dared me to take a second look and allowed me to find a quiet place in your house my entire life.

To Angela Ward: You will never know how much your presence in my education came back to assist me for so many years. Your direction to always take the road less traveled, your consistency in living up to the words you spoke and wrote, and your many years of mentorship and friendship means more to me than words can say. "We know what we are, but we know not what we may be." I count you amongst my heroes.

Many, many thanks to everyone at Page Street Publishing for the opportunity and generosity, and for helping with the entire process. Special thanks to Sarah Monroe, my editor who put up with my barely-on-time deadlines with grace, constructive criticism, and who reached out at the perfect time in my life, as well as Meg and Rosie on design. This book would not have happened without the incredible team you all are.

And, to all those who played a key part in getting there: Tiffani Patton (for being my lifelong best friend, cheerleader, and sister); Ryan Lovett (for being "in" on the Enneagram from the early days); Nick Paton (for being the best Type One eagle-eye reader I could have asked for); Emily, Holly, and Meghan (for asking the hard questions and having the good conversations); and Brennan Fortier (for encouraging me to write—"since it's creative"—during school hours).

None of this would be possible without my Lord and Savior Jesus Christ, whom I would be lost without, and whose overwhelming peace, love, and care weaves divinely through every thread of my life.

About the Author

Sierra Mackenzie began what she describes as one of her life callings at the age of four, when she wrote her first short story. She has since become a singer–songwriter, poet, screenwriter, believer in the Oxford comma, and a nomad-soul at heart who has lived everywhere from Australia to New York City.

Studying Shakespeare and earning a BA in English literature and songwriting helped solidify her love for writing, storytelling as a ministry, and human nature through psychology, and it launched her love for the study of individual personalities. As the founder of Enneagram Enthusiast and her personal brand, SierraMackenzie, *The Complete Guide to the Enneagram* is Sierra's first non-fiction book, written during the COVID-19 pandemic, when we all showed our true colors and found ourselves in our most stripped-back standing.

Sierra currently lives in Sydney, Australia.

Index